# Russia

# Russia

## Great Power, Weakened State

*Second Edition*

Marlene Laruelle
The George Washington University

Jean Radvanyi
National Institute for Oriental
Languages and Cultures

ROWMAN & LITTLEFIELD
*Lanham • Boulder • New York • London*

Published by Rowman & Littlefield
An imprint of The Rowman & Littlefield Publishing Group, Inc.
4501 Forbes Boulevard, Suite 200, Lanham, Maryland 20706
www.rowman.com

86-90 Paul Street, London EC2A 4NE

British Library Cataloguing in Publication Information Available

**Library of Congress Cataloging-in-Publication Data**

Names: Laruelle, Marlene, author. | Radvanyi, Jean, author.
Title: Russia: great power, weakened state / Marlene Laruelle, The George Washington
    University; Jean Radvanyi, National Institute for Oriental Languages and Cultures.
Other titles: Understanding Russia | Great power, weakened state
Description: Second edition. | Lanham: Rowman & Littlefield, [2023] | Includes
    bibliographical references and index.
Identifiers: LCCN 2023019452 (print) | LCCN 2023019453 (ebook) | ISBN
    9781538174784 (cloth) | ISBN 9781538174777 (paperback) | ISBN
    9781538174791 (epub)
Subjects: LCSH: Russia (Federation)—Politics and government—1991- | Russia
    (Federation)—Foreign relations. | Russia (Federation)—Economic conditions—1991-
Classification: LCC DK510.76 .L37 2023 (print) | LCC DK510.76 (ebook) | DDC
    327.47—dc23/eng/20230426
LC record available at https://lccn.loc.gov/2023019452
LC ebook record available at https://lccn.loc.gov/2023019453

∞™ The paper used in this publication meets the minimum requirements of American
National Standard for Information Sciences—Permanence of Paper for Printed Library
Materials, ANSI/NISO Z39.48-1992.

# Contents

# Figures, Maps, and Tables

## FIGURE

## MAPS

# TABLES

# Introduction

The full-scale war launched by Russia against Ukraine on February 24, 2022, constitutes a turning point not only in the history of the postcommunist world since the collapse of the Berlin Wall in 1989 and that of the Soviet Union in 1991 but also, more broadly, in the history of Europe since the end of World War II. Not that it is the only conflict the European continent has known in the past eight decades, but the decades-long Irish conflict and the Yugoslav wars of the 1990s were conducted on a smaller scale, while Russia's is a full-scale, old-fashioned war of conquest. Its extreme violence reminds European publics of World War I: everyday life in the trenches on the front lines in the Donbas region of eastern Ukraine resembles that of Verdun or La Marne, the big battles of 1916–1918, in eastern France.

But more than that, the war is also an earthquake shaking the very foundations of the post–Cold War, rules-based international order, with long-term impacts on already severe global imbalances. Russia's invasion has resulted in a consolidation of the West around NATO—and a new role, both geostrategically and in terms of energy policy, for the United States—but also in a growing decoupling of the West from the Global South, which has refused to take sides in the conflict or cut ties with Russia.

To understand the reasons that have led to the dramatic decision of Russian president Vladimir Putin to invade Ukraine, one has to remember that none of the major conflicts of the twentieth century had a singular cause; each was a result of multiple entangled crises. And indeed, the Russo-Ukrainian War did not happen as the result of just one issue, be it Putin's "irrationality," Russia's "imperial DNA," or even as the West's "mistake," as is stated by realist figures such as John Mearsheimer.[1] The war broke out because of a combination of problems of different scales: three decades of strategic misunderstanding between Russia and the West on the post–Cold War European security architecture; an increasingly resentful and conspiratorial political culture among the Russian elite, impacting their reading of Russia's place on the international scene and in Eurasia and an inability to rethink the lessons of their own history; and the unavoidable isolation of an aging, authoritarian leader whom no one dares inform of the real state of the Russian military and the mindset of Ukrainian society.

The war comes as the culmination of Russia's distrust toward the West but also of the West's negative view of Russia, likewise accumulated over many decades. This negative image has deep roots: this was apparent even before the Marquis de Custine and his famous *Letters from Russia* of 1839, for it was Stendhal who wrote from Smolensk as early as 1812, "In this sea of barbarism, not a sound responds to my soul! Everything is coarse, dirty, putrid, physically and morally."[2] After several decades of the West, and especially the United States, framing the Soviet Union as an "evil empire," the first Ukrainian conflict (Russia's conquest of the Crimean Peninsula and covert destabilization of the Donbas in 2014) as well as "Russiagate" (Russia's meddling in the 2016 US presidential election) both added a new chapter to the framework inherited from the Cold War. In 2014, at the peak of the first Ukrainian crisis, US secretary of state Hillary Clinton compared Vladimir Putin to Adolf Hitler,[3] and since February 2022, the parallels drawn between Putin's Russia and Hitler's Germany have multiplied.

At the same time—and this is a key point of this book—Russia is fearful too. Over thirty years after the end of the Soviet Union, multiple ghosts still haunt both the Russian elite and society at large, from worries about the country's vulnerability to foreign intervention to concerns about demographic and economic decline. Opened up practically overnight under President Boris Yeltsin, the country has had to deal with a rapid and traumatic globalization. Faced with a West that emerged victorious from the Cold War, a shockingly dynamic modern China, and former Soviet republics claiming their right to emancipate themselves from Moscow's stranglehold, Russia has been vacillating between reformist aspirations and a fear of liberal society, between the autarky of the "besieged fortress" and the messianism of a Third Rome,[4] taking upon itself the mission to establish a new world order in the face of a decadent West.

Russian society is at once profoundly European in its history and culture *and* different from Europe. Its existential dilemmas permeate the country's greatest creations, from the novels of Fyodor Dostoevsky and the plays of Anton Chekhov to the symphonies of Dmitri Shostakovich. Throughout the twentieth century and to this day, Russia's ideological and political choices have been regarded with both fascination and repulsion. When the Soviet system disintegrated, many hoped that Russia would magically align itself more closely with the West and "return" to the European fold. This naive expectation was doomed to fail. And even today, many analysts continue to analyze Moscow's supposedly erratic and inexplicable policies from the standpoint that President Boris Yeltsin's Russia was the norm of a pro-Western and liberal Russia. Seen from Russia, however, the Yeltsin years are anything but the norm; they serve as an antimodel, illuminating a path Russia does not wish to go down again.

In this book, we do not see Russia as an "other" that is fundamentally and radically different from "us," and we do not share the essentialist discourse that frames Russia as a civilization antithetical to the Western one; on the contrary, we see Russia as part of a continuum with the West and in a permanent mirror game with it. What was happening in Russia before the war was deeply inscribed into broader global trends that can also be observed in the West. Distrust of the post–World War II global order and established institutions, doubts about the direction taken by the world economy and the processes of globalization, and the rise of conservative values and suspicion of some elements of the liberal system were not unique to Russia; they could also be found in Western societies. The decision to launch the war has partly broken these ideological affinities, but Moscow's voice continues to resonate in the Global South, and its links with Europe are not totally broken.

While this unjustifiable war is the full and sole responsibility of the Russian leadership, the strategic deadlock that preceded it was a cocreation of both the West and Russia. The difficulty of assessing the relationship between that deadlock and the war—that is, could the war have been avoided, or was it that the deadlock was inescapably leading to a military conflict?—is largely based on value judgments and has a normative character. Indeed, the Western view of Russia depends on how each observer looks at their own society. The most vocal critics of Russia are often convinced of the correctness of the Western system and its status as an indisputable international standard, and they read the war as the battle between good and evil, between the forces of light and the forces of darkness. Those with some reservations about the Western model are more nuanced in their assessment of responsibilities and their reading of the war's ultimate ends.

In addition, analysis of Russia's stance is often focused on internal determinants—mostly Putin's personality and KGB background—as if tracing a natural and predestined path, without regard to influential external events that have arguably caused changes to the Russian position. But Russia's path has not been entirely predetermined as though it were written in the DNA of the Putin regime; it resulted from three decades of interaction between Russia and the world, in particular with the West. This calls into question the ideological continuity of the Putin regime and its internal logic. For a long time, the regime was based on an implicit social contract with the population that was continuously renegotiated and limited the leadership's options. The Kremlin was on a permanent quest to draw inspiration from, and co-opt, grassroots trends, and there were many bottom-up dynamics that foreign observers typically did not see. Moreover, the internal configuration of the regime was closer to a plural conglomerate of opinions and ad hoc improvisations rather than a uniform, cohesive group with rigid ideological boundaries. This ad hoc equilibrium has been dramatically shaken by the war and is now more repressive than co-opting, more top-down than bottom-up, with less internal diversity, yet it does not, for now, fit the definition of a totalitarian regime.

While the decision to go to war is often presented as Putin's alone, it may seem counterintuitive to state that one should stop being excessively focused on getting inside "Putin's mind." But Russia is indeed much more than its president, even in wartime, and there is a paradoxical society behind it. Russians—both the ruling elites and a large part of the population—maintain a paranoid relationship with the massive opening that has taken place over the last three decades. This mixture of fascination and fear—interest in, and incomprehension of, the world around them—has resulted in contradictory realities. Before the war, Russian elites were sending their children to the West to study, live, and obtain quality medical care, yet they were criticizing Western lifestyles and behavior. While attracted by autarkic principles, the Russian economy was a genuinely globalized one, interacting especially with Western countries and firms, selling raw materials in exchange for technologies. The decoupling from the West that resulted from the war may have cut that relationship but did not transform Russia into a new North Korea: the country remains wide open to the Global South.

The list of Russia's ambivalences is long. One of them is to see the Russian leadership solely through the Soviet prism while several central points of Putin's policies—such as the defense of a handful of neighboring states that are under Russian influence or neutralized, Moscow's leading role in a crusade for traditional values in the face of a "decadent" West, and its global outreach—cannot be evaluated without highlighting historical continuities that go back long before the Soviet regime and have their roots in the Tsarist period. More importantly, while Russia has faced, even before the war, an undeniable authoritarian streak in the economic, social, and cultural realms, it has also accelerated neoliberal practices far removed from the Soviet model. Many of Russia's paradoxes and ambivalences are the result of precisely this openness to the world and of Russia's maladaptation to what it interprets as its integration into a globalized system.

The decision to go to war has transformed Russia's trajectory both domestically and internationally. It has shed light on an accumulation of miscalculations about the state of the Russian Army in terms of firepower, coordination, logistics, and morale; about the capacity of the Ukrainian Army and society to resist; and about the West's political unity and support for Ukraine. But it has also confirmed Russia's multiple forms of resilience, which include the regime's stability and unity (even if shaken), the population's support (even if by fear), and the capacity of the economy to cope with the sanctions. Writing this second edition of the book at a time when the war continues to rage with no victory in sight for either side, nor even with prospects for ceasefire conditions, is a perilous exercise. But a comprehensive analysis of Russia's trajectory over the last three decades, as well as of its interaction with the rest of the world and especially the West, remains the only possible approach to capturing the systemic causes of this war—and for mapping a way out.

## NOTES

1. John Mearsheimer, "Why the Ukraine Crisis Is the West's Fault," *Foreign Affairs*, September 2014, https://www.foreignaffairs.com/articles/russia-fsu/2014-08-18/why-ukraine-crisis-west-s-fault.

2. Stendhal, to Félix Faure, August 24, 1812.

3. Philip Rucker, "Hillary Clinton Says Putin's Actions Are Like 'What Hitler Did Back in the '30s,'" *Washington Post*, March 5, 2014, https://www.washingtonpost.com/news/post-politics/wp/2014/03/05/hillary-clinton-says-putins-action-are-like-what-hitler-did-back-in-the-30s.

4. "Third Rome" refers to the Russian Orthodox political-religious idea that the collapse of Rome as the first center of Christendom marked the end of the ancient world, followed by the collapse of Byzantium marking the end of the medieval world, leaving Muscovy as Christendom's heir in the modern era.

# 1

# Territorial Fatigue

## *External Borders Challenged and Domestic Development Unbalanced*

Moscow and the city of Peter,[1] and the city of Constantine—
Here are the sacred capitals of the Russian royalty . . .
But where is its limit? Where are its borders—
To the north, east, south, and west?
In times to come, fate will be revealed . . .
Seven internal seas and seven great rivers . . .
From the Nile to the Neva, from Elbe to China,
From the Volga to the Euphrates, from the Ganges to the
Danube . . .
Such is the Russian empire. . . . And it will not pass through the
centuries,
The Spirit foretold it, Daniel prophesied it.

—Fyodor Tyutchev, 1848

In an immense country of some 17,098,246 square kilometers (6,601,670 square miles),[2] Russia's territorial malady tends to be underestimated. To paraphrase the pioneering Soviet documentary film and newsreel director Dziga Vertov, Russia is a veritable continent unto itself, accounting for one-eighth of the world's habitable landmass, and should be sufficient for its inhabitants. However, the annexation of Crimea, following a hastily organized referendum on March 16, 2014, and then the full-scale military invasion of Ukraine launched on February 24, 2022, confirmed that Russia's leadership has not accepted—or did accept and then changed its mind about—the borders that were agreed upon when the Soviet Union disintegrated in late December 1991.

For the third time in less than fifteen years, after recognizing the independence of Georgia's secessionist regions of Abkhazia and South Ossetia in

7

2008 and annexing Crimea in 2014, a Russian president reneged on Boris Yeltsin's commitment (the Alma-Ata Declaration of December 26, 1991) to respect the territorial integrity and inviolability of state borders following the breakup of the Soviet Union.

Yet these difficulties in accepting post-Soviet borders are intimately correlated to other inward-looking concerns about Russia's territorial integrity, its regional development, and the connectedness of its disparate regions. Although Russian public opinion almost unanimously applauded the Federation's annexation of Crimea, the country was already having great difficulty managing its own sprawling territory. Whole regions of Russia are practically unpopulated, especially in rural areas, Siberia, and the Far East, to the point that a bevy of specialists has become obsessed with the problem of maintaining national territorial integrity. The space Russians actually occupy is shrinking for the first time in about five centuries, further underscoring the symptoms of this territorial malady.

## RUSSIA, A STATE WITH NO FINALIZED BORDERS?

For some of its elites, Russia can only be imperial. Nataliya Narochnitskaya, a herald of a politicized reading of Russian Orthodoxy, very early summarized this point of view: "Russia is inconceivable outside of imperial thinking. It can only be an empire. We must have a grand policy, a great national idea—otherwise we cannot be aware of our national interests. We will not understand why it is necessary to have navigable rivers and harbors that do not freeze."[3] Speaking about the annexation of Ukrainian territories in September 2022, Vladimir Putin compared himself with Emperor Peter the Great, presented as a great unifier of Russian lands, saying "[He] waged the Great Northern War for 21 years. It might seem that he was at war with Sweden, he took something from them. He did not take anything from them, he returned what was Russia's."[4]

Already in the 1990s, former national security advisor to Jimmy Carter, Zbigniew Brzezinski, declared that "without Ukraine, Russia ceases to be an empire, but with Ukraine suborned and then subordinated, Russia automatically becomes an empire."[5] But what is an empire without domination of the national core's margins? And what is core, what is periphery? Is Tuva, a small republic near Mongolia that joined the Soviet Union only in 1944, "core" for Russia because it is part of the Russian Federation? And is Ukraine, whose capital Kyiv is "the mother of Russian cities," as every Russian schoolchild learns, a periphery because it was a separate Soviet republic that became independent in 1991? What are legally core and periphery do not always fit Russia's imagination, in which Kiyv matters more than Tuva.

And how can the empire be defined in a continental space without obvious natural boundaries? "From the Volga to the Euphrates, from the Ganges to the Danube": these forgotten words of the Russian poet and diplomat Fyodor Tyutchev (1803–1873) sound familiar today, as two states with renewed geostrategic power, Russia and China, question the limits of their territories. To the west, Moscow no longer accepts the loss of its European sphere of influence, which occurred at its greatest moment of weakness: at the end of the 1980s and in the early 1990s. To the east, Beijing seeks to impose its Nine-Dash Line maritime claims over most of the South China Sea[6] upon its neighbors Vietnam, Malaysia, Brunei, the Philippines, and especially Taiwan. The imperial strategic parallels shared between these two authoritarian partners aimed at destabilizing portions of neighboring states' territorial rights are hard to miss.

## A Postimperial Syndrome

The feeling of being contested on its periphery makes Russia anxious. In turn, its actions have provoked anxiety in others, primarily in neighboring former Soviet republics with significant ethnic Russian or Russian-speaking populations, such as the Baltic states, Belarus, Ukraine, and, to a lesser extent, Kazakhstan, or even those with non-Russian minorities, such as Georgia. The defense of these populations served as the pretext for Russia's annexation of the Crimean Peninsula in 2014 and the full-scale invasion of Ukraine in 2022. Yet some national elites—in Estonia and Latvia, for example—did not wait for the two phases of the Russo-Ukrainian War to paint Russian ethnic minorities as a "fifth column" that could be mobilized by Moscow. A newly powerful Russia, resurgent after decades of weakness, also concerns Western leaders, who, even while intervening around the world, reject the application of power according to what they see as a Monroe Doctrine or Yalta-type sphere of influence.

In the aftermath of the December 1991 accords that ended the Soviet Union and created the Commonwealth of Independent States (CIS), a new expression appeared in Russian media and political discourse: the "near abroad" (*blizhnee zarubezh'e*).[7] Andrei Kozyrev, foreign minister under Boris Yeltsin, and Andranik Migranian, one of Yeltsin's advisers, popularized (and possibly even invented) the term, which refers to the other former Soviet republics. Adopted by most Russian authors as well as many Western commentators, the near abroad was quickly interpreted by the West as an indicator of Russia's neo-imperialist thinking.

By classifying the newly independent states separately from other foreign countries, or the "far abroad" (*dal'nee zarubezh'e*), Russian leaders clearly indicated the existence of a different category of states over which Moscow would reserve a particular role for itself. Yeltsin put forward this idea at the highest level. "Russia," he wrote in 1992, "located at the juncture of Europe and Asia, is obligated to finally fulfill its unique historical mission, that is, to become a link connecting East and West. The resolution of this task presumes two essential conditions: assuring stability within the former Soviet Union and building constructive relations with the other states to strengthen international security."[8]

The minister of foreign affairs and many of his advisers further specified Russia's new strategy. One of the most illuminating texts is a note prepared after a Ministry of Foreign Affairs meeting in 1992:

> As the internationally recognized heir of the Soviet Union, the Russian Federation must base its foreign policy on a doctrine that declares the geopolitical space of the former Soviet Union to be its vital sphere of interest (like the "Monroe Doctrine" of the United States in Latin America); it must obtain international recognition of its role as the guarantor of political and military stability in the entire former Soviet territory.[9]

Between 1992 and 1995, during the many summits that brought together the presidents of all twelve CIS states (the three Baltic states never joined the new organization), Russian leaders offered a wide range of treaties to realize their design of this new community. It became clear that Yeltsin, though treading resolutely down the path of pro-Western liberal reforms, had no intention of giving up his country's role in the post-Soviet space. Moscow, for instance, proposed the creation of a collective force for peacekeeping and a joint mechanism controlling all CIS airspace, as well as the organization of an integrated defense community, a sort of eastern North Atlantic Treaty Organization (NATO). More troublingly, Russian leaders suggested that the twelve CIS states should be regarded as a unique space, with external borders to be guarded and defended by a common force under a single command, and that this same space should also become a wider free trade area. It was obvious to all the partners that these proposals involved keeping Russian border guards in all the signatory states and that the command of these forces and organizations would in large part be given to Russian officers, who had the most training in these functions. Moreover, in several countries (Armenia, Belarus, Kazakhstan, Kyrgyzstan, and Ukraine), Russia did everything possible to maintain control of its military and naval bases.

Even beyond Russia's legitimate strategic interest, it was well understood that these bases carried strong symbolic weight (particularly the Crimean port of Sevastopol and the Baikonur Cosmodrome in Kazakhstan) and embodied Russia's broader influence over its neighbors.[10] In outlining what would become the foundation of their foreign policy in the near abroad, Russian leaders tried to use the legacies of the collapse of the Soviet Union to their advantage. Nine of the fifteen new states are landlocked; in other words, they have no direct access to open seas. In addition to the five Central Asian states, this is true of Armenia and Azerbaijan (since the Caspian Sea is not connected to any ocean), Belarus, and Moldova.[11]

As part of imperial and Soviet policy, most major communication routes, roads, railways, and tunnels were directed toward Russia and its capital cities, Moscow and St. Petersburg/Leningrad. This organization of networks inherited from the Tsarist and Soviet past has given modern Russia leverage in orienting the trade policies of its newly independent neighbors. However, this is a double-edged sword in the case of oil and gas: while several countries (notably Kazakhstan and Turkmenistan) depend on Russia as a transit route for their exports, Russia was long dependent on third countries (the Baltic states and Ukraine) for its deliveries to the European Union (EU)—until it completed the infrastructure necessary to bypass them and reach European markets directly.

Such attempts by the Russian leadership to rearrange the former Soviet space in its favor have faced strong resistance. Many of the new states have sought all possible means of disengaging from what they see as imperial legacies: Uzbekistan, Turkmenistan, Azerbaijan, Georgia, Moldova, and Ukraine were all quick to oppose the presence of Russian guards on their borders. They have found significant support from their new Western partners. Systematically and repeatedly, US diplomats in CIS capitals have reasserted that the organization is useless and a naked tool of Russian policy.

The approach that successive Russian presidents have taken to the territorial conflicts that have arisen in the post-Soviet space only substantiates these fears. Although these conflicts draw on factors that are internal and have often existed since the creation of the Soviet Union, it is obvious that, after 1991, when these issues were exacerbated and became local wars, Moscow systematically intervened to exploit them and gain leverage over its neighbors.[12] In some cases, support for breakaway regions was designed to eliminate the risk of these states' accession to NATO or the EU, since those organizations' statutes require that any territorial dispute be settled before accession. In other places, as in the disputed Nagorno-Karabakh region, Moscow wanted to preserve its sphere of influence so that new actors, in this case Turkey, did not break Russia's strategic monopoly over the Caucasus, which had been well established ever since the 1920s.

Moscow's interventions in this near abroad vary depending on the local situation and Russian interests, but all reflect a strategy of realpolitik.[13] While supporting the Armenians in their dispute with the Azerbaijanis in Nagorno-Karabakh, the Kremlin has maintained an ambiguous neutrality to preserve its interest in Baku, the Azerbaijani capital located on the western

Caspian seashore in an area rich in oil and gas. By supporting the secessionist movements of Transnistria in Moldova, or Abkhazia and South Ossetia in
Georgia, Moscow seeks to weaken states that challenge its geopolitical tutelage. The annexation of Crimea in 2014 and then of other occupied regions
of eastern Ukraine in 2022 reflect an old feeling of ethnic irredentism or
ethnic imperialism: territories populated by Russians, or having belonged at
some point in time to Russia, must return to it. Conversely, as seen during
the political crises in Belarus (in 2020) or in Kazakhstan (January 2022), in
former Soviet states that still accept its tutelage, Moscow supports the powers
that be. For the others, the Kremlin foments already existing local grievances
to weaken reluctant elites and, in the specific case of Ukraine, is ready to go
to war to overthrow them.

## Russia's Ukrainian Obsession

Ukraine occupies a special place in the mind of the Russian elites and
Vladimir Putin himself. The country lies in a very special geographical space,
at the crossroads of two strategic axes, one north–south along the old trade
route between the Baltic and the Black Seas, the other east–west linking
Europe and Russia along the pathways of many past invasions. Crimea and
its port in Sevastopol are crucial for controlling the Black Sea. In this respect,
Russian authorities agree with the words of Brzezinski quoted above, which
justify, according to them, the establishment of a red line on the possibility of
Ukraine's rapprochement with NATO.

But there are more than just geopolitical considerations at play. In July
2021 (just after his meeting with US president Joe Biden in Geneva on June
16), Putin released an astonishing article titled, "On the Historical Unity
of Russians and Ukrainians."[14] Retracing in his own way to the history of
this ancient relationship, the Russian president insisted that the two peoples
were one and the same. According to him, it was Soviet national policy that
split the "large Russian nation, a triune people comprising Velikorussians
(Russians), Malorussians (Ukrainians) and Belorussians." Modern Ukraine
would be entirely the "product of the Soviet era . . . shaped—for a significant
part—on the lands of historical Russia," which was thus stripped of one of
its territories. The entire text reflects one of the deep-rooted trends in Russian
political thought since the demise of the USSR in 1991, namely the belief in
an East Slavic unity that cannot be broken.

And indeed, for two centuries, a large part of the Russian elite has considered Ukrainian territories as part of a whole, that of Great Russia. The Nobel
Prize laureate in Literature, Alexander Solzhenitsyn, had taken up this thesis
in his own way by proposing to integrate Russia, Ukraine, Belarus, and even
the north of Kazakhstan into a single state: the "Union of Russia."[15] A field of

polemics situates Moscow and Kyiv in opposition to one another on the very origins of the Russian state and the existence of a Ukrainian nation. Until the 1990s, this question had almost always been approached from the point of view of the dominant power, Tsarist and then Soviet.

This could be the banal statement of a colonial state in permanent expansion, which imposes its narrative for the purpose of integrating its new conquests. But in this case, nothing is really banal because, since at least the nineteenth century, Kyiv has occupied a unique place in Russian historiography. It is presented as the "mother of all Russian cities" and the territory surrounding it is said to be the space of the origins of the Russian state proper, the ancient *Rus,*' before the Tatar-Mongol invasions subjugated it, forcing the Orthodox metropolitan to take refuge further north, first in Vladimir and then in Moscow in the fourteenth century.

The controversy has never ceased over the term *Rus,*' translated either as Russia (which supports the thesis associating it with today's Russia) or as Ruthenia (which distances it from today's Russia). The debate also concerns the reality of this first East Slavic state, founded by Scandinavian chiefs, the Varangians, who would have mixed with the indigenous Slavic peoples occupying these vast southern steppes. For the Russians—and Putin has repeated this assertion several times—Rus' is indeed the origin of a single state, of a single people that subsequently broke up (the three components of the "triune people") and that he proposes to reconstitute, by force of arms if necessary. For the Ukrainians, on the other hand, this ancient Rus' is a specific construction that extends over a territory other than Russia and cannot be confused with it.[16]

For Putin, the desire to bring Ukraine back under Moscow's tutelage has become a kind of obsession. In the tradition of Peter the Great and Catherine the Great, Putin sees himself becoming "Vladimir the Gatherer of Russian Lands," starting with the reintegration of Ukraine. When announcing the beginning of his "special military operation" at dawn on February 24, 2022, he mixed strategic and (erroneous) historical arguments.[17]

The first justification presented was "the eastward expansion of NATO, which is moving its military infrastructure ever closer to the Russian border." According to Putin, the North Atlantic Alliance is creating, in the historical lands of Russia, a "hostile 'anti-Russia'" that is "fully controlled from the outside" and supports an ultranationalist and neo-Nazi power in Ukraine. Hence the need to organize a form of preventive war against the forces that would be ready to attack Russia (he even speaks of a "genocide of the millions of people who live there and who pinned their hopes on Russia"). He then evokes the treaty of assistance that links his country to the two self-proclaimed People's Republics of Donetsk and Luhansk (the DNR and LNR, respectively), which he has just recognized. The ultimate goal of the special military operation, "to demilitarize and denazify Ukraine," implies that Moscow will overthrow the government in Kyiv and replace it with a puppet regime subservient to Russia.

To justify the war, the highest dignitaries of the regime, such as current deputy chairman of the security council and former president Dmitri Medvedev, Roscosmos director general Dmitri Rogozin, and Foreign Minister Sergey Lavrov, amplified calls on Russian television and social media networks to eliminate all the Ukrainian resistance fighters, whom they called "bastards, degenerates,"[18] or Banderovites.[19]

In a violent article published by the official news agency RIA Novosti in April, just after the revelations of Russian war crimes committed in the Ukrainian city of Bucha, the journalist Timofei Sergeitsev proposed establishing a reign of terror in Ukraine aimed at eliminating all opponents. Sergeitsev called for the suppression of the very name of Ukraine once its territory is occupied and for its "de-ukrainization," since it is "impossible for Ukraine to exist as a nation-state."[20] On November 23, Piotr Tolstoy, vice president of the Duma and a descendant of the novelist, did not hesitate to state on French television, "Russia is not targeting the civilian population of Ukraine; it is targeting its infrastructure. The infrastructure of Ukraine will be demolished and Ukraine will be sent back to the eighteenth century."[21] This violence, both in action and in words, shows that Russia's toolkit of influence has dramatically evolved over the last three decades.

## Will Russia's Borders Ever Be Stabilized?

But beyond the war in Ukraine, all of Russia's borders have become uncertain. According to the 1991 agreement that created the CIS, the new Russian Federation inherited some 60,000 kilometers (37,282 miles) of borders from the RSFSR (Russian Soviet Federative Socialist Republic), of which approximately 40,000 kilometers (24,855 miles) are maritime (see map 1.1). This legacy has sometimes proven problematic, as questions concerning the demarcation of borders with other former Soviet republics, in addition to a number of outstanding disputes with other neighbors, were never settled during the Soviet period. Although Putin managed—as a result of Yeltsin's efforts—to resolve many of these disputes, others appear to reflect the ambiguities of Russia's exercise of power.

The most notable progress was made in the final demarcation of the Russian–Chinese border along the Amur River. In May 1991, when Moscow finally recognized the international rule that makes the thalweg line (the main channel) the decisive factor, Russia surrendered a number of islands to China, ending a feud that had even turned bloody in 1969. In returning about 340 square kilometers of islands, including a part of the Bolshoi Ussuriiskii

Commonwealth of Independent States (CIS)

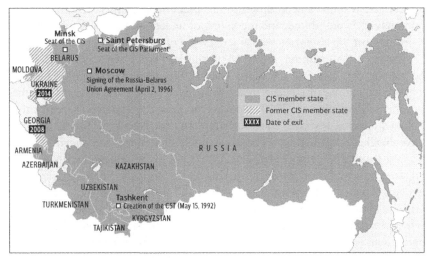

Map 1.1: Commonwealth of Independent States (CIS).

Island across from the border city of Khabarovsk, to China in 2004 (over the objections of regional elites), Putin concluded the negotiations that Mikhail Gorbachev had begun.[22] Officially, there are no more territorial disputes between the two neighbors, although the Chinese still note on many maps that parts of the Russian Far East—and of Central Asia—were under their rule in different eras.

Similarly, in 2010, there was a surprise settlement with Norway of a difficult border dispute in the Barents Sea, in an area deemed to be rich in fish and hydrocarbons.[23] The compromise demonstrates that Moscow can make concessions when it sees fit. In this case, the two countries are a step ahead on the future division of the Arctic, which is a strategic and disputed area. Even if the common border does not reach to the North Pole—as the Russians claim it does—the maps added in the appendix of the agreement show that the latitude of the agreed border goes a long way in this direction.

The same pragmatic attitude can be found in Russia's approach to maritime boundaries in the Caspian Sea. On one side, with two bilateral treaties, Moscow set its maritime borders with Azerbaijan (an area then thought to lack hydrocarbons) and Kazakhstan (with agreements to share neighboring deposits). Yet on the far side, Russia and Iran long blocked negotiations on the Caspian Sea's status in order to hamper the construction of oil and gas pipelines between both of its shores.[24] It was only in 2018, at the Aktau summit on Kazakhstan's Caspian seashore, that the region's five littoral states signed a convention determining the international body of water's hybrid status as both a lake and a sea. The littoral states share and apportion the aquatic and underwater resources according to their predefined sectors, access by third-party navies is prohibited, and the laying of underwater pipes is subject to the agreement of the countries whose territory such pipes must cross.[25]

Among the remaining unsolved territorial issues with non-post-Soviet neighbors, one can find the Kuril Islands, the dispute over which has prevented the signing of a peace treaty with Japan since 1945. The visit of then president Medvedev in 2010 and several Japanese statements reaffirming Tokyo's sovereignty over the four southernmost islands in the archipelago have blocked negotiations. The annexation of Crimea and the imposition of anti-Russian sanctions by Japan following the full-scale invasion of Ukraine now make any progress on this matter unlikely. Some Russian leaders have taken a dim view of any such compromise, just as they continue to criticize the US–Soviet delimitation of the Bering Strait, signed by Eduard Shevardnadze in 1990, as giving too much to the Americans. The Russian parliament has never ratified this treaty, but it functions as an ad hoc border, and both sides have agreed on joint management of fisheries.[26]

The demarcation of borders with post-Soviet neighbors also held many surprises. The borders between Soviet republics had previously been only administrative, and many towns and villages sat on lines that had simply never meant anything. With independence, several major Russian rail lines suddenly found themselves on foreign territory—parts of the famous Trans-Siberian Railway, for instance, crossed into Kazakhstan—which implied the need for special transit arrangements. Although border demarcation has not been a particular problem with Kazakhstan or Belarus, this is not the case everywhere.

Newly independent Estonia and Latvia tried to reclaim some districts that had been forcibly attached to the Russian Soviet Federative Socialist Republic (RSFSR) by Stalin in 1945, invoking treaties signed in 1920 with Bolshevik Russia that assigned the areas to them. The prospect of joining the EU and NATO deterred them from reviving these conflicts, but the Russian Duma (the lower house of the legislature) delayed the ratification of new border agreements, thus exerting leverage over their final outcomes.[27] In these two countries, the war in Ukraine has reignited fears of the Russian threat as well as doubts regarding the loyalty of their important Russian diasporas, sometimes seen as a fifth column. A BBC docufiction program had even taken the Russian minorities in the Baltic states as the point of departure for a fictional World War III.[28]

In negotiations with Azerbaijan, Russia's pragmatic interests likewise prevailed, and the clarification of the boundary along the Samur River saw Moscow surrender two enclaves south of it, whose Lezgin populations were resettled to the neighboring Russian region of Dagestan.[29] Yet the issue of water use remains unresolved, as Moscow has reserved the right to increase its quota. Conversely, disputes with Georgia and Ukraine led to a series of armed conflicts in which Russia was directly involved.

In Abkhazia and South Ossetia, Moscow has continued, ever since Yeltsin's presidency, to support the claims of local secessionist movements (often by drawing parallels with Kosovo's independence being supported by many Western countries)[30] and thereby weakening successive Georgian governments. Tbilisi's discriminatory policies toward national minorities contributed to increasing tensions, but the deadly escalation that led to the five-day war launched by Georgian president Mikheil Saakashvili on August 8, 2008, would not have reached the magnitude it did without constant pressure from Moscow.[31] In Ukraine, after the flight of pro-Kremlin president Viktor Yanukovich and a change of power in Kyiv, the Russian military decisively intervened in Crimea to help the organization of the March 2014 annexation referendum and supported secessionist warlords in Ukraine's eastern Donbas region.

Russia's full-scale invasion of Ukraine on February 24, 2022, constituted a new step in the breaking of the commitments made by Yeltsin in 1991. Yet territorial conquest was not the first goal of the "special military operation." In his speech announcing it, Putin declared, "It is not our plan to occupy Ukrainian territory."[32] And indeed the main goal seems to have been to overthrow Ukrainian president Volodymyr Zelenskyy's government and replace it with a vassal regime. But the plans of the Russian General Staff—a lightning victory based on the hypothesis of a neutral or even favorable reception on the part of the Ukrainian people and the routing of the Ukrainian Army and Zelenskyy's government—were quickly shown to be inoperative.

Unable to bring about this regime change, Russia then moved toward territorial conquest. Putin organized four referendums in September 2022 with the aim of annexing new regions of eastern Ukraine (Luhansk, Donetsk, Zaporizhzhia, and Kherson) as a way of putting them under the same strategic protection (potentially nuclear) as the rest of Russia's territories. However, Russia did not manage to secure them; a few weeks after their "annexation," the city of Kherson was taken back by the Ukrainians. Moreover, Ukrainian forces have been able to attack deep into Russian territory, striking military bases in the Belgorod, Kursk, and Saratov regions and up to Moscow and organizing an attack against the highly symbolic Crimean Bridge linking the peninsula to Russia across the Kerch Strait between the Black Sea and the Sea of Azov.

As for the Russian strategy of contesting post-Soviet borders, Russian officials' justifications have varied, from the right of popular self-determination, to the defense of Russians and Russian-speakers abroad as a strategic interest. Concerning Crimea, Putin added a religious factor: the sanctity of this region as the place where the Russian people were baptized into Orthodoxy.[33] Russia's actions thus confirm the impression of a state that has not yet finished defining its own territory. Yet one may wonder if conquering lost territories has really been a driver of Russia's strategies toward its post-Soviet neighbors: Moscow has always given preference to political control over its neighbors, as in the former socialist bloc, and has resorted to territorial aggression only once it lost political control.

For a long time, Crimea's annexation was seen as an exception, but Putin's language on Ukraine's illegitimacy as an independent nation and state, together with the September 2022 annexations, shows that territorial conquest has now become part of Russia's portfolio of actions. Such a position of challenging the borders inherited from the Soviet Union is not without risk for Russia itself. Were there to be a sustained weakening of Moscow, might some republics in the North Caucasus claim independence, or might other neighbors, such as China, make their own territorial demands?

## A FEDERATION SICK OF ITS HYPERCENTRALISM

### The Paradoxes of a Shrinking Space

While Russia has been expanding its territory at the expense of Ukraine, whole sections of its own space lie abandoned, stirring up major anxieties in public opinion. For decades, a number of regions have been losing population. This phenomenon stems from several factors.

The first is the general demographic crisis, which saw the country's population decline between 1993 and 2010, and once again from 2019 onward, as will be discussed in chapter 2. This decline is uneven across regions and particularly affects the more northern and eastern parts of the country, where natural and economic conditions are toughest. These areas were colonized by methods that combined forced resettlement and deportation (Tsarist exile camps and then the GULAG), as well as economic incentives. A second decisive factor was the end of the Soviet planned system that, with the exception of a few sectors such as hydrocarbons, weakened the benefits (bonuses, wage supplements, etc.) that for decades had allowed the government to attract pioneering young people to those frontiers. The near demise of benefits at the same time as prices spiked (e.g., for transportation, heating, and food) drove a mass exodus to other parts of the country.

In the Russian Far East, depopulation is pervasive (see map 1.2.). This vast area, which covers 36 percent of the country's territory, has lost 23 percent of its population since 1990. Chukotka, the region bordering the Bering Strait across from Alaska, has lost nearly 70 percent. The neighboring Magadan

Regional net migration rate in Russia, 2021.

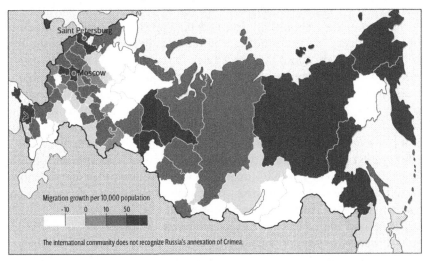

**Map 1.2: Regional net migration rates in Russia, 2021.** *Source: Ezhegodnik* **2022, tab 4.2.**

oblast (region), on the northwest shore of the Sea of Okhotsk, has lost 65 percent, and the Kamchatka Peninsula, which separates that sea from the open Pacific, has lost over 39 percent. Young and old, and especially ethnic Russians, have left these places en masse to return to the European part of the country. In some cities, whole neighborhoods have been drained of signs of life.

This phenomenon can even be found in Primorskii krai along the Sea of Japan (down 17 percent), which remains the most favored region in the Far East; the Pacific port city of Vladivostok, the provincial capital, has lost 6.5 percent of its population. This situation is even more paradoxical given that the Asia-Pacific region has become one of the most dynamic in the world today. This trend, which slowed but continued after 2015, is all the more worrisome to the authorities because the Far Eastern Federal District, with an average population density of only 1.1 inhabitants per square kilometer, is next door to northern China, where population densities and urban dynamism are much higher. This situation has revived ancient fears of the "yellow peril," a Chinese invasion,[34] even if the topic has now disappeared from Russia's public space, given the official honeymoon with Beijing.

Another, less visible, phenomenon reinforces these territorial apprehensions: the bleeding of rural northern Russia, the so-called non-black-soil areas—a name that contrasts these areas to the southern regions, known as Black Earth (*chernozem*) for their rich soil. This is not a new phenomenon:

it appeared as early as the 1960s, as a result of Soviet premier Nikita Khrushchev's disastrous agricultural policies. Young people, then a large part of the working-age population, left underequipped rural areas in search of jobs and a better life in the cities or in the so-called Virgin Lands (the vast pastures in northern Kazakhstan reclaimed for cultivation in the late 1950s).

Since 1991, this depopulation trend has continued at a slower pace but in a way that is affecting more regions in the Ural Mountains, and in Siberia to their east. This has two major consequences. The first is the narrowing of inhabited space, a veritable "shrinking skin" that sees whole villages disappear (wooden houses in the north, if they are not inhabited, rot in place within a few years) or their population reduced to a few elders. The 2021 census found that 59,000 of 153,000 Russian villages had fewer than ten permanent inhabitants; in non-black-soil areas, 70 percent of villages had fewer than one hundred residents, most of whom were beyond working age.[35]

The second consequence is the abandonment of arable land. In many districts, the abandonment of unused gardens and meadows has allowed the forest to reclaim these areas after centuries of clearing. The total sown area fell by 36 percent between 1990 and 2012, from 118 million hectares to 76 million, before beginning a slow recovery that reached 79.9 million hectares in 2020.[36] (Yet one should note that even if the total sown area has shrunk, Russia's agricultural production has increased since last decade thanks to new production methods, state incentives, and a deep institutional reorganization, see chapter 5).

The phenomenon of a shrinking populated space is not limited to the northernmost areas and the Far East; it also affects the European part of the country, including along the Moscow–St. Petersburg corridor. The Pskov and Novgorod oblasts, which lie between Russia's two largest cities, have lost 27 percent and 21 percent of their populations, respectively, since 1989. Other regions are facing a depopulation crisis due to the decline of one-industry towns (*monogorod* in Russian) that owed their growth to a single factory or industrial group. Various initiatives have been proposed to curb these trends by directing immigrants to these areas. However, most of them aspire to settle in the big cities, where they can find jobs and live in a multicultural environment more easily than in historic rural Russia.

Of course, these forms of territorial abandonment do not all have the same significance. In the European part of the country, they reflect economic and demographic adaptation crises, which also exist elsewhere: the North American continent abounds in "shrinking cities," too, and *Paris and the French Desert* was the title of a 1947 book by geographer Jean-François Gravier, who denounced the extreme monopoly of that city over French resources. Yet in the Russian Far East, depopulation trends are likely to undermine the very territorial integrity of the state and have pushed the government to take urgent measures, such as an ambitious program that offers one hectare of land to any new homesteader.[37] The program was sufficiently successful (with 63,000 hectares distributed) for the government to apply it to Arctic regions too.[38] The government's efforts to address territorial issues notwithstanding, the spatial fragility of the Russian Federation should not be underestimated.

## Issues and Taboos of Russia's Internal "Colonialism"

In a book devoted to the post-Soviet space, the famous Russian geographer Vladimir Kagansky wrote,

> An important element of a region is its coherence, the connections of its territory. The Russian Federation is much less "connected" than each of its parts. Numerous nodal regions intersect on its territory, but none match the Federation in its entirety. The preservation of Russia as a state entity requires large ongoing efforts. The opening of the country has made clear the attraction of a large part of its territory to the outside.[39]

Kagansky points out several major elements that are fragility factors in the new Russian state. The first is the weakness of communication networks that cover the whole country. They are often fragmented and outdated. Russia's famous rail network does not cover entire regions of the country and still lacks high-speed trains outside the Moscow–St. Petersburg corridor. Roads are being improved, with a real effort being made to upgrade major federal roads, but the interregional network is still in its infancy, limited to a few sections radiating out of Moscow and surrounding a few large cities.

On main roads, there are still many deficiencies (no city bypasses, unpaved sections, dilapidated bridges and the like), and the thawing of permafrost (deep-frozen soil) in Siberia due to climate change will further complicate matters. Thus Russia's perennial road deficit remains a genuine handicap. Similar problems affect the air transportation network vital to numerous remote regions. Hundreds of local airports closed in the 1990s before a program to restore major regional airports was launched by Putin in the 2000s. Yet despite recent investments, whole areas are cut off from the rest of the country for part of the year or are poorly connected to it, limiting the mobility of people and goods.

One of the main legacies of Putin's terms in office has been his systematic attempt to address the main infrastructure gaps that the country inherited from the Soviet era. In 2009, he became president of the board of trustees of the Russian Geography Society, headed by none other than Sergei Shoigu (at that time the minister of emergency situations and, since 2012, the defense minister). Putin has thereby sought to personally participate in the symbolic mobilization of the Russian population around the natural potential and richness of the national territory. His role in protecting endangered species, from Siberian tigers to Baikal seals, is well known. But his highly publicized trip behind the wheel of a Lada on roads in the Far East in 2010 belongs to a different set of strategic concerns, those related to transportation and communication inside Russia's mainland.[40]

Over the course of his successive terms, a twofold strategy has been at work. On the domestic front, the aim was to modernize all transportation infrastructure. Significant emphasis has been placed on the large railway and road networks, as with the building of the first genuine highways and the first high-speed trains (the Sapsan, which travels from Moscow to St. Petersburg in five hours over 700 km/430 miles, has been operational since 2009). Less eye-catching, but just as essential, is the detailed work being done on the sore spots evoked above: to construct bypasses around the main cities, build or repair bridges over the country's main rivers, and upgrade the main airports to international standards.

At the same time, a particular effort is being made to reorganize the country's main export routes, as seen in the exceptional development of new Russian ports (e.g., Ust-Luga and Primorsk in the Baltic, Novorossiysk and Port Kavkaz on the Black Sea, and Nakhodka and Vanino on the Pacific Ocean); the emphasis placed on the use of the Northern Sea Route in the Arctic; and the way in which Moscow is trying to slot into the Chinese Belt and Road Initiative. Often unnoticed by Western experts, this focus on reinforcing the physical cohesion of Russian territory has been one of the major policy planks of Putin's presidencies.

Another major fragility factor is the enormous disparity between regions. As the heir, with minimal changes, to the administrative divisions of the Russian Soviet Republic, today's Russian Federation comprises eighty-five federal subjects—if we include the Republic of Crimea and the Federal City of Sevastopol, whose annexation in 2014 is not recognized by the international community, but not counting the four Ukrainian regions annexed in September 2022. There are forty-six oblasts (regions) and nine krais (territories), mainly populated by ethnic Russians. But as in the Soviet period, twenty-seven of these federal subjects are based on the presence of some important ethnic minority that gives them its name: twenty-two republics, four autonomous okrugs (districts), and one autonomous oblast. Three federal cities (Moscow, St. Petersburg, and Sevastopol) are also included in this asymmetric federal system.

As seen in tables 1.1 and 1.2, about 55 percent of the value of the country's total regional output is concentrated in the ten richest regions, while the ten

**Table 1.1.** Share of regions in Russia's federal output: Top ten most contributing regions (subjects), (% and million rubles), 2020

|  | Share of Russian GDP | Millions of rubles |
|---|---|---|
| Moscow city & Oblast | 26.77% | 25,122,063 |
| St. Petersburg city & Oblast | 6.90% | 6,481,845 |
| Autonomous Okrug Khanty Mansi | 3.57% | 3,353,302 |
| Autonomous Okrug Iamalo-Nenets | 2.95% | 2,768,191 |
| Krai Krasnoyarsk | 2.90% | 2,722,640 |
| Republic of Tatarstan | 2.80% | 2,633,912 |
| Krai Krasnodar | 2.79% | 2,616,754 |
| Sverdlovsk Oblast | 2.69% | 2,529,781 |
| Republic of Bashkortostan | 1.82% | 1,711,684 |
| Cheliabinsk Oblast | 1.72% | 1,615,149 |
| Total | 54.91% | |

*Source: Rossiiskii Ezhegodnik, 2022.*

**Table 1.2.** Share of regions in Russia's federal output: Bottom ten least-contributing regions (subjects), (% and million rubles), 2020

|  | Share of Russian GDP | Millions of rubles |
|---|---|---|
| Republic of North Ossetia | 0.19% | 186,122 |
| Republic of Kabardino-Balkaria | 0.19% | 183,027 |
| Republic of Adygea | 0.15% | 143,191 |
| Republic of Karachay-Cherkessia | 0.10% | 96,566 |
| Chukotka Autonomous Okrug | 0.10% | 94,884 |
| Republic of Kalmykia | 0.09% | 93,325 |
| Republic of Tuva | 0.08% | 82,810 |
| Republic of Ingushetia | 0.07% | 72,708 |
| Jewish Autonomous Oblast | 0.06% | 63,014 |
| Republic of Altay | 0.06% | 62,520 |
| **Total** | 1.09% | |

*Source: Rossiiskii Ezhegodnik, 2022.*

poorest produce about 1 percent. In 2019, the variation in GDP per capita among Russia's federal subjects ranged from 1.5 million rubles for the richest to 145,700 for the poorest (see tables 1.3 and 1.4). Moscow city and Moscow region, the two most attractive entities of the Federation, alone account for 26 percent of Russia's GDP. Most economic indicators, such as the volume of retail trade and average wages, corroborate these differences. Outside of Moscow and St. Petersburg, the privileged areas produce hydrocarbons or metals, are home to heavy industry, or serve as hubs for the food industry or the transit of hydrocarbons. Only one territory, Krasnodar, is economically "mixed," with intensive agriculture, a transit function (Novorossiysk), and the Black Sea Riviera (Sochi).

**Table 1.3. Russia's top twenty richest regions (subjects), (GDP per capita, in thousands of rubles), 2020**

| Russian average | 640 |
| --- | --- |
| Nenets Autonomous Okrug* | 5,206 |
| Iamalo-Nenets Autonomous Okrug* | 5,072 |
| Autonomous Okrug Chukotka* | 2,404 |
| Sakhalin* | 2,059 |
| Magadan* | 2,035 |
| Khanty-Mansi Autonomous Okrug* | 1,994 |
| Moscow city | 1,567 |
| Sakha Yakutia | 1,168 |
| Murmansk Oblast | 1,072 |
| St. Petersburg city | 971 |
| Krai Krasnoyarsk | 951 |
| Krai Kamchatka | 942 |
| Tiumen Oblast | 757 |
| Republic of Komis | 749 |
| Moscow Oblast | 684 |
| Republic of Tatarstan | 675 |
| Leningrad Oblast | 661 |
| Khabarovsk Krai | 658 |
| Belgorod Oblast | 646 |
| Irkutsk Oblast | 631 |

* The six top richest regions are sparsely populated and produce mineral resources.

*Source: Rossiiskii Ezhegodnik, 2022.*

Conversely, out of the current total of eighty-five constitutive entities, the twenty least prosperous regions include fourteen of the twenty-two national republics, almost all in the North Caucasus and Siberia, as well as typical Russian regions such as Stavoprol, Kostroma, and Ivanovo, which were hit hard by the industrial crisis following the collapse of the USSR and the decline of agriculture. The magnitude of these discrepancies is due to many factors, of course, with natural characteristics (remoteness, climate, and resources) playing a role. But the key lies in economic choices (such as the concentration on raw-material extractive industries) and especially in policy decisions.

Since the early twentieth century, Russia has had only two brief periods of relative decentralization—a very brief one under Khrushchev and a longer one between perestroika and the end of the Yeltsin presidency. The hypertrophy of Moscow, where an abnormally high share of investment, skilled management, and high-level students and researchers is concentrated, was initially due to political hypercentralization. This, in turn, had the effect of weakening regional cities and solidifying their subordinate role, which affected regional development overall.

**Table 1.4. Russia's bottom twenty poorest regions (subjects), (GDP per capita, in thousands of rubles), 2020**

| Russian average | 640 |
|---|---|
| Kostroma Oblast | 323 |
| Kirov Oblast | 315 |
| Republic of Adyghes | 309 |
| Stavropol Krai | 308 |
| Republic of Buryatia | 307 |
| Kurgan Oblast | 294 |
| Altay Krai | 291 |
| Republic of Mari El | 290 |
| Republic of Chouvachia | 287 |
| Republic of Altay | 283 |
| Republic of Sakha-Yakutia | 258 |
| Ivanovo Oblast | 274 |
| Republic of Crimea* | 270 |
| Republic of North Ossetia | 267 |
| Republic of Tuva | 251 |
| Republic of Dagestan | 239 |
| Republic of Kabardino-Balkaria | 210 |
| Republic of Karachaevo-Cherkessia | 207 |
| Republic of Chechnya | 171 |
| Republic of Ingushetia | 142 |

* The international community does not recognize Russia's annexation of Crimea.

*Source: Rossiiskii Ezhegodnik, 2022.*

Without going into detail, many surprising features can be observed that set the Russian case apart from most models worldwide. Border regions are often depressed, which is to say that the "border effect" (asymmetries in trade patterns that favor cities and industries located at the border with another country) does not play its usual dynamic role. Fearing that these particular regions might become autonomous by taking advantage of their role as foreign trade operators (one of the main sources of profit for the Russian economy), the government under Putin's presidencies has imposed significant administrative constraints on them that hinder their development.[41] This was, for instance, the case with the strengthening of state control on imports in the Primorie territory (Vladivostok) or changes in the functioning rules of the free economic zone of Kaliningrad. The same goes for many port cities that were long "closed" (i.e., that required access permissions) and remain unattractive today. Finally, too many medium-sized cities are underdeveloped compared to the Russian average and therefore cannot act as they should as points of support for their surrounding areas.

The magnitude of these differences is all the more worrying because they broadly correlate with ethnicity. Many of Russia's national republics are among the country's most disadvantaged regions, and this weighs on inter-ethnic relations and internal migration patterns. The economic and social developmental deficit of the North Caucasian republics is certainly one of the major drivers of the conflicts and tensions that have arisen there since the late 1980s. These deprived republics have also provided a significant propor-tion of the volunteer soldiers (attracted by the pay and sometimes pressured to join) for the Russian Army in the 2022 invasion of Ukraine, and it will be important to see how these populations react to the number of young men killed on the front. The largest protests reported after the decree on partial mobilization (September 2022) took place in Dagestan, one of the North Caucasian republics with a very young population and a high unemploy-ment rate.[42]

The ethnic factor does strengthen broader criticisms concerning the consol-idation of the hypercentralized policy, which is at the heart of debates on the relationship between the center (the federal government) and the periphery. For two decades, there have been a series of controversies and claims on the topics of regional autonomy and the center's inability to manage the country. Two sensitive issues are at the heart of this debate. The first is how the regions can benefit from their specific advantages—location, natural resources, and potential specializations—rather than seeing them captured by federal lobbies that tend to monopolize these assets. The second issue is the way the federal government tends to limit autonomy in regional decision-making in an array of important areas, from the distribution of tax revenues to the definition of school programs, even as it credits the regions with having greater expertise in these areas.

While this does not translate to the political level, some Russian oblast leaders have joined with republic leaders to denounce the hypertrophy of the center and the lack of economic, fiscal, and cultural autonomy in the peripheries, be they Russian (such as Siberia or Kaliningrad) or nonethnically Russian (such as the Volga and Caucasus). This debate recalls the writings of the "regionalists" of the late nineteenth century, such as the Siberian Nikolai Yadrintsev (1842–1894), who denounced Tsarist policy on the borders of the empire.[43] In 2010 and 2011, an important weekly, *Kommersant Vlast*,' pub-lished a series of surveys on the autonomist tendencies emerging in several regions, and since then, the topic has been regularly relaunched. The war has revived a long-held taboo, the idea of colonial exploitation of the periphery by the "Moscow hydra." Although it is not expressed in the form of politi-cal secessionism, as was the case in Chechnya in the 1990s, these debates point the finger at one of the serious weaknesses of the new Russian state: its overcentralization.

## An Overly Centralized Regional Policy

The Russian authorities are struggling to define a coherent regional strategy. This is apparent in the instability of the central government entity in charge of the matter. The Ministry of Regional Development was dissolved in 2014, and its prerogatives have been redistributed between the Ministries of Economic Development (*Minekonomrazvitiia*), Culture, and Justice. It would be wrong to say that the federal authorities are not interested in these issues. On the contrary, there has been a proliferation of consultation meetings and regional plans for economic and social regional development, a management approach typical of the Soviet era.

Obviously, the center still thinks of these issues as it did during Soviet times—in a purely bureaucratic and hierarchical way. Symptomatically, to accelerate and control the development of the three most sensitive areas of the country (the North Caucasus, the Far East, and the Arctic) the center created three new area-specific administrations.[44] Moreover, the federal government intervenes in individual cases by taking ad hoc decisions to address disparities, extinguish sources of tension through exceptional allocations, or attract foreign investors by creating "special development zones" where ineffective federal standards do not apply.

Although rarely implemented at full scale, the projects included in the development programs for the North Caucasus and the Far East are extremely ambitious, and impressive budgets have been announced for them—a sign of federal concern about regional disparities and development issues.[45] The projects include both major infrastructure modernization (of ports, airports, and road and rail bottlenecks) and spectacular undertakings such as the planned development of international ski resorts in the North Caucasus or priority development areas on the Pacific Rim. Observers are cautious, stung by the profusion of such outlandish plans that have never actually been brought to fruition. One can, of course, single out the successful realization of the 2014 Sochi Olympics, but it took the direct intervention of the president and outsized investment to complete this exceptional site. Yet Russia is not the only country investing in expensive megaprojects today.

Another example of regional issues is the case of border regions where the attractiveness of the neighboring country has become sensitive. This is the case for the Murmansk region and the republic of Karelia, which look to their Scandinavian neighbors for inspiration, and for the Kaliningrad region on the Baltic coast, whose population long benefited from a special visa-free regime allowing them to shop in neighboring districts of Poland (though this was abolished by Polish authorities in 2016). It also includes the inhabitants of the Russian Far East, who are attracted to the Chinese border towns and almost exclusively drive used Japanese cars with the steering wheel on the right.

The development of cross-border trade and employment is common between many countries, but in Russia, these situations are often regarded as a kind of foreign invasion or even a possible challenge to territorial cohesion. While not prohibited, they serve as an example for those who argue in favor of limiting the autonomy of these borderlands—such that, far from being an advantage, being located on a border can actually become a handicap. In the case of the Kaliningrad exclave wedged between two EU states, Poland and Lithuania, there were difficult debates between the majority of the residents, who wanted to see their region serve as a model for better integration of Russia into the European neighborhood, and a Moscow administration that sought above all to better integrate the oblast into the Federation.

The war in Ukraine and resulting sanctions and embargoes have only served to heighten these tensions. In 2022, several companies that had set up shop in the Kaliningrad area to enjoy one of Russia's few effective free economic zones, such as Russian carmaker Avtotor (which has previously partnered with General Motors and BMW), have announced their withdrawal. At the same time, the temptation of the Lithuanian authorities to cut off transit between the exclave and the rest of the Russian territory has rekindled these tensions with the fear that the Russian Army will attack the Suwałki corridor, the narrow strip of land that connects Poland to Lithuania and, by extension, to the other Baltic states.

All of these territorial issues remain highly sensitive for Russian society and its elite. This is partly due to the history of the state, whose borders have fluctuated for centuries. It is also linked to the country's size and the diversity of its territories. The answer to the uneasy question of how to manage Russia's immense size has yet to find a balanced solution. The current strategy of hypercentralization is far from efficient, and it raises many crucial questions for the very future of the federation through the relationship between the center of power and the entities based on the presence of ethnic minorities. As early as 2001, Tatarstan's president (a status now equivalent to that of a governor) Mintimer Shaimiev commented on Putin's first reforms:

> Today it is not necessary to be scared of saying that if we give autonomy to regions, Russia will collapse. If we succeeded in preserving the country's integrity at the most difficult moments of political reforms, there is no more room for such concerns today. Russia can only be strong through strong regions. Such a large country cannot be governed in all its aspects from only one center.[46]

But in his desire to control all of politics, Putin has, on the contrary, reinforced the famous "vertical power" by reducing the autonomy of the cities and regions to the benefit of the upper echelons of the administrative hierarchy.

With the exception of Chechnya, where local power has a special relationship with Putin, the republics are deprived of decision-making autonomy, including in cultural and linguistic areas (learning local languages in school has become optional).[47] In 2017, Moscow refused to renew the power-sharing treaty (signed in 1994 and renewed in 2007) with Tatarstan, putting an end to the republic's increased autonomy.[48]

The prolongation of the war in Ukraine further reinforces this hypercentralizing tendency. While different levels of martial law are applied to the regions bordering the conflict, such as Belgorod, Putin set up in October 2022 a special coordination body of the regions, placed under the responsibility of the mayor of Moscow, Sergey Sobyanin, whose activity is expected to further decrease the autonomy of regions and municipalities.[49] Spatial issues and regional policy are doomed to remain among the major elements of the identity crisis Russia is facing.

## NOTES

1. Meaning Rome (Saint Peter was the first bishop of Rome, according to Roman Catholic and Eastern Orthodox Christian theology).

2. When including Crimea, total Russian territory amounts to 17,125,407 square kilometers (6,612,157 square miles).

3. Nataliia Narochnitskaia, "Za chto nas ne liubiat," Pravoslavie.ru, August 2013, https://pravoslavie.ru/63668.html.

4. Andrew Roth, "Putin Compares Himself to Peter the Great in Quest to Take Back Russian Lands," *The Guardian*, June 10, 2022, https://www.theguardian.com /world/2022/jun/10/putin-compares-himself-to-peter-the-great-in-quest-to-take-back -russian-lands.

5. Z. Brzezinski, *The Premature Partnership* (New York: Foreign Affairs, 1994), n. 73.

6. Most experts consider this to be in open violation of China's own commitments under international law as a signatory to the United Nations Convention on the Law of the Sea, or UNCLOS.

7. Including in the statistical tables of foreign trade, in which, for several years, the data for CIS states were given in rubles, whereas data for the "far abroad" foreign states were denominated in dollars.

8. See, for example, his letter of January 27, 1992, to the new UN secretary-general, Boutros Boutros-Ghali (http://lawru.info/base29/part3/d29ru3539.htm), and his address to the Security Council, on January 31, 1992, https://news.un.org/ru/audio /2013/02/1002851.

9. Cited by Marie Mendras, *Russie: Le débat sur l'intérêt national* (Paris: La Documentation française, 1992), 19.

10. Alexander Cooley, "Scripts of Sovereignty: The Freezing of the Russia–Ukraine Crisis and Dilemmas of Governance in Eurasia," *Center on Global Interests*, January 30, 2015.

11. Moldova no longer had access to the Black Sea after Stalin transferred the south of Bessarabia to the Ukraine. In 2001, only after an exchange of territory with Kiev did Moldova manage to escape its landlocked status, obtaining a kilometer of shoreline along the Danube and the possibility of opening an international port there.

12. Jean Radvanyi, *Russie, un vertige de puissance* (Paris: La Découverte, 2023).

13. Gerard Toal, *Near Abroad: Putin, the West, and the Contest over Ukraine and the Caucasus* (Oxford: Oxford University Press, 2017).

14. Vladimir Putin, "On the Historical Unity of Russians and Ukrainians," Kremlin, July 12, 2021, http://en.kremlin.ru/events/president/news/66181.

15. Alexander Solzhenitsyn, *Rebuilding Russia* (London: Harvill, 1991).

16. On these controversies, see Timothy Snyder, *The Reconstruction of Nations: Poland, Ukraine, Lithuania, Belarus, 1569–1999* (New Haven, CT: Yale University Press, 2004), and Andreas Kappeler, *Russes et Ukrainiens, les frères inégaux* (Paris: CNRS Éditions, 2022).

17. Vladimir Putin, "Address by the President of the Russian Federation," Kremlin, February 24, 2022, http://en.kremlin.ru/events/president/transcripts/67843.

18. Dmitri Medvedev's Telegram channel, June 7, 2022.

19. Supporters of Stefan Bandera (1909–1959), one of the main leaders of the Ukrainian nationalist movement from the end of the 1930s onward and who collaborated with the Nazis against Soviet troops.

20. Timofei Sergeitsev, "Chto Rossiia dozhna sdelat's Ukrainoi," RIA Novosti, April 3, 2022.

21. Piotr Tolstoy, interview on the French channel BFMTV, November 23, 2022, https://www.youtube.com/watch?v=9ZL92LCrQ38.

22. See more in Jeanne Wilson, *Strategic Partners: Russian–Chinese Relations in the Post-Soviet Era* (Armonk, NY: M. E. Sharpe, 2004).

23. Tore Henriksen and Geir Ulfstein, "Maritime Delimitation in the Arctic: The Barents Sea Treaty," *Ocean Development & International Law* 42, no. 1–2 (February 2011): 1–21.

24. Ilias Bantekas, "Bilateral Delimitation of the Caspian Sea and the Exclusion of Third Parties," *International Journal of Marine & Coastal Law* 26, no. 1 (2011): 47–58.

25. "Convention on the Legal Status of the Caspian Sea," Kremlin, August 12, 2018, http://en.kremlin.ru/supplement/5328.

26. Vlad Kaczynski, "US–Russian Bering Sea Marine Border Dispute: Conflict over Strategic Assets, Fisheries, and Energy Resources," *Russian Analytical Digest* 20 (May 1, 2007): 2–5.

27. Lauri Mälksoo, "Which Continuity? The Tartu Peace Treaty of 2 February 1920, the Estonian-Russian Border Treaties of 2005, and the Legal Debate about Estonia's Status in International Law," *Archiv des Völkerrechts* 43, no. 4 (December 2005): 513–24.

28. *World War Three: Inside the War Room* (BBC 2016).

29. "Dagestanu ponadobilos' 900 millionov na pereselenie lezgin iz Azerbaidzhana," *Lenta.ru*, December 26, 2012, https://lenta.ru/news/2012/12/26/resettlement.

30. Mikulas Fabry, "The Contemporary Practice of State Recognition: Kosovo, South Ossetia, Abkhazia, and Their Aftermath," *Nationalities Papers: Journal of Nationalism & Ethnicity* 40, no. 5 (2012): 661–76.

31. On the 2008 war, see Heidi Tagliavini, *Independent International Fact-Finding Mission on Georgia* (Council of Europe, 2009), and Toal, *Near Abroad.*

32. Putin, "Address."

33. Ishaan Tharoor, "Why Putin Says Crimea Is Russia's 'Temple Mount,'" *Washington Post*, December 4, 2014, https://www.washingtonpost.com/news/worldviews/wp/2014/12/04/why-putin-says-crimea-is-russias-temple-mount.

34. Eva-Maria Stolberg, "The Siberian Frontier between 'White Mission' and 'Yellow Peril,' 1890s–1920s," *Nationalities Papers: Journal of Nationalism & Ethnicity* 32, no. 1 (March 2004): 165–81.

35. Rosstat, "Gruppirovka selskikh naselennykh punktov po chislennosti naseleniia po subieektam Rossiiskoi Federatsii," Vol. 1, "Chislennosti i razmeshchenie naseleniia," *Vserossiiskaia perepis naseleniia 2020 goda.*

36. *Rossiiskii statisticheskii ezhegodnik–2021* (Moscow: Rosstat, 2021), 394; *Rossiia v tsifrakh–2016* (Moscow: Rosstat, 2016), 282, http://www.gks.ru/free_doc/doc_2016/rusfig/rus16.pdf.

37. Federal Law 119-FZ, May 1, 2016, http://www.kremlin.ru/acts/bank/40772.

38. "More Than 7,000 Russians Apply for Hectare in Arctic Since Program's Start," TASS, August 16, 2022, https://tass.com/economy/1494291.

39. Vladimir Kaganskii, *Kul'turnyi landshaft i sovetskoe obytaemoe prostranstvo: sbornik statei* (Moscow: NLO, 2001), 304.

40. Jean Radvanyi, "Quand Vladimir Poutine se fait géographe," *Hérodote* 3–4, no. 166–167 (2017): 113–32.

41. See Vladimir Kolosov and Olga Vendina, eds., *Rossiisko-ukrainskoe pogranich'e. Dvadtsat' let razdelennogo edinstva* (Moscow: Novyi Khronograf, 2011).

42. Harold Chambers, "Mobilization in the North Caucasus," *Riddle*, September 26, 2022, https://ridl.io/mobilization-in-the-north-caucasus.

43. Nikolay Yadrintsev, *Sibir' kak koloniia: sovremennoe polozhenie Sibiri, eia nuzhdy i potrebnosti, eia proshloe i budushchee* (St. Petersburg: Izd. M. Stasyulevicha, 1882).

44. See their website: http://www.minkavkaz.gov.ru for the North Caucasus, https://minvr.ru for the Far East, and the Arctic Governmental Commission, https://arctic.gov.ru.

45. "Strategiia sotsial'no-ekonomicheskogo razvitiia Dal'nego Vostoka i Baikal'skogo regiona na period do 2025 goda," December 28, 2009, http://static.government.ru/media/files/L1VhVy1Iw0VrQo9s5vhGPaaiWKBip8B8.pdf; "Natsional'naia programma sotsial'no-ekonomicheskogo razvitiia Dal'nego Vostoka na period do 2024 goda i na perspektivu do 2035 goda," September 24, 2020, http://static.government.ru/media/files/NAISPJ8QMRZUPd9LIMWJoeVhn1l6eGqD.pdf; "Strategiia sotsial'no-ekonomicheskogo razvitiia Severo-Kavkazskogo federal'nogo

okruga na period do 2030 goda," April 30, 2022, http://government.ru/docs/all/140821.

46. *Tatar-inform*, October 10, 2001.

47. For a well-documented analysis of Putin's effort to reduce regional autonomy, see Richat Sabitov, *Le fédéralisme russe contemporain et la République du Tatarstan* (Paris: Fondation Varenne, 2013).

48. See "Tatarstan gotov pogovorit' o dogovore," *Kommersant*, August 4, 2017, https://www.kommersant.ru/doc/3374350 or "Rustam Minnikhanov otkazalsia ot dogovora s Rossiei," *Kommersant*, September 22, 2017, https://www.kommersant.ru/doc/3417048.

49. "Putin poruchil Sobianinu koordinatsiu regionov po voprosam bezopasnosti," RBK, October 19, 2022. https://www.rbc.ru/politics/19/10/2022/634fe54f9a79470ab0148aa2?ysclid=ldiqxi36v3400737199.

## 2

# Russia's Multiple and Troubled Identities

## Diversity, Decline, and Migration

The breakup of the Soviet Union and the emergence of Russia as a new state named the "Russian Federation (Russia)" (*Rossiiskaia Federatsiia-Rossiia*) caught the Russian population by surprise. Historically, such a state had never existed within these borders. During the Soviet era, the authorities increased their efforts to prevent the Russian Socialist Federal Soviet Republic (RSFSR) from being anything other than an administrative entity without a particular national identity. In tandem with the rapid redefinition of political, economic, and institutional systems, precipitated by the Soviet collapse, concerns about the country's identity came to the fore.

Not only is Russia a territorial and cultural archipelago, characterized by large regional differences in living standards and socioeconomic dynamics, it is also an ethnic mosaic that reproduces the ethnic diversity of the former Soviet Union on a smaller scale. While debates over national identity are by no means specific to Russia, the multiplicity of challenges facing the country and its citizens has no equal on the European scene. The unstable relationship between state and nation inherited from the imperial tradition, the demographic crisis, internal and external migration flows, citizenship policies, xenophobic tensions, the COVID-19 pandemic, and then the war against Ukraine have laid bare a country in transformation.

## RUSSIA'S CHALLENGING NATION BUILDING

Each state has its own coding of difference—by race, ethnicity, religion, or class—that can be explained by the country's history and political culture and that largely shapes debates on national identity and citizenship.[1]

Russia inherited a prerevolutionary, imperial scheme that for centuries assigned differentiated statuses to conquered peoples based on how they became a part of the empire, and the Russian administration's ability to co-opt their indigenous elites. Less-numerous Siberian ethnic groups were pushed to assimilate with Russians and convert to Orthodox Christianity. Occupied territories in Europe, such as Poland and Finland, were given for some time their own constitution, more liberal than the autocratic regime in place in the imperial capital at St. Petersburg, while at the same time being gradually pressured to russify. The lands of Ukraine, the Caucasus, and Central Asia were all treated differently depending on their elite systems.

Today's Russia is also heir to the Soviet system, which, beginning in the 1920s, made ethnolinguistic identity a key marker of individuals and communities, sometimes with benevolent results (mass literacy being the main positive result of the Soviet regime), but often with tragic ones (the deportation of "punished peoples," accused of collaboration with the Soviet Union's enemies, unofficial quotas limiting Jews' access to intellectual professions, and a general Russification of all national cultures).[2]

Russia is not managing solely the legacies of previous regimes. Since the collapse of the Soviet Union, the identity debates that rage in Europe and the United States have also influenced discussions on the domestic scene. Samuel Huntington's "clash of civilizations" theory,[3] the success or failure of the American melting pot and European multiculturalism, the uprisings in the French suburbs in 2005, the terrorist attacks against *Charlie Hebdo* in 2015, the refugee crisis in Europe, the Black Lives Matter movement in the United States—all have been widely discussed in Russia, fueling controversy among intellectuals, influencing decision-makers' framing of the national identity question, and being heavily instrumentalized by state-led media as examples of the West's cultural failures.[4]

## How to Name the Nation?

The first question that needed to be resolved at the collapse of the Soviet Union was the very designation of the nation. There were two options from which to choose: a new Russian nation-state (*russkoe gosudarstvo*), as proposed by the Russian nationalists who had been very active since the 1960s, or a Russian Federation (*Rossiiskaia Federatsiia*) with a more inclusive nationhood.[5] It was this second option that reformers, such as then prime minister Yegor Gaidar, supported in order to mitigate the risk of marginalizing non-Russian ethnic minorities and encouraging secessionism and which Boris Yeltsin chose when he signed the Minsk Agreements that announced the end of the Soviet Union on December 8, 1991.

The choice to promote a civic identity for the new Russian Federation aimed at following the path of Western liberal democracies but also, more pragmatically, at mitigating the risk of the country dividing along ethnic fault lines and repeating the USSR's dissolution. The fear of Russia's collapse reverberated with Chechen demands for independence and autonomist pressures from Tatarstan,[6] pushing the Kremlin to quickly develop the project of a civic identity modeled on the Russian term *rossiiskii*, or "Rossian," which refers to everything related to the Russian state, as opposed to *russkii*, which applies specifically to Russian language, culture, or ethnicity. This Rossian identity was meant to unite all citizens of the Federation around civic patriotism and was symbolized by the dropping (in 1997) of the mention of ethnicity (*natsional'nost'*) from the Russian internal passport.[7]

In the Russian doctrine, as promoted by its founders, such as Valery Tishkov, then director of the Institute of Anthropology and Ethnology, ethnicity belongs to the private sphere. Yet this Rossian civic identity does not eliminate the multiplicity of local ethnic identities, which are still recognized with disparate rights inherited from the Soviet system. This is why Russia has thus far remained a federal state consisting of eighty-three or eighty-five subjects (depending on whether one includes Crimea and Sevastopol, annexed from Ukraine), of which twenty-seven originate directly from the ethnic specificities of their populations. Several of these national entities pertain to dual ethnicities, such as Kabardino-Balkaria or Khanty-Mansi; a few are multiethnic, such as Dagestan, with thirteen recognized constitutive ethnic groups.

Altogether, about fifty ethnic groups benefit from public policies that preserve, at least on paper (realities on the ground have more mixed results), their vernacular language and ethnic culture in the local education system, as well as give "titular" individuals (representatives of eponymous peoples) priority access to high positions in local government.[8] But those which do not have a titular territorial entity find themselves in a more fragile situation, even if some republics, such as Sakha (Yakutia) in eastern Siberia, also give them some protective rights. The 2021 census distinguished in Russia about 150 "nationalities," a heterogeneous category that includes indigenous ethnic groups as well as a variety of diasporas and expatriate communities.[9]

Nonethnic Russian citizens of the Federation, representing about 20 percent of the population, have various symbolic status. Ukrainians and Belarusians form significant minorities: Ukrainians counted for two million before 2014, and about one million joined Russia as refugees between 2014 and 2021, mostly from the Donbas region. With the 2022 war, Russia officially declared almost three million Ukrainian refugees on its territory to the UN High Committee on Refugees, but it is difficult to know how many fled voluntarily, had no choice, or were captured and brought to Russia by Russian occupation forces. Belarusians accounted for about half a million people in 2014 but only two hundred thousand at the time of the 2021 census.[10]

Both Ukrainians and Belarusians are considered "brother Slavs" who are so well integrated that public opinion does not view them as ethnic minorities. Mixed marriages, assimilation, and Russification are common, but the tensions with Ukraine since the 2004 Orange Revolution, the first conflict in 2014, and then the full-scale war have also pushed many Ukrainians to reidentify as Russians in the census (there are only eight hundred thousand self-identifying Ukrainians recorded in the 2021 Russian census). While the Russian and Ukrainian nations have been historically closely interconnected, important migration flows (Ukrainians "going back" to Ukraine, and Russians of Ukraine to Russia) have also gradually reduced this interconnectivity, and obviously the 2022 war largely broke people-to-people links.

Russia is also home to several Finno-Ugric populations (Karelians, Mordvins, Chuvash, Udmurts, Maris, and Komis), as well as peoples of Siberia and the Far North (Yakuts, Tuvans, Buryats, Nenets, Chuktches, etc.). They are largely Russified linguistically; some were converted to Russian Orthodoxy, while others maintain Buddhist or shamanistic beliefs. Their unique identity is seen first and foremost in linguistic and folk expressions, but there have been regular cases of political tensions around language and environmental issues as well as around their degree of autonomy from the center.

The feeling of otherness is more consistently expressed toward nominally Muslim peoples (in the sense that they belong to a traditionally Muslim culture, which does not automatically equate to religious belief or practice). About 17 million Russian citizens are of traditionally Muslim ethnicities; among them, the Tatars are the most numerous (4.7 million), followed by the Chechens (1.7 million), Bashkirs (1.6 million), and smaller groups mostly in Dagestan.[11] Political tensions in the North Caucasus and Volga, coupled with a growing sense of Islamic otherness, made these minorities the main ones deemed potentially problematic for Russia's national cohesion.

The Russian civic identity promoted during the Yeltsin era was both a success and a failure. It was a success inasmuch as the citizens of the Russian Federation widely recognized themselves as a part of the Russian state and since then have not really displayed different levels of patriotism based on their ethnicity. It was a failure because the term *rossiiskii* did not take root and found itself increasingly challenged, initially by Chechen leaders seeking independence and nationalist elites in the ethnic republics, for whom Russia's state identity remained too "Russian" and insufficiently "Rossian"—that is, it was lacking in federalism and multiethnicity.

It also sparked harsh criticism from Russian nationalists, who denounced the civic identity as a "de-Russification" of Russia and a submission of ethnic Russians to minorities' diktat, an old theme already present in some semidissident circles.[12] More generally, the use of *rossiiskii*, while still dominant in many official documents and in the media, is often associated with the negative image of the 1990s decade,[13] and since the onset of the war in 2022, Putin tends to speak more about the "multinational people of Russia" (*mnogonatsional'nyi narod*) to insist on the country's diversity without having to refer to the term *rossiiskii*.

## Tensions between Unity and Diversity

In the 2000s, the debate between Russian and Rossian narratives underwent a series of semantic evolutions. First came the formalization of a new political language that expanded the space for patriotism, based primarily on the rehabilitation of the imperial and Soviet past, and the engine of social consensus (see chapter 4). The state committed significant funds to commemorating the great symbolic battles of Russian history (Alexander Nevsky against the Teutonic Knights, Dmitry Donskoy against the Mongols, Mikhail Kutuzov against Napoleon, Alexey Yermolov commanding the imperial army in the Caucasus, etc.).

The Russian authorities also gave new rights to Cossacks, the descendants of the peasant soldiers who formed the backbone of the Russian force that colonized the Caucasus and Siberia between the seventeenth and nineteenth centuries and who are now integrated into the army and in all law enforcement agencies.[14] This rehabilitation of the Tsarist colonial past does not happen without generating negative reactions from local peoples: for instance, in 2010, the inauguration by Cossacks of a monument devoted to Yermorlov in the North Caucasian city of Piatigorsk was very negatively received by local ethnic minorities.

Second, some influential intellectuals and politicians, tapping into Russian nationalist sensitivities, have continued to raise the specter of the de-Russification of Russia. Many proposed laws have identified ethnic Russians as the only carriers of statehood and have formalized Russian culture as first among equals. The elites of the national republics and most minorities have reacted strongly to what they interpret as the breakdown of the Rossian civic contract. Many advocate a proactive policy of preserving ethnic languages. The question became particularly sensitive in Tatarstan after 2017, when Moscow decided that Tatar language instruction would not be mandatory anymore.[15]

Some want the reintroduction of ethnicity in passports, in order to protect minorities from assimilation or, in the case of Russian nationalists, to avoid a possible "dissolution" of Russianness. Others argue for strengthening federalism to give more autonomy to the national republics. Some claim to be given a voice in the deciding of Russia's economic choices: Indigenous nations of the Far North have, for instance, been asking for the right to be involved in decisions made by extractive industries on their traditional lands.[16]

Not only has the federal nature of Russia de facto largely disappeared under Putin's presidencies but the existence of some ethnic districts has been challenged. Putin has mentioned several times the need to eliminate all administrative differences between subjects of the Federation, and, in 2004–2008, the incorporation of several small Siberian autonomous districts (Nenets, Khanti-Mansi, Yamalo-Nenets, as well as two Buryat districts) into neighboring regions looked like the first step toward simplifying the administrative map at the expense of ethnic minorities. Yet this process ceased, as it generated grassroots tensions and resistance.

Despite the centralizing will of Moscow, local situations are very diverse. In the North Caucasus, in Tatarstan and Bashkortostan, Islam is increasingly taught in public schools or in numerous private madrassas—some of them may spread radical Salafi views even if they are heavily controlled by law-enforcement agencies. In several republics, textbooks offer a differentiated reading of history, presenting the federal perspective—"peaceful integration" of the territory into the Russian Empire—in the class on Russian history but celebrating local resistance to "Russian colonialism" in the class on local history. Chechnya benefits from a special dispensation allowing it to diverge from federal laws. For instance, Russia's official state secularism no longer applies there, and a version of Sharia (Islamic law) has been partially introduced, forcing women to veil themselves and allowing polygamy.

State identity and the place of ethnic Russians in it have been further complicated by the strategies Moscow has developed to maintain its influence in the "near abroad." In gradually implying that ethnic Russians living abroad and, even more broadly, Russian-speaking populations could potentially (re)join Russia, the regime has blurred the relationship between the civic nature of the Russian Federation and the notion of Russianness.[17]

In the 1990s, and more significantly into the following decade, Moscow developed the concept of "compatriot" (*sootechestvennik*) to refer to Russian minorities living in Soviet successor states, as well as to former Soviet citizens and descendants of the waves of outward migration that Russia has experienced since the nineteenth century more broadly.[18] Moscow initially facilitated the rapid acquisition of Russian citizenship for any former Soviet citizen who wanted it[19] and then took up a more selective policy until the Ukrainian crisis of 2014, after which the policy became more inclusive again. Although the term "compatriot" does not guarantee any legal status, it allows Moscow to concretely practice asymmetric policies. For example, Russia distributed passports to Abkhazians and South Ossetians in Georgia (as well as to the inhabitants of the breakaway region of Transnistria in Moldova and Donbas in Ukraine) and then used this fact to justify its intervention in Georgia in August 2008 as undertaken in defense of its "citizens."

With the annexation of Crimea in 2014 and the onset of the war in 2022, the internationally recognized borders of Ukraine have been forcibly changed to accommodate the symbolic boundaries of Russianness. In defense of its actions, Moscow has variously invoked its strategic security against NATO's advances, its right to defend Russians abroad or all those who identify with Russia, and even the baptism of Russia in Chersonese (Crimea) in 988. This mixing of categories disrupts the identity repertoires created in the 1990s and 2000s. This expansion of Russianness—real and symbolic—weakens the internal consensus between the majority and the country's minorities and accelerates the progressive erasure of the difference between *Rossian* and *Russian*. These identity hesitations are exacerbated by fears of a changing ethnic balance within the Federation itself.

## A COUNTRY PROFOUNDLY
## TRANSFORMED BY MIGRATION

Debates about Russia's national identity are indeed directly associated with migration controversies. A land of emigration since the nineteenth century, Russia is now a country of immigration as well. It has the fourth-largest immigrant population in the world (after the United States, Germany, and Saudi Arabia) at 11.6 million. Yet this amounts to only 8 percent of its population which is low by present-day European standards (the figures for Germany, the UK, and France are, respectively, 18.8 percent, 13.8 percent, and 13.1 percent for 2020).[20]

### A Major Destination for Labor Migration

For decades, from Tsarist times until after World War II, the Russian population was in a state of expansion, with authorities pushing people to move to newly conquered territories in Siberia, the Caucasus, and Central Asia, whether by promises of more freedom or by forced relocation, exile, or forced labor. Since the 1979 Soviet census, well before the end of the USSR, there has been a reversal of migration flows, with people tending to "return" to Russia from the southern Soviet republics. The first to leave were young Russians or Russian-speakers (Slavs and Balts) who, born in the Caucasus and Central Asia in the context of the major industrial and agricultural projects of the Stalin and Khrushchev eras, did not belong to the local titular nationality and had difficulties finding good jobs, which were reserved for the titular nationality of the respective Soviet socialist republic in question.

Upon the collapse of the Soviet Union, migration to Russia was accelerated by conflicts in the South Caucasus and the civil war in Tajikistan. Poorly-equipped Russian authorities had to learn to manage refugee camps in border areas and adopt international standards on the status of refugees and asylum seekers.[21]

Compounding these flows was the influx of Russians and Russian-speakers who were fearful of staying in the newly independent states. They were not fleeing anti-Russian pogroms but rather difficult economic conditions and identity anxieties related to the fear of having no future in the new nation-states of which they did not know the national language. Of the twenty-five million people identified as ethnic Russians who lived in Soviet republics other than Russia at the time of the 1989 census, many millions "returned" to Russia (which was often a symbolic homeland, since most of these individuals had been born in the republics). There are no definitive figures, but around half of this group left the republics for Russia or more distant destinations (see table 2.1).[22]

Since the early 2000s and the revival of the Russian economy, the nature of migration has changed. Labor migrants in search of wages to send home have largely replaced the former "identity migrants." Among the sending countries of these economic migrants, Uzbekistan tops the list, with about 3 million citizens in Russia, followed by Ukraine (1.5 million before 2014), Tajikistan (about 1 million), Azerbaijan (800,000), and Kyrgyzstan, Armenia,

**Table 2.1. Russians in the former Soviet states**

|  | Total Population 1989 (millions) | Total Population 2020 (millions) | Russians in 1989 (%) | Russians in 2020* (%) |
|---|---|---|---|---|
| Estonia | 1.5 | 1.3 | 30.3 | 25.1 |
| Latvia | 2.7 | 1.9 | 34.0 | 25.2 |
| Lithuania | 3.7 | 2.7 | 9.4 | 5.8 |
| Belarus | 10.2 | 9.4 | 13.2 | 7.5 |
| Moldova | 4.3 | 3.4 | 13.0 | 4.1 |
| Ukraine | 51.7 | 43.9 | 22.1 | 17.3** |
| Armenia | 3.2 | 2.9 | 1.6 | 0.4 |
| Azerbaijan | 7.0 | 10.0 | 5.6 | 1.3 |
| Georgia | 5.4 | 3.7 | 6.3 | 0.7 |
| Kazakhstan | 16.5 | 19.2 | 37.8 | 15.5 |
| Kyrgyzstan | 4.3 | 6.4 | 21.5 | 5.1 |
| Uzbekistan | 19.9 | 30.5 | 8.3 | 2.7 |
| Tajikistan | 5.1 | 9.5 | 7.6 | 0.4 |
| Turkmenistan | 3.6 | 5.0 | 9.5 | 3.2 |

* Last known value, between 2015 and 2020.

** Last Ukrainian census, 2001.

*Sources:* Soviet census of 1989 and different statistical committees.

and Moldova (each of which has about half a million citizens in Russia). Evidently, Russia attracts mostly former Soviet citizens, although there are also immigrant communities from Afghanistan, China, and Vietnam, with the latter two communities mainly located in the Far East.

As in Europe, these migrants fill specific economic niches scorned by Russian citizens: construction, road services, minor commercial activities, hotel and restaurant work, taxi driving, and, increasingly, human services (as home health aides or caregivers for children and the elderly). Some nationalities specialize in certain sectors: young Ukrainian and Moldovan women dominate the market for home health aides, Kyrgyz invest in restaurants, Tajiks are mostly in construction, and Azerbaijanis and Uzbeks have pursued petty commercial activities, such as fresh fruit and vegetable stands in Soviet-era markets and now supermarket chains in Russia's major cities.[23]

These labor migrants have become an integral part of the economy. Ads call for "Tajiks"—now a generic term designating a low-skilled worker—to work at construction sites, taxi and bus drivers speak "accented" Russian, "people of color" (several derogatory terms exist in Russian) clean the sidewalks, and women in colorful clothing run the market stalls. Migrants have fundamentally changed the urban landscape, with the emergence of ethnic neighborhoods (not on a par with the segregation of American cities, but a new phenomenon for Russia nonetheless), often in the suburbs of large cities, and the development of ethnic restaurants and mosques including in Russian regions without traditional Muslim populations.[24] Most migrants work in difficult conditions without official contracts or health insurance, putting them at the mercy of their employers. Workers at construction sites and wholesale markets tend to live in barracks or other units, segregated from the rest of the population.

Whatever the exact number of migrants, Russian authorities are struggling to establish a functional migration policy. The country remains liberal on the matter, as CIS citizens can enter Russia without a visa, and those whose country is a member of the Eurasian Economic Union (Belarus, Armenia, Kazakhstan, and Kyrgyzstan; see chapter 6) can be hired without excessive red tape. The others CIS citizens have one month to declare themselves to the immigration services and register their place of residence and employment contract before they become "illegal."[25]

At their own expense, migrants drive another part of the Russian economy: the corruption of law enforcement agencies and migration services. Those who can afford to do so purchase Russian passports; the less fortunate secure fake registrations, work permits, and health insurance certificates. The departments in charge of migrants (beginning in 2016, the Federal Migration Service has been integrated into the Ministry of the Interior) are so intimately involved with administrative malfeasance that it becomes almost impossible to know whether migrants have proper papers, hence the emergence of the term "real-fake" documents, which the official services create but do not actually record.[26]

Since 2007, Russian authorities have tried several times to improve the regulation of migration.[27] Controlling flows at the borders is illusory; no customs service can even operate effectively along the entire 7,000-kilometer (4,350-mile) border with Kazakhstan alone and, in any case, Russia wants to remain an open space for citizens of Eurasian Economic Union member states. Instead, it is through integration into the national economy that the authorities try to regulate migrants. They initially introduced a quota system requiring companies to notify the municipal and regional administration of their labor needs for the forthcoming year. However, this system was both too rigid (a company could not know the number of employees it would need in a year) and maladaptive (companies preferred to hire underpaid, undocumented migrants rather than play the costly and time-consuming game of legalization). In addition, the penalty measures for businesses that employ illegal labor were largely inefficient, given the endemic corruption of law enforcement agencies.[28]

Since 2015, Russia has replaced the quota system with a duty system (*patent* in Russian) that is easier, because each migrant can become their own employer. The authorities also introduced a Russian-language test for legalization, but documents satisfying this requirement were available for sale on the growing market for false documents before it ever took effect.[29] Highly specialized professionals whose knowledge is in demand benefit from simplified procedures, and the list of specializations is revised every year.

Even in today's context of economic downturn and long-term contraction, the country will continue to need cheap and undemanding labor. In addition, a growing number of migrants settle permanently in Russia and obtain dual citizenship. Between the 1989 and 2021 censuses, the number of Russian residents of Tajik, Kyrgyz, Uzbek, and Armenian ethnicity multiplied by about 8.9, 3.5, 2.8, and 2 times, respectively.[30] In 2021 alone, 104,000 citizens of Tajikistan, 50,000 of Kazakhstan, 47,000 of Armenia, 32,000 of Uzbekistan (and even 376,000 of Ukraine) were naturalized as Russian citizens.[31] These migrants see Russia as their second home and bring their families, which implies the increasing entry of migrant women into the labor market and the need to adapt the Russian school system for the arrival of non-Russian-speaking children.

## Dealing with Xenophobia and Racism

With migration now part of the everyday social fabric, Russia is in tune with broader, pan-European societal evolutions. And, as in Europe, the influx of migrants attracts the attention of public opinion and media and has given rise to an unprecedented increase in xenophobia. This xenophobia takes place in a specific cultural context, in which race issues were rarely formulated as such and considered taboo by the Soviet regime. Yet Soviet nations harbored strong ethnic prejudices while also living together in the context of shared cultural values.[32] Compared to Western Europe and the United States, today's Russian society is marked by a lack of debate about accumulated colonial perceptions and a still strong disdain for those belonging to what are identified as "lesser" or "backward" nations.

In the early 1990s, polls showed strong ethnic sentiment among minorities, whereas the majority of ethnic Russians seemed relatively indifferent to ethnic classifications and instead clung to Soviet symbols and the slogan of "friendship of the peoples." With the First Chechen War, xenophobic discourse directed against Chechens—and North Caucasians in general—gained in popularity, with the idea that North Caucasians were "unable" to assimilate into Russian cultural values—even if they are citizens of Russia. Symptomatically, in the late 1990s, several Russian leaders believed it would be better to grant Chechens independence and erect a wall between the region and the rest of the country.[33] In the 2000s, this xenophobia was transformed with the arrival of labor migrants. Sociological surveys conducted by polling agencies such as the Levada Center showed the gradual transformation of the "threat": people from the North Caucasus and other groups that had traditionally faced discrimination (Jews, expatriates or students from sub-Saharan Africa and Asia, and Roma, known as *Tsigany* in Russian vernacular language) were gradually overtaken by Tajiks and Uzbeks, who had become more easily identifiable targets for violence.[34] This trend was even given a new term in Russian: *migrantofobiia.*

In a 2019 survey, 72 percent of respondents said they wished to reduce immigration, compared to only 9 percent who wished to facilitate it. And two-thirds described the presence of migrants in their region as "excessive," a figure that reached 91 percent in Moscow.[35] Many Russians support a policy of deporting undocumented immigrants and the establishment of a visa regime with the southern former Soviet republics. Migrants are generally accused of being unwilling or unable to integrate and of not respecting Russian values and lifestyles.[36]

Many ambiguities accompany this xenophobia.[37] As we saw, it concerns not only foreigners but also North Caucasians, who, though full citizens of the Russian Federation, are considered culturally foreign. While national republics such as Dagestan are experiencing massive departures of people heading for other parts of Russia, given high youth unemployment,[38] polls show that mainstream public opinion wants them to be "parked" in their republics and not settled elsewhere in the country. In the late 2000s to early 2010s, one of the most popular slogans was "Stop feeding the Caucasus," alluding to the massive federal investments geared toward the North Caucasus and especially Chechnya's reconstruction. Nowadays, the main institutions representing Islam in Russia, in particular the Moscow-based Council of Muftis, consider it their religious duty to meet the needs of migrants and therefore increasingly play a mediating role between the government and diaspora Muslim communities. The conflation of migrants and Muslims and the rise of Islamophobia have also taken root in Russia, yet to a lesser extent than in Europe.[39]

This xenophobia is not only expressed in discourse and attitudes but has led to violence. In the 1990s, only the Roma and sub-Saharan and Asian expatriates were victims of aggression, and some Jewish cemeteries were desecrated. In the following decade, the extent of the phenomenon and its victims grew, with skinhead groups—up to fifty thousand members at the peak of their popularity—taking the lead in this street violence.[40] Between 2004 and 2007, the number of racist attacks exploded from 270 (of which 47 were fatal) to 632 (67 of them fatal) without the authorities taking measures to combat or prevent this rising tide of violence. The riots in Kondopoga in the northwestern region of Karelia in the fall of 2006, which followed a brawl between ethnic Chechens and Russians, ignited Russian nationalist movements and increased clashes between skinhead groups and security forces in the Moscow metro area, pushing the authorities toward a more repressive policy. The laxity that had previously characterized police attitudes toward skinhead groups was called into question.

The incidence of street violence initiated by skinheads declined in the years that followed—even if it remains underrecorded, especially in the provinces.[41] For several years, another type of violence emerged: mass clashes between Russian nationalist and North Caucasian groups following large xenophobic demonstrations. In 2010, some 5,000 young Russian nationalists and football (soccer) fans occupied Manege Square near the Kremlin, shouting neo-Nazi slogans never before heard in the country on such a vast scale. In 2011, street militias organized to violently expel Azeris and Roma who were suspected of being members of an organized crime syndicate from the village of Sagra in the eastern foothills of the southern Ural Mountains, near Yekaterinburg. In 2013, Biryulyovo, a Moscow suburb, ignited after a bloody settling of scores between a victim, who was identified as Russian, and the killers, identified as North Caucasians. Youth gangs fighting in the streets took the opportunity to loot neighboring stores, especially those belonging to ethnic minorities.[42]

For a long time, the authorities were not just neutral spectators of the rise of xenophobia. The mayors of some cities even quietly backed skinhead groups as "street cleaners" and celebrated their willingness to restore law and order. The Moscow municipality—under its former mayor, Yuri Luzhkov, as well as under his successor, Sergey Sobyanin—have openly played to xenophobic slogans and conducted media campaigns celebrating the arrest of undocumented migrants in the city's markets. The presidential party's youth movements, Young Guard and Nashi ("ours"), have set up "training sessions" to explain to migrants how to "behave" in Russia and respect its "national traditions."

Several official figures, meanwhile, expressed concern about migrants bringing about a deterioration in the quality of spoken Russian and the fact that ethnic Russians are accused of racist violence but never recognized as victims of minorities. Assertions that migrants were responsible for the reactions they generate—a topic largely cultivated by the media—and that the country was threatened by a creeping Islamization were then mainstream. In 2009, Moscow authorities closed down the Cherkizovsky market—known as Europe's largest marketplace, employing about 100,000 workers, mostly from China and Central Asia—overnight in order to showcase the state retaking control over informal economic flows.

After 2014, the authorities took a much more restrictive approach toward ethnic violence. They strengthened legislation against it, broke up the majority of skinhead groups that instigated this violence, as well as the main Russian nationalist groups, and shut down internet websites propagating ethnic hatred, so that fatalities stemming from ethnic violence fell from 724 in 2007 to 71 in 2021.[43] Of course, the new strategy taken by the authorities should not be interpreted as a desire to protect migrants and ethnic minorities from xenophobic aggression but as acknowledgment that Russian ethnic nationalism has been seen as a potential challenge to the Putin regime's legitimacy and therefore has been brought under control.[44] Xenophobia, too, appears heavily correlated with broader issues of threat perception and the identification of Russia's "foes": in the great moment of near-unanimous anti-Westernism that followed the annexation of Crimea, propelling Putin to record popularity, antimigrant feelings suddenly fell.

## DEMOGRAPHY: RUSSIA'S EXCEPTIONALISM

Russia's migration debates and xenophobic violence cannot be understood without looking at the country's nationwide demographic challenge. The breakup of the Soviet Union had a radical influence on population flows. In total, between 1991 and 2011, four to six million people left Russia for Europe (primarily Germany), the United States, Israel, and Canada.[45] Ethnic Germans and Jews, who during Soviet times were mostly denied the right to emigrate, left in huge numbers. These emigration flows were massive in the early 1990s and then slowed.

However, they resumed at a brisk pace after 2012, with the clouding of the country's "modernization" outlook: 150,000 to 450,000 per year between 2014 and 2021.[46] Emigrants are often younger and more educated than average citizens, contributing to the brain drain that has afflicted the country over the course of the whole twentieth century. The war-related emigration of 2022 has been the biggest exodus of Russian citizens since the collapse of the Soviet Union: at least 700,000 people (about 200,000 in the spring, likely around 500,000 in the fall, even if data is difficult to collect), though many who left as a result of the "partial mobilization" of September 2022 came back later. Theirs is an emigration even more specific in terms of socioeconomic groups, representing mostly the urban, educated middle-classes, especially information technology workers who can easily work remotely for a largely globalized market. Russia's history of emigration impacts the way the fear of demographic disappearance is addressed, even if the core reasons for demographic decline are more socioeconomic than purely migration related.

## The Fear of Demographic Collapse . . .

Since his rise to power, Vladimir Putin has made frequent mentions of the grim demographic situation in Russia as constituting a threat to the very survival of the nation and the sovereignty of the state. Russia is indeed the only developed country to experience a population decline with such severe potential consequences. Japan has maintained very low fertility rates and a near absence of immigration, but given long life expectancies, it has been able, until recently, to avoid significant population decline. For comparison, life expectancies are also declining in the United States for public health reasons (though they remain higher than in Russia), but migration and relatively high fertility rates guarantee the country's continued demographic growth.

Russia is a unique case on the world demographic landscape. Throughout the twentieth century, the country's political upheavals impacted its demographics. Years of civil war, collectivization, Stalin's purges, and the massive losses during World War II cost tens of millions of human lives, compounded by the fact that the shrunken generations of the 1920s through the 1950s themselves had fewer children. During the years under the leadership of Soviet premier Leonid Brezhnev (1964–1982), falling fertility rates and excess mortality among working-age cohorts of Slavs were partly obscured by the vitality of the Soviet Union's southern peoples. The reversal that occurred after the disintegration of the Soviet Union was thus particularly noticeable: the Russian population declined from 148.5 million in 1992 to 142.7 million in 2009.[47] The correlation between this decline and the economic and political crisis in the country struck a chord with public opinion. The population issue became a major point of political contention, with conservative politicians linking demographic decline to liberal reforms.

Figures stabilized at the turn of the 2010s, with a minor increase in the population and, in 2013, a positive natural increase for the first time since 1992. In 2017, the authorities welcomed this success, loudly announcing a population of 146.8 million, including 2.3 million new citizens following the annexation of Crimea. Fertility rose from its lowest level in 1999, at 1.17 children per woman, to 1.54 in 2009 and 1.78 in 2015, and since then has declined and stagnated at around 1.5.[48] The increase happening up to 2015 was supported by improvements in middle-class living standards, social optimism in young households, and the establishment of a pronatalist policy, which includes financial support for families (a "baby bonus" allocated beginning with the second child), programs promoting large families, and a collapse of abortions, long used in Soviet culture as a means of contraception.[49]

The authorities celebrated this rise in the birth rate with great pomp, interpreting it as Russia's awaited demographic rebirth and rightly highlighting an improvement in the welfare of households of childbearing age. But despite this modest demographic recovery, now over, the outlook remains somber. Like many European countries, since the 1960s Russia has never attained the 2.1 fertility rate needed for replacement, with the exception of a few years in the 1980s. The rebound of the early 2010s was primarily due to the arrival of the larger cohorts into childbearing age and the naturalization of immigrants. But the number of women of childbearing age will decline again by 20 percent around 2025 due to the age-cohort effect, and it is too early to know the effect that the war in Ukraine will have on Russian citizens' desire for creating families.

The government also avoids lingering too long on the rise of regional differences, at least in the public arena. In fact, demography is doing well in some areas of the country (see map 2.1). This growing gap between ethnic Russians and minorities has been confirmed with the release of the 2021 census data, which took note of a major collapse in the number of ethnic Russians (from 111 million in 2010 to 105.5 million in 2021), while ethnic republics account for almost half of the 26 regions that grew, led by Chechnya and Ingushetia, followed by Adygea, Dagestan (all in the North Caucasus), and then Tuva, in southern Siberia.[50]

## ... And More Global Public Health Issues

Beyond the issue of demographic renewal, Russian society faces many other public health issues. The main one, which makes Russia really stand out from the rest of Europe, is excess male mortality.[51] Life expectancy for men at birth declined from 63 years in 1990 to 58 in 1996 (which was lower than the rate

Regional population increase in Russia, 1989–2020

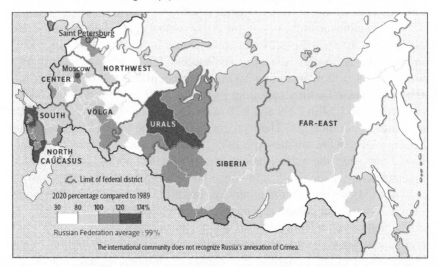

**Map 2.1: Regional population increase in Russia, 1989–2020.** *Source:* Goskomstat Russia.

under Soviet premier Nikita Khrushchev, who ruled from 1953–1964), before slowly rising to 68 in 2019 before the COVID-19 pandemic. The gap between both sexes grows with age cohorts: there are 105 males for every 100 females under the age of 15, but only 92 men per 100 women between the ages of 15 and 65, and 44 men per 100 women over the age of 65.[52] According to the World Health Organization, Russia still has the world's highest age-adjusted rate in terms of mortality due to external causes (that is, not related to disease). Yet the situation has improved over the years, with a decline of mortality due to external causes per 100,000 from 237 in 2002 to 94 in 2019.[53]

This excess male mortality is directly and indirectly explained by alcohol abuse (diseases related to alcohol consumption and poisoning with adulterated liquor), a very high number of accidents at work and on the road, and suicides—all, to a large extent, caused by alcohol. Government programs designed to combat male mortality are few, but recent years have seen a slight decline in vodka consumption (though consumption rose again in 2022 with the war), greater control over its production, and the launch of some road safety policies. Little has been done regarding Russia's drug problems: about eight million Russian citizens were estimated to be drug users in the mid-2010s,[54] and the country ranks ninth in the world for prevalence of opiate use.[55] This consumption also influences the growth of the AIDS epidemic, with Russia's infection rate being thirty-first in the world, behind mostly sub-Saharan countries.[56] However, the authorities continue to ban alternative treatments such as methadone and syringe programs for at-risk groups.

The COVID-19 pandemic further deteriorated the country's global health standings, albeit with strong regional variation (see map 2.2). Officially, 400,000 people died from the coronavirus, meaning a proportional level of 270 deaths for 100,000 inhabitants, below that for the United States and Europe (mostly because Russia has fewer elderly people to begin with).[57] But when accounting for associated deaths (including all those who did not get treatment while the pandemic was overstretching medical facilities), the numbers rise to around 600,000 more people who died in 2021 compared to 2019, especially among the elderly, many of whom could likely be considered as collateral victims of the pandemic.[58] As in Europe, neoliberal reforms that transformed the previous, more generous, public health culture and hospital fabric across the country contributed to making the reaction to the pandemic more difficult to manage. But the lack of commitment of the Russian administration in implementing safety measures and the hesitations of Orthodox clergy toward vaccination have contributed to the death toll, which is among the highest in the developed world.

The Russian state agency for statistics, Rosstat, calculates that there will be 144 million inhabitants in the country by 2030 (including Crimea)[59]; the UN projects 142 million (excluding Crimea),[60] so both institutions are more or less in agreement about population statistics for the near term. These numbers are quite different from the grim forecasts from the early 2000s, which were

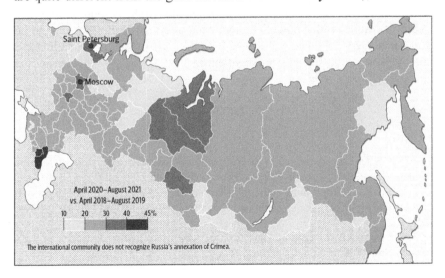

Map 2.2:   COVID excess mortality per region. *Source:* Rosstat.

calculating only about 120 to 130 million people for Russia.[61] But in the longer term, the demographic balance will be difficult to keep.

As European countries are, Russia is faced with a policy dilemma: the only way for the country to increase its population will be to accept and naturalize the many migrants who come to its borders, or—a matter more complex—to raise its fertility rate and reduce male mortality. Higher School of Economics demographers have calculated that Russia needs to take in between 400,000 (in an optimistic scenario) and one million (in a pessimistic scenario) immigrants a year for the next half century in order for the country to remain at around 146 million inhabitants, or else the country's population around the year 2100 could fall by as much as half.[62]

Russia's demographic future is also linked to the issue of its working-age population. Rosstat has a median projection for it to increase from 82 million in 2021 to 87 million in 2030.[63] Yet even if Rosstat's predictions come true, this will not solve the lack of the highly specialized cadres that Russian industry needs in the medium and long terms. In 2022, Russia lost about a million young qualified workers under age thirty-five—a number that will deprive Russian businesses of the brainpower they need.[64]

Demography and migration are only two pieces of the puzzle of Russia's complex nation building. Internal ethnic and regional diversity, as well as the ambiguous status of ethnic Russians in the symbolic politics of Russia's nationhood, will continue to create tensions both in government narratives and in the relationship between the state and some segments of society. The war in Ukraine, because it is justified by a language of imperial revanchism and sometimes of ethnic irredentism, makes the whole nation-building project more fragile, with a potential boomerang effect difficult to forecast so far. Russian society is indeed confronted with multiple other fragmentations, yet it still shows forms of unity and resilience.

## NOTES

1. See Riva Kastoryano, ed., *Les codes de la différence. Race, origine, religion. France, Allemagne, États-Unis* (Paris: Presses de Sciences Po, 2005).

2. See Ronald Grigor Suny and Terry Martin, eds., *A State of Nations: Empire and Nation-Making in the Age of Lenin and Stalin* (New York: Oxford University Press, 2001).

3. See Samuel P. Huntington, *The Clash of Civilizations and the Remaking of World Order* (New York: Simon & Schuster, 1996).

4. Lukasz Jurczyszyn, "Russian Radical Nationalist Interpretation of the French Riots of November 2005," *Demokratizatsiya: Journal of Post-Soviet Democratization* 19, no. 3 (Summer 2011): 277–85.

5. Oxana Shevel, "Russian Nation-Building from Yeltsin to Medvedev: Ethnic, Civic, or Purposefully Ambiguous?" *Europe-Asia Studies* 63, no. 1 (2011): 179–202.

6. See Dmitry Gorenburg, *Minority Ethnic Mobilization in the Russian Federation* (New York: Cambridge University Press, 2003).

7. The Soviet identity card (internal passport, or *vnutrennyi passport*) registered the ethnic origin (*natsionalnost'*) of each individual.

8. Valerii Tishkov, *Rossiiskii narod. Istoriia i smysl natsional'nogo samosoznaniia* (Moscow: Nauka, 2013).

9. All Russian censuses are available from *Demoskop Weekly*, published by the Higher School of Economics, http://www.demoscope.ru.

10. Adam Lenton, "Russia's Changing Ethnic Landscape: Three Takeaways from the 2021 Census," *Russia.Post*, January 30, 2023, https://russiapost.info/society/ethnic_landscape.

11. Estimates of ethnicities' sizes were arrived at by extrapolating the shares of the population that indicated ethnicity (130.6m) to the population as a whole (147.2m): Table 1, "Natsionalnyi sostav naseleniia," Vol. 5, "Natsionalnyi sostav i vladenie iazykami," Vserossiiskaia perepis naseleniia 2020. The estimate of the Muslim population is also supported by the Pew Research Center's 2017 survey, in which 10 percent of the Russian population (being about 14.5 million people, slightly under the number belonging to traditionally Muslim ethnicities) self-identified as Muslim; "Religious Belief and National Belonging in Central and Eastern Europe," Pew Research Center, May 10, 2017, http://www.pewforum.org/2017/05/10/religious-belief-and-national-belonging-in-central-and-eastern-europe.

12. Yitzhak M. Brudny, *Reinventing Russia: Russian Nationalism and the Soviet State, 1953–1991* (Cambridge, MA: Harvard University Press, 2000); Nikolai Mitrokhin, *"Russkaia partiia": dvizhenie russkikh natsionalistov v SSSR 1953–1985 gg* (Moscow: NLO, 2003).

13. Marlene Laruelle, Ivan Grek, and Sergey Davydov, "Culturalizing the Nation: A Quantitative Approach to the Russkii/Rossiiskii Semantic Space in Russia's Political Discourse," *Demokratizatsiya: The Journal of Post-Soviet Democratization*, no. 1 (2023): 3–28.

14. Richard Arnold, "Testing Constructivism: Why Not More 'Cossacks' in Krasnodar Kray?" *Post-Soviet Affairs* 30, no. 6 (2014): 481–502.

15. "Mandatory Tatar-Language Classes Scaled Back in Russia's Tatarstan," *RFE/RL*, November 9, 2017, https://www.rferl.org/a/russia-tatarstan-tatar-classes-scaled-back/28844162.html.

16. Marlene Laruelle, "Indigenous Peoples, Urbanization Processes, and Interactions with Extraction Firms in Russia's Arctic," *Sibirica* 18, no. 3 (2019): 1–8.

17. Mikhail Suslov, *Geopolitical Imagination* (Stuttgart, Germany: Ibidem, 2020).

18. Marlene Laruelle, "Russia as a 'Divided Nation,' from Compatriots to Crimea: A Contribution to the Discussion on Nationalism and Foreign Policy," *Problems of Post-Communism* 62, no. 2 (2015): 88–97.

19. Oxana Shevel, "The Politics of Citizenship Policy in Post-Soviet Russia," *Post-Soviet Affairs* 28, no. 1 (2012): 111–47.

20. "Destination," *International Migrant Stock 2020*, Population Division, Department of Economic and Social Affairs, UN, https://www.un.org/development/desa/pd/sites/www.un.org.development.desa.pd/files/undesa_pd_2020_ims_stock_by_sex_and_destination.xlsx.

21. Anne de Tinguy, *La grande migration* (Paris: Plon, 2004).

22. Sébastien Peyrouse, "Former 'Colonists' on the Move? The Migration of Russian-Speaking Populations," in *Migration and Social Upheaval as the Face of Globalization in Central Asia*, ed. Marlene Laruelle (London: Brill, 2013), 215–38; and Julien Thorez, "*Khorosho, gde nas net*. L'émigration des 'Russophones' d'Asie centrale," *EchoGéo*, no. 9 (2009): 1–25.

23. More in Marlene Laruelle, ed., *Migration and Social Upheaval as the Face of Globalization in Central Asia* (London: Brill, 2013).

24. See, for example, Zhanna Zaionchkovskaya, ed., *Migranty v Moskve* (Moscow: Tri kvadrata, 2009).

25. Galina G. Karpova and Maria A. Vorona, "Labour Migration in Russia: Issues and Policies," *International Social Work* 57, no. 5 (September 2014): 535–46.

26. Madeleine Reeves, "Clean Fake: Authenticating Documents and Persons in Migrant Moscow," *American Ethnologist* 40, no. 3 (2013): 508–24.

27. Esther Tetruashvily, "How Did We Become Illegal? Impacts of Post-Soviet Shifting Migration Politics on Labor Migration Law in Russia," *Region* 1, no. 1 (January 2012): 53–74.

28. Caress Schenk, "Controlling Immigration Manually: Lessons from Moscow (Russia)," *Europe-Asia Studies* 65, no. 7 (2013): 1444–65.

29. Umida Hashimova, "What 2015 Is Promising for Labor Migrants from Central Asia," *Central Asia Policy Brief*, no. 23 (March 2015), http://centralasiaprogram.org/archives/7380.

30. 1989 and 2020 Censuses; figures estimated by extrapolating ethnicities' shares of the ethnicity-indicating population the total population.

31. "Otdelnye pokazateli migratsionnoi situatsii v Rossiiskoi Federatsii za ianvar—dekabr 2021 goda s raspredeleniem po stranam mira," Russian Ministry of Internal Affairs.

32. See Eugene Avrutin, *Racism in Modern Russia: From the Romanovs to Putin* (London: Bloomsbury, 2022).

33. "Mozhet, ikh prosto otgorodit,'" *Kommersant Vlast*,' September 21, 1999, http://www.kommersant.ru/doc/15937.

34. For more details, see Marlene Laruelle, *In the Name of the Nation: Nationalism and Politics in Contemporary Russia* (New York: Palgrave Macmillan, 2009), 35–47.

35. "Monitoring ksenofobskikh nastroenii," Levada Center, September 18, 2019, https://www.levada.ru/2019/09/18/monitoring-ksenofobskih-nastroenij-2.

36. Caress Schenk, "Open Borders, Closed Minds: Russia's Changing Migration Policies: Liberalization or Xenophobia?" *Demokratizatsiya: Journal of Post-Soviet Democratization* 18, no. 2 (April 2010): 101–21.

37. Theodore Gerber, "Beyond Putin? Nationalism and Xenophobia in Russian Public Opinion," *Washington Quarterly* 37, no. 3 (2014): 113–34.

38. Edward Holland and Eldar Eldarov, "'Going Away on Foot' Once Again: The Revival of Temporary Labour Migration from Russia's Dagestan," *Central Asian Survey* 31, no. 4 (2012): 379–93.

39. Marlene Laruelle and Natalia Yudina, "Islamophobia in Russia: Trends and Societal Context," in *Religious Violence in Russia*, ed. Olga Oliker (Washington, DC: CSIS, 2018), 43–63.

40. Hilary Pilkington, Elena Omel'chenko, and Al'bina Garifzianova, *Russia's Skinheads: Exploring and Rethinking Subcultural Lives* (London: Routledge, 2010).

41. See the annual reports by the Moscow-based SOVA-Center, sova-center.ru.

42. On radical violence, see Richard Arnold, "Visions of Hate: Explaining Neo-Nazi Violence in the Russian Federation," *Problems of Post-Communism* 57, no. 2 (2010): 37–59.

43. "Baza dannykh: akty nasiliia," Sova Center, www.sova-center.ru/database/ violence.

44. Pål Kolstø, "Marriage of Convenience? Collaboration between Nationalists and Liberals in the Russian Opposition, 2011–2012," *Russian Review* 75, no. 4 (2016): 645–63.

45. "Migration Profile: Russia," Migration Policy Centre, Robert Schuman Centre for Advanced Studies, European University Institute, June 2013, https:// migrationpolicycentre.eu/docs/migration_profiles/Russia.pdf.

46. Ankit Panda, "Russian Emigration Spikes in 2013–2014," *The Diplomat*, July 25, 2014, http://thediplomat.com/2014/07/russian-emigration-spikes-in-2013-2014. See also *The Demographic Yearbook of Russia* (Moscow: Rosstat, 2021) 204.

47. Rosstat, "Chislennost' postoiannogo naseleniia v srednem za god," Rosstat, https://showdata.gks.ru/report/278930.

48. Rosstat, "Summarnyi koeffitsient rozhdaemosti," 2022, https://rosstat.gov.ru/ storage/mediabank/demo27(1).xlsx.

49. Olga A. Avdeyeva, "Policy Experiment in Russia: Cash-for-Babies and Fertility Change," *Social Politics: International Studies in Gender, State & Society* 18, no. 3 (2011): 361–86.

50. Lenton, "Russia's Changing Ethnic Landscape."

51. Michel Guillot, Natalia Gavrilova, and Tetyana Pudrovska, "Understanding the 'Russian Mortality Paradox' in Central Asia: Evidence from Kyrgyzstan," *Demography* 48, no. 3 (August 2011): 1081–1104.

52. See Rosstat, *2010 Vserossiiskaia perepis' naseleniia*, https://www.gks.ru/free _doc/new_site/perepis2010/croc/results.html.

53. "Deaths by Sex and Age Group for a Selected Country or Area and Year [caused by injury]," WHO Mortality Database, https://platform.who.int/mortality/themes/ theme-details/MDB/injuries.

54. "Strategy Report 2015," US Bureau for International Narcotics and Law Enforcement Affairs, International Narcotics Control, 279, https://2009-2017.state .gov/j/inl/rls/nrcrpt/2015/index.htm.

55. "Annual Prevalence of Use as a Percentage of the Population Aged 15–64 (Unless Otherwise Noted), [tab] Opiates," in "Prevalence of Drug Use in the General Population," Office on Drugs and Crime, UN, 2020, https://www.unodc.org/documents/data-and-analysis/WDR2021/1.2_Prevalence_of_drug_use_in_the_general_population_including_NPS_-_national_data.xlsx.

56. *Global Burden of Disease Study 2019*, Institute for Health Metrics and Evaluation, University of Washington School of Medicine, http://ghdx.healthdata.org/gbd-results-tool.

57. "Latest Reported Counts of Cases and Deaths," WHO Coronavirus (COVID-19) Dashboard, accessed December 2022, https://covid19.who.int/WHO-COVID-19-global-table-data.csv.

58. "Vozrastnye koeffitsienty smertnosti," EMISS.

59. "Izmenenie chislennosti naselenie po variantam prognoza," "Demograficheskii prognoz do 2036 goda," Rosstat, 2021, https://rosstat.gov.ru/storage/mediabank/progn1.xls.

60. "Russian Federation: Total Population, Probabilistic Projections," World Population Prospects 2022, Population Division, Department of Economic and Social Affairs, UN, https://population.un.org/wpp/Graphs/Probabilistic/POP/TOT/643.

61. See the different UN scenarios at United Nations Population Division, "Replacement Migration," https://www.un.org/development/desa/pd/sites/www.un.org.development.desa.pd/files/unpd-egm_200010_un_2001_replacementmigration.pdf.

62. "Demografy nazvali chislo migrantov dlia stabilizatsiia naseleniia Rossii," *RBC*, April 13, 2023, https://www.rbc.ru/economics/13/04/2023/64368b0a9a7947a647a61a2c.

63. "Demograficheskii prognoz do 2035 goda," Rosstat, 2020, https://rosstat.gov.ru/storage/mediabank/progn1.xls.

64. "Rossiia lishilas' bolee milliona molodykh rabotnikov iz-za voiny i massovoi emigratsii," *Moscow Times*, April 11, 2023, https://www.moscowtimes.ru/2023/04/11/rossiya-lishilas-bolee-milliona-molodih-rabotnikov-iz-za-voini-i-massovoi-emigratsii-a39641. See also "Nerabochii variant," *Kommersant*, December 27, 2022, https://www.kommersant.ru/doc/5748057.

3

# Russian Society

## *Fragmented but Resilient*

Russian society has profoundly changed over the past three decades. The data published by Rosstat and hundreds of sociological surveys conducted by the main polling centers, such as FOM, VTsIOM, Romir, and the independent Levada Center, have sketched the contours of a society disrupted by mutations of a scale and speed so great that, in many cases, one can speak of genuine social trauma. Three global features characterize post-Soviet Russian society: its high level of adaptability, its need for stability, and calls for predictability.

The first finding of all these sociological studies is the incredible reservoir of resilience in Russian society. The December 2022 Levada Center poll shows, for instance, a society that has adapted to wartime by staying out of politics, withdrawing into private life, focusing on everyday problems, and communicating with loved ones.[1] While Russians see the "special military operation" and the mobilization as the main events of the year, slightly more than half of citizens called 2022 "average," while only 30 percent called it a "bad" year, making 2022 a better year than 2020 (during the onset of the pandemic) and 1998 (during the economic crash)—a view that contrasts with Western interpretations of the war as a turning point.

Two-thirds of the population report not feeling the impact of sanctions directly, which one can interpret as a success of the authorities' skillful management of the crisis and the government spending done in favor of the poorest demographics. While public opinion panicked at the commencement of the war, the introduction of Western sanctions and the resulting plunge in the ruble's exchange rate, and then a second time at the announcement of the partial mobilization in September 2022, it nevertheless recovered rapidly. The Russian people expect 2023 to be a difficult year for them personally and for the country, yet the majority continue to believe Russia has survived worse crises. One can, of course, consider these surveys problematic in their answers, as the level of self-censorship is difficult to assess, but they fit what cultural anthropologist Jeremy Morris has been calling the "negative consolidation" of Russian society, habituated to facing and surviving hardship.[2]

Over the years, the index of fears of Russian citizens has remained amazingly stable: on a scale of 1 to 5, where 5 represents the public's worst fear, the fear that a new world war will happen stands at 3.5, second after the fear of losing loved ones. Fear of state arbitrariness has risen again to the level of the early 1990s, after having decreased in the 2000s to early 2010s (around 3.5), followed by fear of poverty, and state repression.[3] However, this adaptation also obscures a real divide in the population. In the mid-2010s, 25 percent still indicated they had "to get used to deprivation," and nearly 10 percent felt they could not adapt at all.[4] Even if the Levada Center noted the resilience of what it called the "stability reserve" (the ratio of those for whom it is possible to live under or bear difficult conditions, to those who say that these are not bearable), all these years were marked by anxieties in much of the population.

The other finding is the overwhelming need for stability and predictability. To the question of feeling confident about the future, those responding no (50 percent to 60 percent) always outnumbered the yeses (40 percent to 45 percent), with the exception of a short period between 2010 and 2012 and in the first months of 2014, after Crimea's annexation.[5] The number of those who say they feel reassured about their futures in the next one or two years increased from 15 percent in the early 1990s to 40 percent in 2014. While over 60 percent of those surveyed in 1990–1991 said they did not know where they would be in a few months, this number diminished to 37 percent in 2014.[6] With the war, the negative consolidation of society has modified perceptions: geopolitical fears have increased (the fear of a new world war dominated for 54 percent of the population in December 2022), while nonpersonal fears have decreased, and confidence in one's own future has increased (from 40 percent in December 2021 to 52 percent in December 2022).[7]

## ONE RUSSIA, SEVERAL RUSSIAS

If one looks beyond the traumas of the early post-Soviet years, the exceptional cohesion of public opinion around the figure of the president obscures one of the fundamental characteristics of Russian society: its fragmentation into several parallel realities.

## Adaptability to Social Traumas

During the 1980s and 1990s, the whole of society underwent radical changes: the impact of perestroika and the end of the Soviet system, a sharp reduction in Russia's territorial dominion over its neighbors, major political and economic reforms accompanied by hyperinflation and the evaporation of accumulated savings, the emergence of unemployment in the context of a newly free market for labor without the old government job guarantees, the devaluation of certain skills, and the loss of ideological certainties. It is very difficult to comprehensively assess the effects of these physical and psychological shocks (that is, the loss of jobs for some and loss of purchasing power for most).

While we should be cautious about drawing direct links between a deep economic and social crisis and its demographic impact, it appears certain that the 1991 crisis has had a lasting effect. Two indicators are often cited to measure some of these effects. As we saw in chapter 2, the general fertility rate reached a low of 1.1–1.2 in 1999–2000 before slowly rising. At the same time, the suicide rate per 100,000 people, at 23–24 in the mid-1980s, spiked to a peak of 46 in 1992, remained above 35 until the early 2000s, and fell to 15.4 in 2015.[8] Many saw these abrupt discontinuities as two symptoms of Russians' massive psychological trauma induced by rapid changes of the late 1980s through the early 1990s.

However, traditional macroeconomic and demographic indicators shed little light on the significant variation between regions, social classes, or families. The range of individual reactions to this tumultuous period has been impressively diverse. Some Russians, especially the elderly and those in rural areas, truly fell into a state of destitution. Those visiting Russia in the early 1990s can recall cohorts of women and retirees reduced to selling goods, clothing, or everyday objects on sidewalks or at Sunday markets in order to support themselves. At the same time, many former party officials and administrators, teachers, medical professionals, technicians, and researchers left their posts, often letting their skills fall into disuse as they sought more gainful employment, particularly in the service sector. Trade, banking, insurance, and private agencies of all kinds formed in the early 1990s (notaries, lawyers, consulting, advertising, and travel), and attracted thousands of defectors from formerly state-sponsored sectors.

One of the fascinating aspects of these changes is the speed with which some individuals, beginning in 1988–1989, resolutely embraced the emergence of new market-oriented careers, such as in trade, banking, and start-up companies—even in the absence of certainty about the management, legislative, and regulatory guidelines that would govern these activities. The first laws on cooperatives and the timid beginnings of privatization were initiated under the last Soviet premier, Mikhail Gorbachev. Former Communist Party cadres and members of the Communist youth organization Komsomol, who were relatively well informed, well connected, and trained as accountants or engineers, launched new ventures during this particularly troubled period. Some would go on to become oligarchs, others simply traders or owners of small and medium-sized enterprises. Many would lose their businesses as a result of score settling or forced mergers, which were common throughout the 1990s. But the massive scale of these vocational shifts is an unmistakable sign of the adaptability of a part of Russian society and of the maturation of aspirations for change under the late Soviet system.

Three decades after the onset of these ruptures, one can sketch out the new Russian society and its key features. The primary difference from Soviet society is the impressive increase in inequality, which has brought Russia closer to, if not higher than, most European countries on this metric. Of course, the equality claimed by Soviet ideology was only a facade that concealed a variety of situations. The Brezhnev era was based on the stabilization and reproduction of elites; members of the *nomenklatura* (the country's administrative elite) and their families had privileged networks (special shops, hospitals, and holiday resorts) and thus a very different way of life than common citizens had. Most Soviets had to adapt to living with a modest range of choices as well as shortages, but the regime offered a level of security that explains why nostalgic attitudes persist: free compulsory education, a basic guaranteed health system, the virtual absence of unemployment, and a highly monitored but largely accessible cultural infrastructure.

### From the Extreme Poor to the Extreme Rich

After the collapse of the Soviet Union, social differences quickly emerged. Russia's Gini coefficient (a measurement of income inequality, whereby 0 represents complete equality and 1 represents complete inequality, with all income accrued by a single individual) leapt from an estimated 0.289 in 1992 to 0.395 in 2000 and then peaked at around 0.421 beginning in 2010, before declining to 0.403 in 2020.[9] This put Russia's level of income inequality slightly higher than that in the countries of Western Europe but less than in the United States.

One can observe the presence of a sizable class of the extremely poor, those with incomes below the subsistence level, in each region of the country. This group declined significantly, from 29 percent of the population in 2000 to 12.5 percent in 2010 and 12 percent by 2020.[10] This reduction is due in large part to the proactive body of social policy initiated by the authorities, which has resulted in a substantial increase in pension payments and in purchasing power. Adding to this effective remedial policy is the maternity allowance, which has helped reduce the number of the extremely poor. However, the fact remains that the poorest 20 percent receive only 5.2 percent of total income, while the richest 20 percent collect more than 47 percent.[11]

According to survey data, the poor live mostly either in rural areas (49.5 percent) or in small towns of under fifty thousand people (24.8 percent). In 2021, the average monthly wage in the agriculture, hunting, fishing, and forestry sector was 69 percent the size of the overall average in the economy (although this is an improvement from 53 percent in 2010).[12] It is not surprising that many members of these impoverished social classes reported individual agricultural plots as one of their sources of income.

Such extreme precariousness has become a constant for this part of the Russian population, with the same consequences as in the West: deteriorating housing conditions, lack of access to certain types of care (such as dental) or services (such as culture and travel), spending a significant share of income on food, and an inability to help their children become established as independent adults. Russia's 44.7 million retirees (as of 2022) constitute an important share of the poor,[13] with monthly incomes often around US $200 to $300 in purchasing-power parity (PPP) terms. The extreme poverty and social trauma of the most fragile segments of the Russian population have played a central role in supporting the regime's paternalism, associated not so much with authoritarianism as with generous public policies.

At the same time, attention has been focused on the emergence of the small group of the super rich: the oligarchs, whose activities and lifestyles continuously arouse media curiosity. If one restricts the definition of this group to the criterion of net worth, their numbers have exploded since Putin's rise to power. According to the Russian edition of *Forbes* magazine, there were 7 Russian billionaires (in nominal US dollars) in 2002, 30 in 2005, and 111 in early 2014, before the onset of the Ukraine crisis and sanctions.[14] Contrary to Western expectations of sanctions' impact, the full-scale war with Ukraine seems to have enriched them: the total fortune of Russia's billionaires has increased from $353 billion to $505 billion between 2022 and 2023, and their numbers rose by 22 to 115 (not including the five of them who renounced their citizenship).[15] When lowering the threshold for defining the super rich down to US $500 million, this brings the figure to over 200 as of 2021.[16] Their lifestyles have made headlines, with purchases of yachts, football clubs, and sumptuous residences on the French Riviera, in Switzerland, and in London.

But more important than this jet-setting lifestyle is the oligarchs' role in the economy and society. The sources of their wealth are known. Under various conditions, they have benefited from the privatization (Russians have coined the term *prikhvatizatsiya*, a combination of the words for *privatization* and *seizure*) of the most profitable sectors of the economy: rent-generating sectors (such as oil and gas, minerals, metallurgy, and chemistry), the military-industrial complex (which benefits from government orders), and some service industries (such as banking, telecommunications, and media). They took advantage of offshore investments and globalized financial speculation early on, and their wealth became closely associated with corruption scandals and their permeation of the public and private sectors. Almost all have benefited one way or another from their proximity to political power, either during the Yeltsin era or later under Putin.

It is hardly surprising that in Levada Center polls, about three-quarters of respondents consider it is impossible to become a millionaire in Russia by honest means.[17] This explains why Russian public opinion did not feel sorry (80 percent did not care) about the seizure of oligarchs' wealth or assets in the West within the framework of the 2022 sanctions.[18] In addition, the media sensationalized the fact that many of the early oligarchs were of Jewish origin, feeding implicit anti-Semitism.

## The Difficult Consolidation of Russia's Middle Class

Naturally, the vast majority of the population falls between these extremes of abject poverty and extravagant wealth. Observers' attention has long focused on the emergence of a true middle class, the boundaries of which are disputed. The Russian middle class is commonly understood as being made up of families earning approximately US $2,500 (more in Moscow), but the definition of the category has as much to do with lifestyle as with income.

The average representative of this class is an executive or manager in a private firm who not only earns a relatively high salary but also has a retirement system and supplemental health insurance that provides access to good private clinics. They reside in a large city, own a home in a downtown neighborhood or in one of the protected suburbs as well as a *dacha* (vacation home), are able to invest in their children's education (including one or two years abroad for the better off), and can buy quality consumer goods. The family owns a car and spends some time abroad: summer and winter trips to Turkey or Egypt, and Europe or Southeast Asia for the wealthier. The number of Russians traveling to the "far abroad" (i.e., outside of the former Soviet Union) increased from ten million in 2000 to thirty-eight million in 2014 and forty-eight million in 2019.[19]

According to the calculation methods used by the sociological institutes, the middle class represents 25 percent to 40 percent of Russia's population. Enamored with stability, it has played, at least until the war, a growing role in public opinion, a point to which we will return in chapter 4. Despite the undeniable emergence of this new middle class, the country lacks the professions—skilled personnel and executives—that are traditionally associated with it. Russia is the only country in the world with such a high number of young people engaged in postsecondary or tertiary education and such a low number of new scientific or technical patents.[20]

This lack of a qualified labor force has weighed on the Russian economy since the mid-2000s. Major business leaders such as Alexey Mordashov, the head of the steel holding company Severstal, as well as representatives of business associations, have emphasized the dire need to educate new engineers and specialists and to revitalize the hard and applied sciences.[21] In 2009, a survey conducted among business leaders revealed that more than half of them could not recruit enough staff. The country's largest mining holding company, Nornickel, was forced to conduct recruitment campaigns in Ukraine and Kazakhstan in order to overcome the lack of qualified engineers.[22] The situation has obviously gotten worse with the war-related waves of emigration.

This shortage is even more acute in the area of new technologies and applied sciences. During his presidency (2008–2012), Dmitry Medvedev launched Skolkovo, a major technology innovation center located just outside of Moscow, as a symbol of his signature "modernization." Through it Russia was supposed to make its mark on the global market for new technologies and the deepen its partnerships with Western firms. Yet the country has not been able to produce a new generation of specialists in this highly competitive field, and the war-related sanctions have now reversed the country's technological progress.

Over the past three decades, brain drain has hit Russia hard. Between the collapse of the Soviet Union and the 2014 crisis, nearly thirty thousand researchers left the country, and the Soviet scientific heritage has been reduced to a minimum.[23] Advances remain in some theoretical subjects (such as mathematics and physics), but there are worrying gaps in most applied areas, with the exception of the information technology (IT) sector. In 2010, in parallel to Skolkovo, the authorities launched a major project to finance scientific institutions in the hope of attracting foreign talent and bringing back some expatriates, but without much success.[24]

Since Putin returned to the presidency in 2012, the marginalization of the country following the first Ukrainian conflict in 2014 and strained relations with the West have directly affected foreign investment and scientific partnerships, and the 2022 large-scale sanction waves have largely put an end to them. Symbolizing the brain drain of the early 2010s were the departures of the dean of the Higher School of Economics, Sergey Guriev, and the founder of the main Russian social media platform, equivalent to Facebook, Vkontakte (http://vk.com), Pavel Durov. With the full-scale war, the mobilization, and the new sanctions, the IT sector, which was flourishing in Russia these last years, has been badly impacted. The private sector–based middle class has found itself in challenging situations in the last three decades, yet the massive decoupling with the West that has followed the 2022 invasion of Ukraine has been of a totally different scale and has forced the Russian private sector to largely reinvent itself.

Of course, this new social stratification of the Russian population has a significant impact on the range of values and political attitudes that the different strata share. But before analyzing them, it is necessary to linger on another differentiating factor: the complex differences between types of geographical environments that strengthen these features.

## THE ENTRENCHED URBAN-RURAL DIVIDE

In analyzing the social and professional changes in progress, many Russian scholars insist on spatial divisions within Russian society. Nataliya Zubarevich, director of a major program on regional studies,[25] divides the country into four categories according to a given region's degree of social modernization. Building on this classification, one can clarify the tangible operating conditions of this new Russian society.

### Successful Regions and Cities

The first Russia is composed of the two capitals, Moscow and St. Petersburg (the present capital and the imperial capital, respectively). Moscow certainly holds a special place in the country and is the undisputed modern capital in all regards, a showcase for both the country and the regime, and a model of the economic transformations from which it directly benefits, with Moscow city and its wider region earning more than a quarter of the country's GDP. A few weeks before the beginning of the full-scale war, Moscow was even named the third most prosperous city in the world by the UN-Habitat's City Prosperity Index.[26] St. Petersburg is seeking to bring itself in line with its old rival; but although it can claim cultural and tourist assets, the northern metropolis remains provincial in many ways. It is Moscow that defines all political trends, as well as cultural ones, from architecture to the art market and fashion.

Profoundly transformed by the privatization of real estate and the application of a liberal model of development, the city is now socially and functionally segregated. Gentrification has gradually won out in the downtown area, Moscow's administrative and commercial core. The wealthier segments of the population are concentrated in protected virtual islands, luxury buildings in some central areas such as Ostozhenka, or, more often, in the gated communities and new residential neighborhoods that have mushroomed in the western part of the city. They are well-preserved from an ecological point of view, especially around the lakes of Serebriannyi Bor or toward Rublevka, where most of the official residences of the country's political elite are located. Other central areas, where prices have soared, focus on the new middle classes, who benefited from a dense network of services until the 2022 war; foreign chains such as Swedish furniture giant IKEA or French home and garden retailer Leroy-Merlin, Russia's own Azbuka Vkusa ("alphabet of taste") network of luxury stores, and the popular French Auchan superstores; restaurants and trendy cafes; theaters and cinemas; and agencies of various sorts.

The rapid privatization of housing benefited the tenants installed at the end of the Soviet era, initially providing some social diversity. But the rapid rise in prices has made access to Moscow difficult for newcomers, the young, and the lower-middle classes from the suburbs. Life on the wide margins of the urban area, whether inside or outside the administrative boundaries of the city, is more difficult, with significant commutes made longer by seemingly permanent traffic jams. The communal apartments (former "bourgeois" apartments shared by several families) that were once a part of Soviet daily life have disappeared downtown but have proliferated on the outskirts in new ways. Migrants from Central Asia and from Russian ethnic regions are crammed ten or twenty people to an apartment, often of the same sex and grouped by region of origin. Social tensions related to ethnicity, which were virtually unknown in Soviet times, but are now beginning to be felt, take, for instance, the form of unease about the crowds of young Muslims who fill the streets and squares adjacent to the Grand Mosque in downtown Moscow on every major Islamic holiday.

A second Russia consists of the dynamic regions that are not only home to promising economic sectors—oil or other mineral production industries, large, modernized companies, and rich agriculture (in the south)—but also benefit from the driving role of their regional metropolis. This category encompasses the fifteen cities with more than one million inhabitants (called "millionaire cities" in Russia, *millioniki*), as well as some less populated regional administrative capitals (see map 3.1). Although the difference in comparison to Moscow is still marked, rapid and major changes can be observed all around: the transformation of downtown areas into trendy neighborhoods that are partly pedestrian, reserved for shops, restaurants, cultural facilities, and services; the construction on the outskirts of town of US-style commercial malls; and the development of service sectors for qualified professionals.

An important element of this success is that many people from the provinces are unwilling to live in Moscow, which they consider unfriendly, polluted, and exhausting. They want to maintain a balanced life that involves limited commuting times, being close to nature, and more direct forms of

Population increase in the major cities of Russia, 2010–2022 (2010 = 100).

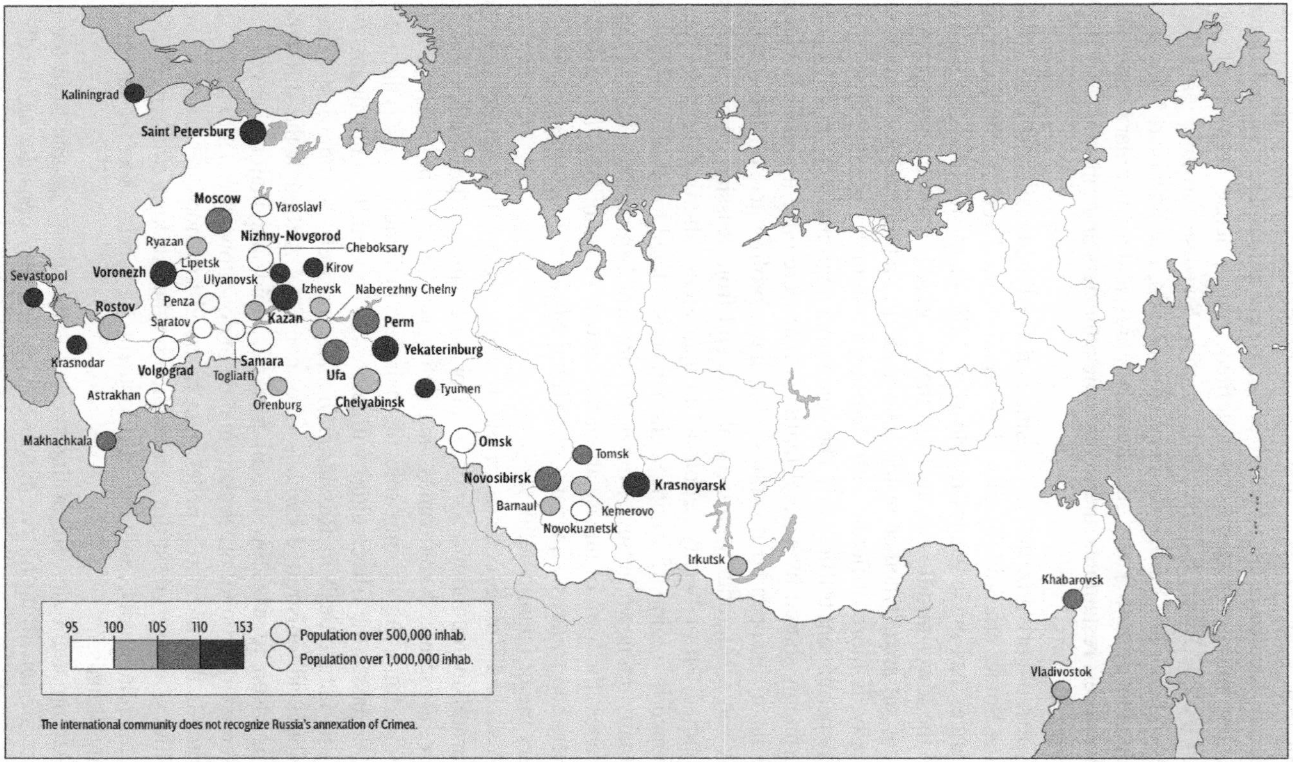


**Map 3.1: Population increase in the major cities of Russia, 2010–2022 (2010 = 100).** ***Source:*** **Rosstat.**

participation in neighborhood life and interaction with local authorities. This provincial dynamism is essential to understanding an under-studied aspect of "deep" Russia. Some lively cities are image conscious and concerned about their branding, such as Tatarstan's capital Kazan and Sverdlovsk's capital Yekaterinburg, which are perpetually vying for the title of "third capital city"; Krasnodar and Rostov-on-Don, which compete for the title of Russia's "southern gateway"; or Vladivostok, which has claimed the mantle of "gateway to the East," as its own name in Russian (literally, "East-rule") implies. The most vibrant examples of these cities' dynamism rely on fairs and festivals, which create annual forums and become important dates on the national calendar, or academic centers and federal universities supposed to attract new elites. As always, much depends on the personality of the governor and having a team that knows how to seize opportunity and resist the temptation of patronage networks that divert a share of resources from the actual needs of the public.

## Depressed and Remote Regions

The third territorial category is the mass of intermediate regions, in which a few vibrant cities manage to thrive by taking advantage of a resource or local company that has resisted the many post-Soviet crises—like Norilsk in the Far North or, closer to Moscow, Kaluga—or simply by having a more entrepreneurial mayor or "city manager." On the contrary, many midsize cities with good reputations in terms of living conditions during the Soviet period now suffer from reliance on a single industry, especially when it is based on manufacturing or textiles. Many blue-collar cities, sometimes linked to the military-industrial complex, have also found themselves in dire straits when government orders stopped and impacted the whole region around them.[27]

The majority of rural areas and small towns (classified in Russian statistics as those with fewer than fifty thousand inhabitants), however, fall into the fourth Russian territorial category: depressed regions. This includes northern Russian villages and Siberian towns, which continue to suffer from dying industries and a weak road network that prevents any modernization. As already mentioned, the elderly tend to populate these small villages or hamlets. At best, the nearest urban centers become *dacha* villages that are popular among urban dwellers; this may save a few old wooden houses but does not change the overall balance. For decades, there has been a little more dynamism in peripheral areas closer to towns, while the most distant outlying areas have withered both economically and demographically.

The cities of these depressed areas often make for a worrying picture. Signs of modernization are everywhere: a hotel or mansion, a couple of restaurants, a few shops that are much better stocked than at the end of the Soviet era, and widely available internet access. But this does not dispel the impression of abandonment: streets pockmarked with potholes, broken sidewalks, and historic buildings left in ruins (with the exception of restored churches). In some public housing neighborhoods in depressed workers' cities, it is not uncommon to lack running water or district heating, such that residents must resort to fetching water from pumps on the street and heating apartments with wood-burning stoves.

Next to this, and sometimes in the same region, it is possible to find villages or small towns that have escaped this curse thanks to a savvy mayor or a dynamic collective movement that took over the affairs of the city and was able to draw on—or develop—economic resources in the form of tourism or agro-industrial activity. The facades of houses have been restored, streets have been paved, and some museums and new shops have opened. In Russia's south, much more compact and densely-populated large rural towns have maintained collective functions, family assets, and mutual assistance mechanisms that are more common among Caucasians and Cossacks. Houses have been enlarged and enhanced with new additions, large courtyards are planted with fruit trees, and cars and trucks are omnipresent—all testaments to these households' commitment to successful interregional trade.

These differences in development and modernization, coupled with the sense of abandonment that the inhabitants of many villages and small towns feel, feed high levels of disillusionment and depression. Against such a background, it is easy to understand the nostalgia expressed for the Soviet era, when the material aspects of life seemed more assured. These feelings often reflect a rejection of Moscow and Muscovites, a mixture of jealousy and envy that was present in Soviet times but has been revived by differences in income and lifestyles. The flashes of frustration born from such disparities can quickly turn toward convenient scapegoats—the Roma, Caucasians, and migrants, who are accused of benefiting from this situation. Xenophobic actions bear witness to the growing gap in lifestyles and cultural values in a society that has become increasingly complex over the past three decades.

## THE WIDENING GAP IN CULTURAL VALUES

The socioeconomic fragmentation of Russian society directly impacts the diversity of cultural values expressed by different social groups. It is difficult to identify dominant trends, as the variety of reactions to openness to the world and globalization has led to myriad complex processes in a country that was long closed to outside influences.

## Cultural Globalization and Reactions to It

The first massive reaction was the extraordinarily rapid spread of a number of foreign models, largely dominated by US examples, once seen only through the distorted prism of the Soviet media. One can easily date this craze to the January 1990 opening of the first McDonald's, on Pushkin Square in downtown Moscow, which created incredibly long lines. At the beginning of 2022, before the invasion of Ukraine, the company had 850 stores in Russia.[28] There are many other examples of the "Westernization" of Russian consumer society, from the IKEA and Auchan networks already mentioned to the presence in virtually all cities of companies such as Pizza Hut, Le Pain Quotidien, Starbucks, Coca-Cola, and Apple, as well as many foreign luxury brands.

It is important to note that this openness is not only to the West. The country has also experienced strong Asian influences, including Chinese and Japanese food, the Japanese cars that make up the bulk of the automotive fleet east of the Urals, the affinity for martial arts, K-pop music, and a craze for Caucasian and Central Asian cuisine (exemplified by the Alaverdi and Chaikhona No. 1 restaurant chains). Far from being limited to trade or food, this trend is also reflected in architecture: the new Sochi ski resort resembles the major resorts of the Rocky Mountains, and the amusement park adjacent to the Olympic Stadium is a Russian copy of Disney World. Television (including Brazilian, Turkish, and South Korean series) and women's magazines (such as the Russian versions of *Elle*, *Cosmopolitan*, and *Vogue*) are part of the same globalizing trend.

The war in Ukraine has reshaped this foreign brand landscape: the most famous Western brands have left or paused their activities in Russia under boycott campaigns by activists and concerns for their reputation (see chapter 5). While fancy neighborhoods of Moscow have indeed seen commercial malls emptied of their Western brands, the Russian retail business, especially in agribusiness and catering services, clothes, and so forth, has enough to offer to compensate for the disappearance of Western brands, and newcomers from Asia or the Middle East fill out the abandoned niches.

The results of thirty years of opening are contradictory. One often has the feeling of a sort of disorganized copy-and-paste of the most popular and commercial Western models, a mix of European hipness and Disney esthetics, somewhere between New York, Berlin, and Dubai but with a Russian coloration. Yet a closer look reveals other trends. The globalization of food, for example, quickly sparked resistance that can be seen in the appearance of new, typically Russian fast-food networks, such as Mu-Mu or Yolki-Palki. During the Olympic Games in Sochi, the impressive Olympic Park restaurant served more Russian specialties—soups, *pirogi* (pies), *pelmeni* (Siberian dumplings), and *blini* (pancakes)—than global dishes (pizzas, hamburgers, hot dogs, and rolls). A strong patriotic movement resurfaced, demanding a return to "real" Russian values.

This current, riding the wave of nostalgia induced by the destabilizing effects of the reforms, has continued to assert itself in all areas. In architecture, it is seen in the revival of wooden buildings, the proliferation of churches and chapels on the urban landscape, and the overwhelming presence of icons and other Orthodox religious symbols. It is also exemplified by the reappropriation of reinvented traditional crafts: linen and felt, leather and wood, ceramic and porcelain. On top of this, there have been attempts to make space for products marked "Made in Russia" in the hope of reviving economic nationalism—and these are now accelerating as a way of dealing with the decoupling from the West as a result of the 2022 war.

## Beyond the Russian Orthodox Church: Russia's Religious Diversity

Foreign influences over Russian society in the last three decades have also been found at much deeper levels. By the late 1990s, there was virtually no city, large or small, that did not have a Protestant church started by an Adventist, Baptist, or Pentecostal proselytizing group. This took advantage of people's critical need for new points of reference in the wake of the disappearance of the Soviet ideological system but also relied on funding from American, German, or Korean parent organizations.[29] Their aggressive activities in the spiritual realm, as well as with school programs (they circulated textbooks translated into Russian) and charities, soon disturbed the Russian Orthodox Church, which tried to prohibit their expansion by promoting the adoption of restrictive laws. The authorities came to view the new churches as a Western attempt to subvert Russian society.

Russia's religious landscape has widely diversified, despite thundering declarations from the Orthodox Church, which claims to represent the Russian nation as a whole.[30] Since the collapse of the Soviet Union, the number of people who openly say they consider themselves Orthodox Christians has certainly grown. Between 1991 and 2020, the proportion of those professing belief in God increased by 2.5 times, from 14 percent to 35 percent; the share of avowed atheists decreased from 18 percent to 9 percent; and the number of those not knowing, or believing intermittently, or believing in a higher force but not in God, remained more or less stable.[31]

The proportion of Russian citizens declaring themselves to be Orthodox (an ambiguous formulation that does not necessarily imply belief in God or adherence to specific practices) has stabilized at around 65 percent, making it lower than the share of people identifying as ethnic Russians (80 percent), as some belong to another faith or denomination or do not feel attached to any faith, but higher than the share of those who believe in God, with the implication that many self-described Orthodox Christians are nonbelievers. A survey conducted in 2021 found that only 55 percent of respondents said they belonged to a religion, of whom 81 percent identified Orthodoxy as their religion, meaning only 40.5 percent of Russian citizens identified as Orthodox believers.[32]

Religious practice remains even more minimal, at numbers close to the most secular countries in Europe. Church attendance is very low, estimated at between 2 percent and 6 percent, depending on how the question is framed. This confirms that Russia shares with Europe the trend of "Identitarian Christianism,"[33] referring to Christian roots as part of national culture and identity to oppose Islam, migrants, or, in the Russian case, the supposedly decadent West, but without any religious practice.

Yet the Church has secured the respect of a large part of the population. More than 90 percent of the public has a positive attitude toward it, a figure that includes members of ethnic minorities belonging to other faiths.[34] A slight majority of Russians support the idea of protecting the Church from symbolic degradation and consider insulting religious values inappropriate. According to a 2013 survey conducted by the pooling agency FOM (Public Opinion Foundation) at the time of the Duma discussions on a law against blasphemy in the wake of the Pussy Riot affair (a Russian feminist protest and performance punk group that sang an anti-Putin song in the famous Orthodox Cathedral in Moscow before getting arrested), 55 percent of respondents supported imposing fines for offending religious feelings, while only 8 percent were opposed.[35] Interestingly, people with higher education and residents of big cities (Moscow excluded) tended to be more in favor of the law, while young people (eighteen- to twenty-four-year-olds) and Muscovites took a less supportive stance.

Outside of Orthodoxy, Russia counts about 300,000 Protestants, 140,000 Catholics, 90,000 Jews (a drastic decrease from the 537,000 at the last Soviet census of 1989), around 150,000 Hindus and Krishna worshippers (both expatriates from South Asia as well as converts), and over a million neo-pagans.[36] But more important are the two other main religious traditions within Russia: Buddhism in Buryatia and Tuva (both just north of Mongolia) as well as in Kalmykia (on the northwest shore of the Caspian Sea), and obviously Islam, the second-largest religion in the country.

Like the rest of their fellow citizens, Muslim Russians live in diverse socioeconomic and cultural situations. One can distinguish at least four different contexts for Muslim Russians. First and second are the North Caucasus and the Volga-Urals regions, where Muslims live on their ancestral territories. The North Caucasus is set apart from the rest of Russia in many respects, including due to its remoteness and the low number of ethnic Russians

still living there: they still represent about 30 percent of the population in
the western North Caucasus regions of Karachay-Cherkessia and about 22
percent in Kabardino-Balkaria, but only 3 percent in Dagestan and less than
1 percent in Chechnya, which form the eastern half of the North Caucasus
border territories.[37] In the Volga-Urals region, Tatars and Bashkirs (both local
Turkic peoples) are almost as numerous as ethnic Russians. Both are better
integrated into the Federation framework and Russian culture than their North
Caucasian counterparts are, but they, too, live on ancestral Muslim soil, the
region having converted as early as the ninth century.

More recently, two other regions have come to host important Muslim
communities: the Moscow region and western Siberia. The Moscow region
is home to about two million Muslims, both citizens and immigrants, and
has become one of the capitals of Russian Islam: it hosts one of the country's main Islamic institutions, the Spiritual Administration of Muslims of
the Russian Federation (DUM RF); has erected Russia's main Cathedral
Mosque[38]; and serves as a hub for the production of halal goods to be sent
across Russia and the post-Soviet space. Western Siberia, and especially
the rich Yamalo-Nenets and Khanty-Mansi Autonomous Okrugs (to the
immediate northwest and center-west of the Ural Mountains, respectively),
has become the new home of tens of thousands of Muslims from the North
Caucasus, Volga-Urals, Azerbaijan, and Central Asia, who have been migrat-
ing there since the 1960s to work in the oil and gas fields. These migrants,
who now control a large proportion of western Siberia's informal and retail
markets (such as in transportation, food, clothing, and everyday furniture),
have been financially successful enough that it has become fashionable in
their countries or regions of origin to marry a "northern guy" (*Severianin*), a
migrant who has succeeded in western Siberia.[39]

Beyond these four regions, Muslims have settled in all of Russia's major
cities, including Vladivostok and Yuzhno-Sakhalin Island on the Pacific
coast. Islamic communities prosper in Far North cities such as Norilsk, to
the point that Russia can brand itself as having the world's northernmost
mosque—a title for which it competes with Canada, as the booming oil province of Alberta hosts several small mosques.[40]

## From Old Believers to Hipsters, Diverse Ways of Life

Despite the authorities' desire to control society, a growing number of communities are coalescing around specific practices, cults, and ideas outside
of the mainstream favored by the regime and the official media. From time
to time, on the occasion of some scandal or diversion, the press refers to
the existence of these various groups and sects, from fire worshippers of
Ramakrishna to environmentalist communities. The two extremes of this

wide spectrum are the Old Believers, on one side, and the "bobos" (bourgeois bohemians) or hipsters, on the other.

Russia's territorial vastness makes it possible for certain religious communities to preserve their lifestyles and operate almost hermetically, like the Amish in the United States. This is the case for Old Believer communities. Born of an internal schism in the Russian Orthodox world in the seventeenth century, they managed to survive Tsarist and Soviet persecution due to their isolation. It is estimated that there are as many as two million Old Believers in the world today, including the descendants of relatively large groups that emigrated to North America. In Russia, these communities total around four hundred thousand people and are concentrated mainly in eastern Siberia and the Far North. The Old Believers, divided into several subbranches, are now out of hiding; the main groups have returned to the bosom of the Orthodox Church and recognize the authority of the Moscow Patriarchate[41] but have preserved the specificity of their rituals and even inspired some Russian nationalists to convert.

There are also some communities belonging to another schismatic movement, the Dukhobors (often presented as folk-protestants inside the Orthodox realm, as they reject priesthood and rituals). Several hundred Dukhobor families were repatriated from Georgia to Russia, mainly to the Tambov region (due southeast of Moscow), in a publicized but relatively marginal move.[42] Orthodox traditionalists are easily recognized by their appearance—long dresses for women, and beards and old-fashioned shirts for men—and their large families.

In addition, there are some New Age communities that call for a return to nature and the rehabilitation of pre-Christian rites derived from neo-Druidism, Wicca, and so forth. Some of these movements advocate for a doctrinal neo-paganism with books of faith, priests, and rituals, and they often incorporate nationalist elements. Others are more eclectic and remain faithful to the New Age principle that a holistic spiritual quest can only be an individual path.[43] The archaeological site of Arkaim, near Chelyabinsk (at the southeastern end of the Urals), has become the Russian Stonehenge. Dating from the seventeenth century BCE, the site is particularly well preserved, but its historical value has been completely overtaken by the New Age cult that has established itself there. Presented as "the city of the swastika," the ancient capital of a so-called Aryan civilization, the site receives tens of thousands of curious visitors in search of esoteric mysticism and holistic medicines every year. The tourist draw is so strong that even the regional administration has gotten into the game, emphasizing the exceptional nature of the place as "connected" to higher powers.[44]

At the other end of the ideological spectrum, the upper-middle classes of large cities have seen the slow emergence of "bobos," or hipster communities, a phenomenon that Russia shares with Europe. These families are financially comfortable, have considerable cultural capital, possess advanced degrees, and are accustomed to consuming cultural goods (books, films, music, and art). Before the war, they were well integrated into the global world, regularly traveling abroad and sending their children there to study. They promote eclectic Western or liberal values—environmentalism, feminism, antiracism, the rejection of established hierarchies, and cultural diversity—though without necessarily seeing these as entailing politicization against the regime. The war has hit these communities hard at all levels, with many emigrating, with cultural spaces and habits shrinking, and with an ideological tightening that has made the authorities consider them as part of the political opposition.

## Which Shared Values?

Beyond this diversity, a product of both Russia's territory and history, what do Russian citizens share? The European Values Survey gives us a good overview of Russian society as a whole: Russians have a high rate of "conservation," defined as security, conformity, and tradition (these being the opposed to the contrary notions of independence, stimulation, and hedonism) when compared to other European nations. They exhibit "security" values, find themselves in the middle on "conformity" and "tradition," and rank particularly low on "risk and novelty." However, in terms of "openness to change" versus "conservation," Russia is basically the same as many other Western and Central European countries. The only value on which it clearly stands out is a preference for "self-enhancement" (power, wealth, achievement) over "self-transcendence" (universalism and benevolence), probably a product of what had then been three decades of liberal reforms that had shrunk the welfare state and eroded horizontal ties.[45]

While Russian society is very fragmented in its ways of life, one can still identify a majority unified around some key shared values. The memory of the Great Patriotic War (as World War II is called by Russians) has been the cornerstone of the social and cultural consensus, reinforced over the years by state-backed narratives. Linked to this, Soviet nostalgia has been one of these unifying elements for a large part of the society, rising up to more than 70 percent in the mid-1990s, shrinking to 50 percent around 2012, and since then rising again to around 60 percent today.[46]

Yet this nostalgia should be interpreted with caution, as it more often describes a cultural nostalgia that allows for indirectly expressing dissatisfaction with today's global values, especially neoliberal reforms, more than any form of political nostalgia for the Soviet regime. When asked about what has been lost with the disappearance of the Soviet Union, Russian citizens remember first and foremost a unified economic system (49 percent), the feeling of belonging to a great power (46 percent), and mutual support (36 percent).[47] Renewed interest for everything Soviet, from food to everyday items and design, as well as for Soviet cultural production, in particular movies and music, has thus offered a form of identity safety net for a society facing full-scale cultural and value readjustments.

Nostalgia for some forms of moral order translated later into massive support for patriotic and paramilitary training for youth: in 2016, 78 percent of Russians supported reinstating a military preparation course in schools. It can also explain popular support for a state ideology. In 2021, the question "Do you believe that Russia needs a state ideology?" was answered in the affirmative by 79 percent of those surveyed, while only 14 percent responded negatively.[48] These numbers confirm that, for many Russians, today's Russia is still in need of a new societal order, translated into the language of a "state ideology"—a narrative obviously strongly endorsed by the regime and the Church, as we will discuss in chapter 4.

In terms of moral values, Russian society remains plural, even if it has become more conservative over the years.[49] Russians have, for instance, become polarized on abortion, with 46 percent in support of and 47 percent opposed to it in 2021.[50] Yet this rise in opposition has not translated into pushing for a full ban but, instead, into the view that it should be authorized only in some circumstances (medical and socioeconomic). The same trend, yet less divisive, is noticeable on the issue of divorce, with an increase in those categorically condemning it, from 16 percent in 2012 to 36 percent in 2021.[51]

On both these issues, the gap between attitudes and behaviors is important. Although some conservative values may prevail discursively, actual behavior tends to be far more liberal, especially when it comes to practices inherited from the Soviet era. For instance, even though an increasing number of Russians describe divorce as reprehensible in public opinion polls, it remains fairly common: Russia's ratio of marriages to divorces is in line with the European average. Putin even divorced his wife when he was already in office, a risk no American president has ever taken. Moreover, people across the country largely accept common-law relationships and single motherhood. On abortion, there has been a marked change in practice: in the past thirty years, the number of abortions has dropped by 80 percent.[52] Today Russia's current abortion legislation is more restrictive than its Soviet counterpart was, but the restrictions are still in line with those of many progressive European countries.

The LegitRuss survey, conducted in 2021, paints a picture of a society with mixed attitudes toward conservative values. Two-thirds favor equality of women and men in the job market, but only half support gender equality in politics; childcare duties are seen almost unanimously as a shared responsibility between parents; sex before marriage is accepted by a little more than half of the population; and the ideal family size is two or three children. Conservative values appear especially in relation to sexuality, with a huge majority in favor of a heterosexual family.

Indeed, one of the crystallizing issues reflecting Russia's societal transformations has been the status of homosexuality, heavily instrumentalized by the regime in its fight against the West (see chapter 4). For a long time, Russia was only moderately conservative in terms of public attitudes toward homosexuality: in 2005, 51 percent of its population agreed fully or partly with the idea that homosexuals should have the same rights as other citizens. Between the decriminalization of homosexuality in 1993 and the first so-called anti–homosexual propaganda law in 2013, Russia passed no specific legislation either against homosexuals or to protect them from discrimination. Homosexuality was considered a private matter: it was not forbidden, but LGBTQ+ individuals were asked to remain invisible, with very few activists fighting for recognition.[53]

The peak of homophobic attitudes was reached in 2013, yet two caveats must be noted. The first is that homophobia may express different things in the popular vernacular than at the level of state rhetoric: it may relate more to citizens' relationship to cynical elites and nostalgia for Soviet cultural homogeneity than to an existential Russia–West binary. It is also often an expression of social distress on the part of the lower and middle classes and a way of coming to terms with economic inequalities without using the language of class (LGBTQ+ culture is seen as a product of hipster upper classes).[54]

Second, it seems that popular homophobia is on the decline. In 2019, Levada registered the highest level of support for LGBTQ+ rights, with 59 percent of respondents agreeing with the statement "Gays and lesbians should enjoy the same rights as other citizens" compared to 43 percent who disagreed.[55] Yet when the question is asked in a more precise manner, for instance, authorizing same-sex marriage, only 12 percent supported it—a rise after falling to 4 percent in 2013, albeit still low.[56] Homophobia thus appears to be a highly ideological point of tension around Russia's own representation as a specific nation and its ideological competition with the West, which explains its salience in state-backed conservatism.

After the division between urbans and rural dwellers, generational gaps form another major line of divide in Russian public opinion. Born into an individualistic and less oppressive culture, younger cohorts are more inclined to accept individual differences and are more tolerant of individuals' sexual orientations than older generations. The 2018 Levada survey on Soviet nostalgia showed that Russian youth are the least nostalgic of all age cohorts.[57] Urban students are more opposition-minded than older generations or rural youth are, more favorable toward liberal parties such as Yabloko, and more positive toward dissident leader Alexey Navalny.

The youth also tend to be more critical of Soviet child-rearing practices: young people oppose patriotic education in school twice as much as the average person (48 percent and 24 percent, respectively), while older people are the most supportive (with 81 percent in favor).[58] And while the entire population has been affected by a rise in anti-Americanism since the 2014 Ukraine crisis, young people remain largely more positive about the United States (and the West more broadly) than older generations: in 2018, 60 percent of those aged eighteen to twenty-four had a positive view of the United States, compared to an average of 33 percent for the country as a whole.[59]

The LegitRuss survey confirmed this trend, finding that young people (defined as those under thirty-four) are more likely to agree that people can have sex before marriage, are more tolerant toward homosexuality, and are less likely to agree that a course on the basics of Orthodox culture should be taught in schools. The same generational divide is visible in relation to the death penalty: the youngest cohort (ages eighteen to twenty-four) supports its having been abolished, while older generations (age fifty-five and older) are more supportive of restoring the death penalty as it existed in the 1990s.[60] Young people also have more faith in the court system: 49 percent of those up to age twenty-nine trust the courts "a great deal" or "quite a lot," compared to 40 percent of those between thirty and forty-nine.[61]

The generational divide became particularly visible with the onset of the war in Ukraine: young people are less supportive of the war than the Russian average, especially as compared to their grandparents' generation, likely since they may be the ones at risk of being sent to the front line but also because they watch less televised propaganda and consume a more diverse array of news sources.[62]

In the four decades of transformation that have followed the onset of perestroika in 1985, Russian society has been fractured to its core. To a large extent, it has adopted Western societies' consumerism, values, and ways of living. This is, in part, the acceleration of a natural trend that was delayed by the ideological and material barriers once imposed by the Soviet system. But this process uncovers much deeper contradictions. When the Levada Center asked, before Crimea's annexation, how current Russians differ from Soviets, 26 percent said that they understand the world better, 29 percent that they are freer, and 30 percent that they are poorer—but 35 percent also indicated that they are more intolerant of others, and 58 percent said that they have become more cold and calculating.[63]

As political and social rights have shrunk in Russia over the last two decades, adherence to norms, values, and cultural practices has become the glue that holds citizens together and preserves the social contract with the state. At a time when Russian society remains very diverse in terms of ways of life and cultural consumption, some forms of discursive moral conservatism allow for the sharing of common values.

When asked in March 2014 about what historical path Russia should take, 21 percent responded that it should take the path of European civilization, while 22 percent would prefer to return to the path forged by the Soviet Union, and 46 percent believed that Russia must choose its own, special way. In 2020,[64] the results were 14 percent, 30 percent, and 47 percent, respectively.[65] This is the paradox of the current situation. While the population largely identifies with Europeans' lifestyles and dreams of a European-style welfare state, surveys note the rise of anti-Americanism and wider anti-Westernism as well as genuine debate over which values to defend. It is these rifts that are instrumentalized by the Kremlin and of which Putin takes advantage when he celebrates Russia's supposed defense of so-called traditional values and the need to protect Russia from Western normative intrusion.

# NOTES

1. Denis Volkov, "Reservoir for Resilience: Why Russians Do Not See 2022 as a Disaster," *Russia Post*, January 11, 2023, https://russiapost.info/page33166724.html.

2. Jeremy Morris, "Russians in Wartime and Defensive Consolidation," *Current History* 121, no. 837 (2022): 258–63.

3. "Strakhi," Levada Center, December 2022, https://www.levada.ru/tag/strahi.

4. *Obshchestvennoie mnenie—2014* (Moscow: Levada Center, 2015), 15.

5. *Obshchestvennoie mnenie—2014*, 14.

6. *Obshchestvennoie mnenie—2014*, 22.

7. "Predvstavleniia o budushchem: gorizont planirovaniia i nastroienia," Levada Center, January 11, 2023, https://www.levada.ru/2023/01/11/predstavleniya-o-budushhem-gorizont-planirovaniya-i-nastroeniya.

8. Il'nur Aminov, "Smertnost' ot samoubiistv v Rossii i v mire," *Demoskop Weekly*, 705–6 (November 14–27, 2016), http://demoscope.ru/weekly/2016/0705/tema03.php.

9. *Rossiia v tsifrakh—2016* (Moscow: Rosstat, 2016), 129; *Rossiia v tsifrakh—2021* (Moscow: Rosstat, 2021), 64. See also World Bank, "GINI Index: Russian Federation, United States," https://data.worldbank.org/indicator/SI.POV.GINI?locations=US-RU&most_recent_value_desc=true.

10. *Rossiia v tsifrakh—2021*, 56.

11. *Rossiiskii statisticheskii ezhegodnik—2015* (Moscow: Rosstat, 2015), 158.

12. *Rossiiskii statisticheskii ezhegodnik—2022* (Moscow: Rosstat, 2022), 156.

13. "Obshchaia chislennost pensionerov v Rossiiskoi Federatsii," Rosstat, 2022, https://rosstat.gov.ru/storage/mediabank/sp_2.1.docx.

14. "88 rossiiskikh milliarderov. Reiting Forbes—2022," *Forbes*, 2022, https://www.forbes.ru/milliardery/463151-88-rossijskih-milliarderov-rejting-forbes-2022.

15. Igor Terent'ev, Mariia Abakumova, "V reitinge bogateishikh rossian stalo na 22 millardera bol'she," *Forbes*, April 19, 2023, https://www.forbes.ru/milliardery /487880-v-rejtinge-bogatejsih-rossian-stalo-na-22-milliardera-bol-se.

16. "200 bogateishikh biznesmenov Rossii—2021. Reiting Forbes," *Forbes*, 2021, https://www.forbes.ru/rating/397799-200-bogateyshih-biznesmenov-rossii-2020 -reyting-forbes.

17. *Obshchestvennoie mnenie—2013* (Moscow: Levada Center, 2014), 25.

18. "Sanktsii zapada," Levada Center, June 8, 2022, https://www.levada.ru/2022 /06/08/sanktsii-zapada.

19. *Rossiiskii statisticheskii ezhegodnik—2015*, 254; "Statistika vyezda rossiian za rubezh v 2019 godu. Ofitsialnye dannye," Association of Tour Operators of Russia, February 17, 2020, https://www.atorus.ru/news/press-centre/new/50475.html.

20. More in Eberstadt, *Russia's Peacetime Demographic Crisis*.

21. "Staff Shortages Cripple Russian Business," *Russia Today*, April 9, 2008, http: //rt.com/business/news/staff-shortages-cripple-russian-business.

22. Marlene Laruelle and Sophie Hohmann, "Biography of a Polar City: Population Flows and Urban Identity in Norilsk," *Polar Geography* 40, no. 4 (2017): 306–23.

23. Robert Ferris, "Putin's Other Problem: Russia's Brain Drain," CNBC, December 17, 2014, http://www.cnbc.com/2014/12/17/putins-other-problem-russias-brain -drain.html.

24. Alexander Chyernich and Lolita Grusdeva, "Russia Looking to Reverse Brain Drain of Young Scientists," *Time*, November 18, 2011, http://content.time.com/time/ world/article/0,8599,2099861,00.html.

25. *Sotsial'nyi atlas rossiiskikh regionov* (Moscow: Nezavisimyi institut sotsial'noi politiki, 2017), http://www.socpol.ru/atlas/overviews/social_sphere/kris.shtml.

26. "Moscow Named World's Third-Most 'Prosperous' City—UN," *Moscow Times*, February 4, 2022, https://www.themoscowtimes.com/2022/02/04/moscow -named-worlds-third-most-prosperous-city-un-a76253.

27. Jeremy Morris, *Everyday Post-Socialism: Working-Class Communities in the Russian Margins* (London: Palgrave Macmillan, 2016).

28. Ielena Ganzhur, "Doshli do 'tochki': chto stalo s setiu McDonald's v Rossii," *Forbes*, January 3, 2023, https://www.forbes.ru/biznes/483155-dosli-do-tocki-cto -stalo-s-set-u-mcdonald-s-v-rossii.

29. John Witte and Michael Bourdeaux, *Proselytism and Orthodoxy in Russia: The New War for Souls* (Ossining, NY: Orbis Books, 1999).

30. Olga Filina, "Mapping Russia's Religious Landscape," *Russia & India Report*, September 1, 2012, https://www.rbth.com/articles/2012/08/30/mapping_russias_ religious_landscape_17819.html.

31. "Velikii post i religioznost,'" Levada Center, March 3, 2020, https://www .levada.ru/2020/03/03/velikij-post-i-religioznost.

32. LegitRuss: Values-Based Legitimation in Authoritarian States: Top-Down versus Bottom-Up Strategies, the Case of Russia, Survey, 2021, conducted by VTsIOM, funded by the Research Council of Norway, Project number 300997.

33. Rogers Brubaker, "Between Nationalism and Civilizationism: The European Populist Moment in Comparative Perspective," *Ethnic and Racial Studies* 40, no. 8 (2017): 1191–1226.

34. LegitRuss.

35. "Otnosheniie k zakonoproektu o chuvstvakh veruiushchikh," FOM, January 22, 2013, https://fom.ru/Bezopasnost-i-pravo/10782.

36. See *Atlas religii i natsional'snostei Rossii*, 2012, http://sreda.org/arena/maps.

37. Jean Radvanyi and Nicolas Beroutchachvili, *Atlas géopolitique du Caucase* (Paris: Autrement, 2010).

38. Rano Turaeva, "Imagined Mosque Communities in Russia: Central Asian Migrants in Moscow," *Asian Ethnicity* 20, no. 2 (2019): 131–47.

39. Akhmet Yarlykapov, "Divisions and Unity of the Novy Urengoy Muslim Community," *Problems of Post-Communism* 67, no. 4–5 (2020): 338–47.

40. Marlene Laruelle and Sophie Hohmann, "Polar Islam: Muslim Communities in Russia's Arctic Cities," *Problems of Post-Communism* 67, no. 4–5 (2020): 327–37.

41. "Russian Orthodox Church Seeks to Heal Centuries-Old Schism," *Orthodox Christian Laity*, December 25, 2013, http://ocl.org/russian-orthodox-church-seeks-to -heal-centuries-old-schism.

42. Koozma J. Tarasoff, "More Doukhobors Moving from Georgia to Russia," April 1, 1999, http://doukhoborology.tripod.com/gdoukh.html.

43. Oleg Kavykin, *"Rodnovery": Samoidentifikatsiia neo-iazychnikov v sovremennoi Rossii* (Moscow: Institut Afriki RAN, 2007). See also Kaarina Aitamurto, "Reviving the Native Faith: Nationalism in Contemporary Slavic Paganism Rodnoverie," *Forum für osteuropäische Ideen und Zeitgeschichte* 1, no. 2 (2011): 167–84.

44. Victor Shnirel'man, "Arkaim: arkheologiia, ezotericheskii turizm i natsional'naia ideia," *Antropologicheskii forum*, no. 114 (2014): 134–67.

45. Vladimir Magun and Maksim Rudnev, "Basic Values of Russians and Other Europeans: (According to the Materials of Surveys in 2008)." *Problems of Economic Transition* 54, no. 10 (2012): 31–64.

46. *Obshchestvennoie mneniie—2021*, Levada Center, 2021, https://levada.ru/cp/wp-content/uploads/2022/04/OM-2021.pdf, 149–50.

47. *Obshchestvennoie mneniie—2021*, 149–50.

48. LegitRuss.

49. For more on this, see Marlene Laruelle, "A Grassroots Conservatism? Taking a Fine-Grained View of Conservative Attitudes among Russians," *East European Politics* (March 2022).

50. LegitRuss.

51. Table 13.1.3, *Obshchestvennoie mnenie—2021*, 116.

52. Ekaterina Kochergina, "Predstavleniia o gendernykh roliakh i gendernom ravnopravii v Rossii. Analiz dannykh massovykh oprosov za 30 let," *Vestnik obschestvennogo mneniia Dannye. Analiz. Diskussii* 3–4 (2018), 127.

53. Alexander Kondakov, "The Silenced Citizens of Russia: Exclusion of Non-Heterosexual Subjects from Rights-Based Citizenship," *Social & Legal Studies* 23, no. 2 (2014): 151–74; Irina Soboleva and Yaroslav Bakhmetjev, "Political Awareness and Self-Blame in the Explanatory Narratives of LGBT People amid the

Anti-LGBT Campaign in Russia," *Sexuality & Culture* 19, no. 2 (2015): 275–96; Francesca Stella, "The Right to Be Different? Sexual Citizenship and Its Politics in Post-Soviet Russia," in *Gender, Equality and Difference during and after State Socialism*, ed. Rebecca Kay (London: Palgrave Macmillan, 2007), 146–66; Connor O'Dwyer, "Gay Rights and Political Homophobia in Postcommunist Europe: Is There an EU Effect?" in *Global Homophobia: States, Movements, and the Politics of Oppression*, ed. Meredith Weiss and Michael Bosia (Champaign: University of Illinois Press, 2013), 103–26.

54. Jeremy Morris and Masha Garibyan, "Russian Cultural Conservatism Critiqued: Translating the Tropes of 'Gayropa' and 'Juvenile Justice' in Everyday Life," *Europe-Asia Studies* 73, no. 8 (2021): 1487–1507.

55. "Otnosheniie rossiian k LGBT liudiam," Levada Center, October 15, 2021, https://www.levada.ru/2021/10/15/otnoshenie-rossiyan-k-lgbt-lyudyam.

56. "Odnopolyie braki: tabu ili novaia norma?," VTsIOM, July 23, 2021, https://wciom.ru/analytical-reviews/analiticheskii-obzor/odnopolye-braki-tabu-ili-novaja-norma.

57. "Nostal'giya po SSSR," Levada Center, December 19, 2018, https://www.levada.ru/2018/12/19/nostalgiya-po-sssr-2/?fromtg=1

58. "Nuzhno-li patrioticheskoe vospitanie?," FOM, July 20, 2020, https://fom.ru/TSennosti/14411.

59. Maria Lipman and Denis Volkov, "Russian Youth: How Are They Different from Other Russians?," *PONARS Eurasia Point & Counterpoint*, January 18, 2019, https://www.ponarseurasia.org/russian-youth-how-are-they-different-from-other-russians.

60. "Smertnaia kazn,'" Levada Center, November 7, 2019, https://www.levada.ru/2019/11/07/smertnaya-kazn-2.

61. "World Values Survey," 2017–2020.

62. "Konflikt s Ukrainoi: otsenki dekabria 2022ogo goda," Levada Center, December 23, 2022, https://www.levada.ru/2022/12/23/konflikt-s-ukrainoj-otsenki-dekabrya-2022-goda.

63. *Obshchestvennoie mnenie—2013*, 52.

64. *Obshchestvennoie mnenie—2014*, 36.

65. Table 3.1.1, *Obshchestvennoie mnenie—2020* (Moscow: Levada Center, 2021), 28.

# 4

# The Political System

## *A Consensus Undermined by Fear and Repression*

Nearly forty years after the onset of perestroika, the Russian political regime still relies on the deep traumas that shaped the Russian society. These have been numerous: the sudden disappearance of the Soviet system, the bloody confrontation between Boris Yeltsin and the Supreme Soviet (the parliament) in October 1993, during which the president fired on the legislature with tanks and killed and injured hundreds of people, the two Chechen Wars, numerous terrorist attacks, several economic shocks that weakened the stability of the middle classes, a revival of tensions with the West . . . and simply the unknown: *Everything Was Forever, Until It Was No More* is the title of a book by cultural anthropologist Alexei Yurchak on the last Soviet generation and the impossibility of imagining the collapse of the Soviet Union.[1] On the other hand, the Russian political system itself has cultivated a situation of fear and chronic instability, exerting constant pressure on representatives of the critical opposition and oligarchs who have refused to play by the regime's rules, and then gradually broadening the pressures put on reluctant segments of the population.

This complex interplay between the exploitation of popular fears born in this new time of troubles and the exercise of state violence is a major feature of Putin's system. These fears explain much of the Russian regime's capacity to cultivate consensus and avoid serious questions about its methods of exercising power, but they cannot hide the various forms of resistance that have emerged. Growing discontent cannot be controlled indefinitely simply by pulling off historic feats such as the annexation of the Crimea, or by increasing repressive measures and establishing an ever more rigid and standard-setting discourse. The full-scale war against Ukraine has deeply shaken the implicit social contract between citizens and the state and strained intra-elite cohesion, yet the regime seems able to continue navigating these new troubled waters.

## THE 1990S: HOPES AND DISILLUSIONMENT

### The "European Home" and the Delegitimation of Liberalism (1989–1993)

From the last years of perestroika until 1993, the Russian elite engaged in a discourse that advocated for the establishment of a "normal country" (read: Western), revealing how they were anxious to make up for what was seen as lost time and to terminate as soon as possible the development path taken by the Soviet Union. Seeing Europe as a model, Gorbachev himself sang the praises of the Soviet Union joining the "European home." The conservative putsch of August 19, 1991, which ousted the general secretary from office for three days, did not enjoy the population's support; rather, it served to discredit proponents of the status quo and strengthened the reformers' position.

The supporters of liberal "shock therapy" gathered around Boris Yeltsin, who was elected chairman of the Supreme Soviet of Russia in March 1990 and then president of Russia on June 12, 1991. In the midst of this pro-Western consensus, only two dissenting voices asserted themselves: those of the Communist Party of the Russian Federation (CPRF), which was formed from the ashes of the old Communist Party of the Soviet Union, and the Moscow Patriarchate (the administrative body of the Russian Orthodox Church). Both sought continued consideration of Russian civilization's specific character, thought to be unassimilable into the Western model and to require preservation from it.

After the Soviet Union was dissolved in December 1991, however, the violent impact of social and economic change was such that the widespread support enjoyed by what was seen as the march toward a dual process of Westernization, both economic and political (the introduction of a market economy and the establishment of a parliamentary system), weakened quickly. Soaring prices, the loss of savings accumulated during the Soviet period, the collapse of living standards, massive closures of factories and businesses, the elimination of social benefits (especially for pensioners), and late payment of salaries, all broke the pro-Western consensus in 1992 and 1993. A brutally impoverished society, the wild privatization of large industrial enterprises, and the birth of a privileged class enjoying social success based on its control of the shadow economy all deeply offended a population accustomed to Soviet uniformity of ways of life.

Unlike in Central Europe, in Russia the Communist *nomenklatura* was the main agent of the transition to a market economy. While former dissidents were largely absent from the post-Soviet political scene, former Communist Party members easily benefited from privatization, fueling the view that the Soviet collapse had been programmed and plotted by elites who had betrayed the egalitarian ideal of the Soviet regime.[2] As a result of these unprecedented changes, "democracy" was equated with the ravages of capitalism and gradually became a negative, even insulting, term in a system that refused to recognize the oligarchs' pillaging of wealth for what it was: the Russian word *dermokratiya*, revealingly coined around this time, mixes the words for "democracy" and "shit." The discourse on the absence of a new ideology for the country was also seen as hypocrisy. The presence of Western donors was interpreted as a proof of "Western economic diktat," and liberalism, especially economic, was perceived as a new ideology imposed by force. References to the "European example" faded, and political rights were considered secondary to dealing with the material issues of individual survival and social justice.

The first political shock to hit the fledgling Russian democracy came in the fall of 1993, after Yeltsin won a hard-fought referendum on continued reforms (though he garnered 58 percent of the vote, turnout was only 53 percent). The president presented a draft constitution to the Supreme Soviet, then dominated by Communists and nationalists, which rejected it. Yeltsin decided to dissolve parliament, which responded by voting for his impeachment. A state of emergency was declared on September 24, and military troops loyal to the president stormed the parliament building on October 4, officially leaving more than 150 dead.[3]

This bloody event has played an important role in the collective memory of post-Soviet Russia, as it seemed that the democratic project ended in bloodshed, and the country nearly descended into civil war. The event also marked the beginning of the presidentialization of the regime: to avoid what was perceived as a step backward, democratic and liberal parties—supported by Western countries—backed Yeltsin in his muscular demonstration of power and demonization of the Communist opposition. They propagated the idea that in its march toward the West, Russia needed to maintain an authoritarian regime—legitimate because it supported liberal values—that would disregard defiant conservative Communist opinion.

The crisis in the fall of 1993 also revealed the new Russian Federation's fragility. Local leaders took to heart the famous phrase that Yeltsin had uttered to regional leaders in August 1990, when he was first elected president of the Russian Soviet Socialist Republic, and struggling with still existing Soviet president Gorbachev: "Take as much autonomy as you can swallow." The situation in many regions was grave due to the brutal economic crisis and rampant embezzlement by those in power, who took advantage of the situation to capture what remained of profitable businesses. In Russia's republics, the new nationalist parties tried to capitalize on their influence by mobilizing minorities sensitive to growing inequalities.[4] To protect the considerably weakened regional markets, some did not hesitate to propose radical measures such as creating local currencies, imposing customs barriers inside Russia's regions, and setting credit limits for their regions. Added to the battle between democratic reformers and Communist conservatives was the so-called revolt of the regions. In September 1993, a motley union of regional leaders hostile to President Yeltsin was set to initiate proceedings to remove him from office.[5] The specter of the Soviet Union's implosion was everywhere.

Concerns about the identity of the new Russian state were accentuated by the situation in two key regions. In 1993, the republics of Tatarstan and Chechnya defied the Russian president and refused to sign a new federal treaty intended to redefine the balance of power between the center and the regions. In fact, Tatar authorities, under the leadership of then president Mintimer Shaimiev, had voted for their own constitution in a March 1992 referendum. The document proposed federalism from below, whereby the subjects of the Federation would delegate sovereign powers (military, security, monetary policy, etc.) to the federal center while retaining control of any regional economic, political, and cultural issues. But the situation was even more dangerous in Chechnya. Since the collapse of the Soviet Union, this small North Caucasian republic had been demanding its independence. Taking advantage of the withdrawal of the federal center, Chechnya existed almost independently of Moscow, with a criminal economy (complete with bombings and kidnappings) marked by significant intra-Chechen rivalries.

## GETTING BACK ON THE PATH OF POLITICAL CONSENSUS (1994–2000)

Over the course of 1994, a transformational year, Russia's two main regional conflicts resulted in two totally different outcomes that would profoundly affect Russian society for years to come. In February, a political compromise was reached between Moscow and Kazan with the signing of a treaty on the division of powers. The Tatar leadership agreed to enter the more centralized institutional framework defined by the 1993 Constitution of the Russian Federation in exchange for some concessions: participation in the management of Tatarstan's large enterprises, control of domestic politics and cultural life, and the right to engage in some diplomatic activities to promote the republic's economic interests abroad.[6]

But Chechnya would not have the same fate as Tatarstan. In December 1994, for reasons mainly related to the internal balance of power in the Kremlin and to internal fighting between Chechen groups,[7] Yeltsin sided with the hawks in his government and launched an attack on Chechnya. The largest military operation organized by Moscow since its intervention in Afghanistan in 1979, the war would be a military and humanitarian disaster in which Russian forces would get bogged down. In 1996, during the presidential election campaign, a peace agreement signed in Khasavyurt (in the neighboring region of Dagestan) allowed Chechnya, renamed the Islamic Republic of Ichkeria, to obtain de facto autonomy and the promise of independence talks in the future, which was seen as a deep humiliation for Russia. Chechnya became the nexus of Russian fears, and the threat to national unity one of the leitmotifs of power.

In this context, Yeltsin tried to erase the deep divisions that had led to the fall 1993 violence and sought to limit the polarization between "liberals," on the one hand, and "Communist-nationalists" (or the "red-brown" coalition) on the other. Prime Minister Viktor Chernomyrdin, representing the interests of the military-industrial complex and the oil and gas industry, granted amnesty to the August 1991 coup plotters and the October 1993 insurgents, allowing conservative figures, such as Alexander Rutskoy and Ruslan Khasbulatov, to return to the political scene. In May 1995, the celebration of the fiftieth anniversary of the end of the Great Patriotic War—the name given in Russia to the period of the country's involvement in the Second World War (1941–1945)—was an opportunity to strengthen national unity by reigniting the flame of patriotism.[8]

Yeltsin's reelection campaign was marked by an implicit agreement with the oligarchs and their media companies that they would back his candidacy in exchange for financial advantages—all with the unspoken support of the Western powers, who feared the Communists' possible return to power. Upon his election to a second term in 1996, Yeltsin accelerated the quest for consensus. For the celebration of Russia Day on June 12 (commemorating Russia's Declaration of Sovereignty in 1990), he declared, "The most important thing for Russia is looking for a national idea, a national ideology."[9] The government newspaper *Rossiiskaia gazeta* launched a contest on the new Russian idea and collected hundreds of slogans submitted by readers.[10] The campaign did not result in anything concrete but signaled that the theme of national identity and need for unity was back on the authorities' radar.

The 1998 economic crisis also came to cast doubt on the market economy and wiped out the first middle-class stabilization efforts, with most Russian citizens losing their life savings for the second time in less than ten years. The feeling that nascent Russian capitalism was a sham spread rapidly in the population, while the wealth and political power of the oligarch bankers close to Yeltsin aroused criticism. In this context, the so-called democratic and liberal parties were largely discredited. Yabloko and the factions that went on to form the Union of Right Forces were denigrated because they were associated with the West's "diktat" (even if Yabloko, as a social-democratic party, was quite concerned about the social cost of reforms) and critical of the Kremlin's management of the Chechen question. In the public's eyes, these parties embodied the brutality of the changes of the Yeltsin years, the negative impact of privatization in the 1990s, and the oligarchs' monopolization of national wealth.

Russian society traveled a long road in that first decade after independence. At the time of the Soviet collapse and into Yeltsin's early years, all surveys showed that Russians held a negative view of themselves. According to the public polling institution VTsIOM, between the beginning and end of 1991, agreement with the statements "We are worse than anyone else" and "We bring only negative things to the world" rose from 7 percent to 57 percent.[11] This feeling was soon combined with the idea that only a return to a powerful state could overcome this shame. Surveys conducted in 1995–1996 confirmed that the majority of Russians were ashamed of the state of their country and viewed the reign of Peter the Great (r. 1682–1725) as the golden age of Russian history. Nearly half of respondents saw the notion of Russia's being a "great power" (*derzhava*) as a unifying element that transcended partisan divisions.[12]

All the elements that would give birth to Putinism indeed took shape during the second half of the 1990s. New personalities gained visibility on the political stage: General Alexander Lebed, former prime minister and minister of foreign affairs Yevgeny Primakov, and Moscow mayor Yuri Luzhkov. For them, the dangers of the two extremes—pro-Western liberalism and Communism—had to be avoided, and the country needed to find a middle way that put the Russian state's interests above all else. By stating that there was no shame in thinking of Russia as a strong state in domestic politics and a great power in foreign policy, these advocates of a "third way" strengthened their patriotic rhetoric and marginalized the last remaining liberals' pro-Western stance.

In 1999, the domestic situation worsened again with respect to Chechnya. In August, local Chechen warlords announced that they wanted to establish an Islamic state in Dagestan. A few days later, several attacks on suburban Moscow apartment buildings led to the deaths of over three hundred people (the Kremlin blamed separatists, while Western observers blamed the FSB, the security agency that was heir to the KGB, although the real planners remain unknown). In the fall legislative elections, the idea of a specific Russian path of development became consensual even within some liberal parties such as the Union of Right Forces, as all were critically analyzing the country's situation and recognizing the need for more authoritarian policies that could meet the Chechen security challenge.[13]

The stage was set for Vladimir Putin—a virtual unknown before Yeltsin appointed him prime minister a few months before his resignation on December 31, 1999—and the bombings served as a pretext for the new leader to embark on what became the Second Chechen War. The new presidential party, Unity, deftly hijacked the need for consensus and security, co-opting the election niche established by Primakov and Luzhkov's rival Fatherland (*Otechestvo*) Party to make Putin the embodiment of national consensus. His "millennium manifesto," published on December 31, 1999, spells out what he sees as his mission for the country:

> The experience of the '90s vividly shows that our country's genuine renewal without any excessive costs cannot be assured by a mere experimentation in Russian conditions with abstract models and schemes taken from foreign textbooks. The mechanical copying of other nations' experience will not guarantee success, either. . . . I am against the restoration of an official state ideology in Russia in any form. There should be no forced civil accord in a democratic Russia. Social accord can only be voluntary. That is why it is so important to achieve social accord on such basic issues as the aims, values and orientations of development, which would be desirable for and attractive to the overwhelming majority of Russians. [These values are:] belief in the greatness of Russia . . . , statism . . . , social solidarity.[14]

## THE 2000s: CONSOLIDATING THE NEW RUSSIA

### Putin I: The Power Vertical

Vladimir Putin very quickly achieved the dual feats of bringing about Russia's economic recovery and restoring its social stability. Pursuing the logic of "patriotic centrism" pioneered by Primakov and Luzhkov, the new president started the official reconciliation with the Soviet past. In December 2000, a new law on Russia's emblem, flag, and anthem brought about an ideological compromise that reconciled the three major periods of the nation's history: the Tsarist regime, the Soviet Union, and modern Russia. The former red flag of the Soviet Army, with its golden hammer and sickle, was newly unfurled as the flag of the Armed Forces of the Russian Federation, with a golden double-headed eagle. The government launched its first patriotic education program for citizens to give a "new impetus to the spiritual rebirth of the people of Russia" and for the purposes of "maintaining social stability, restoring the national economy, and strengthening the defense capability of the country."[15]

Putin's first term (2000–2004) was organized around stabilization and recovery, with themes such as order, authority, and government effectiveness, and two slogans: the "power vertical" and the "dictatorship of the law." The president complained about society's and the elites' lack of political and moral conscience but refused to claim any ideology, instead citing his pragmatism and qualities as a "technologist" of power charged with righting the boat. Several traumas fed into the authorities' will to strengthen the state. The sinking of the nuclear submarine *Kursk* (and the inability to save its crew) in August 2000, a few months after the inauguration of the new president, was experienced as a humiliation that confirmed the decline of the country's military and industrial capacity. Public opinion condemned the investigation procedure's opacity and the military leadership's general contempt for soldiers. Putin promised to tackle the military's leadership and reinvest in the military-industrial complex.

With North Caucasian violence reaching Moscow through the hostage taking at the Dubrovka Theater in October 2002, the Kremlin called for a return to "constitutional order" across the entire national territory. This legitimized Putin's tough talk about Chechen terrorists ("we'll whack them in the outhouse") and his promotion of security slogans, reinforced by the global atmosphere that followed the 9/11 attacks, including the George W. Bush administration's discourse of a "war on terror." However, the regime remained careful not to overcorrelate acts of terrorism with Islam in general, so as not to offend the country's Muslim minorities. The authorities thus created a double-edged discourse on religion: they emphasized the secular nature of Russia but attributed a growing symbolic role to the Orthodox Church; they recognized the rights of the country's four "traditional" religions (Orthodox Christianity, Sunni Islam, Buddhism, and Judaism) but disparaged and limited the others as "non-traditional,"[16] especially proselytizing groups (Protestant, Islamic, as well as Jehovah's Witnesses).

The Kremlin also sought to recentralize the country by ending the asymmetric federalism that had emerged in the 1990s. The first step was limiting the role of the Federation Council, the upper house of parliament, whose members consisted of regional leaders and had originally counted republic presidents and regional governors among their number. In May 2000, Putin established seven superdistricts (*federal'nyi okrug*; see map 2.1 on p. 48), which overlapped with the military regions and were led by plenipotentiary representatives of the president. These were responsible for restoring a unified constitutional space and confirming the supremacy of federal laws over the republics' constitutions and charters. The superdistricts, revised to remove oversize spaces of autonomy that had been granted to Federation subjects, moved the system for nominating heads of regional agencies (customs, tax, and police) away from the regions (where, under Yeltsin, governors had often exchanged their support for political and economic benefits), back toward the federal center.[17]

The regime also reduced the space for political parties by redefining their registration rules while putting in place a structured and hierarchical partisan machine, United Russia (*Edinaia Rossiia*), in order to assert control over parliamentary institutions and guard against the independence of the legislative branch. Last but not least, the Kremlin led the offensive against oligarchs who sought to use the media they controlled to stop this takeover by the central government. In 2001, the government raided the main opposition media channels—ORT, NTV, and TV-6. Oligarchs expressing any hint of opposition that could harm the president saw their economic empires dismantled. Media tycoons Boris Berezovsky and Vladimir Gusinsky were forced into exile; Mikhail Khodorkovsky, the head of Yukos, then the largest Russian oil company, resisted the new rules of the game and was arrested in 2003.

The exceptional popularity of Putin, who attained unprecedently high approval ratings, allowed him to win reelection in March 2004 in the first round, with 71 percent of the vote. In this paradoxical campaign, the country's other political leaders (Gennady Zyuganov for the Communists, Vladimir Zhirinovsky for the nationalists, and Grigory Yavlinsky for the liberals) chose not to run, leaving little-known personalities to stand against the incumbent president.[18] The liberal party Yabloko did not even manage to win representation in the Duma; its successor, the Union of Right Forces, moved away from the government and was marginalized.

## Putin II: The Challenge of Color Revolutions

In Putin's second term (2004–2008), the regime went on the political offensive. The bloody hostage taking at a school in Beslan (in North Ossetia, on the border with Georgia) in September 2004 stoked popular fears and increased demands for security. Putin announced his desire to further weaken the power of governors, whom he framed as sources of corruption and negligence. Governors would no longer be elected by popular vote but appointed by the regional assembly at the request of the president.

This decision, which allowed Putin to dismiss resistant individuals, spurred regional elites to become members of United Russia in droves, such that the party of the president also became the party of governors. The twenty-nine Duma committees moved, without exception, into the hands of United Russia members; the Duma chairman, former interior minister Boris Gryzlov, was the president of both the party and a parliamentary group of the same name. The system of selective coercion and intimidation of opposition forces, already well established, was now accompanied by a growing manipulation of the associative spectrum, embodied by the creation of a third consultative chamber, the so-called Social Chamber, to co-opt civil society's patriotic elements.

The "power vertical" initiated during Putin's first term was reinforced with the progressive structuring of the president's inner circles and their step-by-step conquest of Russia's high-level official functions, especially in the economic sectors. A Russian analyst, Evgeny Minchenko, describes this network as "Politburo 2.0," a reference to the highest body in the Soviet system.[19] However, in our view, this comparison is irrelevant. Except during the Stalinist period, the Soviet Politburo was a collegial body, based on the rules of the Communist Party, and it functioned through rather precise operation mechanics. As far as we can tell, the "consortium" around Putin has rested on different bases, namely, loyalty to the president and a form of co-optation under his direction, thus ensuring its coherence, its ad hoc nature, and its fragility. The "consortium" bridges positions of economic management and explicitly political posts, with the two functions performed simultaneously or successively. It offers a multifaceted career path that can pass through major state bodies (the presidential administration, government, various ministries and committees, and regional governments) and large enterprises.

This "Russia, Inc.," as several Russian scholars delineate it, consists of a narrow group of fifty to sixty people whom Putin had selected to direct all the key branches of the economy and the state: banking and finance, the fuel and energy complex, transportation and infrastructure, and the military-industrial complex, along with metallurgy and chemistry, media and communications, sports and tourism, and the alcohol market. "The president's men," as Yevgenia Albats and Anatoly Yermolin dubbed them in a *Novoe vremia* newspaper article from 2011,[20] can be classified into four categories according to the origin and duration of their personal relationships with Putin.

The most numerous are the "men in uniform," commonly referred to as *siloviki* (from *sila*, "force"), who come mainly from the KGB and its successor the FSB, from the military intelligence agency (GRU), from the foreign intelligence service (SVR), and, to a lesser extent, from the army and police. Among those in the president's inner circle are men who worked with Putin in the KGB's foreign service in East Germany. Since 2000, the Russian press has repeatedly highlighted the increasing number of former KGB/FSB members who have been promoted to executive functions in the state or economy. According to *Novoe vremia*, in 2011 they already occupied about 40 percent of the upper echelons of power of the leading Russian firms.

A second, slightly smaller category consists of the "men of St. Petersburg," whose leading ranks include Putin's colleagues from the time when he held various administrative positions in that city under the leadership of Mayor Anatoly Sobchak (1990–1996). From this period, too, comes the third group, a few members of the Ozero ("lake") cooperative, an association created with the future president to build a series of dachas.[21] They remain close to Putin and have occupied decisive positions in his regime as ministers, financiers, and traders of petroleum products. A final, diversified category consists of other family members and friends from these three circles.[22]

Putin's second term also saw the beginning of political assassinations, the most prominent being the murder of journalist Anna Politkovskaya and the poisoning of former KGB agent Alexander Litvinenko in London in 2006. Putin's second term was also a turning point in terms of ideology. The 2004 Orange Revolution in Kyiv, with a pro-Western Ukrainian administration taking office, took the Kremlin by surprise and drastically influenced the Russian presidential administration's interpretation that revolutions can only happen with external support and funding.

The change of regime in Kyiv also revealed the impossibility of continuing to present the Russian state as "nonideological." The Russian presidential administration, then led by Alexander Voloshin and Vladislav Surkov, its deputy director and Putin's "gray cardinal,"[23] set about reconstructing the Russian regime's image. The Putin administration developed the concept of "sovereign democracy" (*suverennaia demokratiia*) to describe Russia's right to forge its own development path without interference from the West. More successful was the Kremlin's response to the popular dynamics of the color revolutions in the form of pro-Putin youth movements, such as Nashi ("Ours"). The patriotic education program was strengthened in the hope of motivating young men to complete their compulsory military service (which many avoid) and, more generally, to "make the patriotic consciousness of Russian citizens one of the most important values, one of the foundations of spiritual and moral unity," such that patriotism would become the "spiritual backbone of the country."[24]

The government also decided to invest heavily in culture, which it considered an important means of cultivating consensus and consolidating implicit support for the regime. Although outright *political* nostalgia for the Soviet regime has been diminishing (the Communist Party receiving fewer votes than in the 1990s), *cultural* nostalgia for the Brezhnev era (1964–1982), seen as the golden age of Soviet culture, has been massive and exists across class and age divisions.[25] Movies, songs, and literature from that time have been largely rehabilitated, as have some fashions and consumer products; Soviet vintage has been a commercial success. The presidential administration has used this wave of Soviet nostalgia to its advantage, offering generous funding for major historical anniversaries (especially military ones), patriotic concerts, and the development of movies and television series, often of very good quality, to promote national sentiment by revisiting the Tsarist and Soviet past.[26]

Although the rehabilitation of the Brezhnev years has been widely consensual, the Stalin years has been interpreted in contrasting manners. In
2004, Boris Gryzlov, state Duma spokesman and the leader of United Russia,
laid flowers on Stalin's grave and called on Russians not to forget his con-
tributions in difficult times, implying that at this pivotal time, the country
needed an authoritarian leader more than ever.[27] The same year, Putin asked
that in preparation for the sixtieth anniversary of the end of the war, the
name Stalingrad replace Volgograd at the Tomb of the Unknown Soldier in
Moscow, to "respect the heroism of the defenders of Stalingrad in order to
preserve the history of the Russian state."[28] In March 2005, the municipality of Volgograd took this one step further, deciding to erect a monument to
Stalin alongside Franklin D. Roosevelt and Winston Churchill as the victors
of the Second World War.[29] Yet the Orthodox Church has maintained a reverse
reading of Stalinism by canonizing the victims of state repressions, even
while positioning itself as a staunch supporter of the Putin's regime. In 2007,
Putin went to Butovo, a large memorial on the southern outskirts of Moscow
dedicated to the victims of the Stalinist purges, for the seventieth anniversary
of the great trials,[30] with the goal of speaking to both sides—those in favor of
forgetting Stalin's crimes and those calling for remembrance and mourning.

## Dmitry Medvedev: A Liberal Interlude?

In 2008, Dmitry Medvedev, who had been Putin's prime minister, became
Russia's new president, while Putin became his prime minister. Medvedev's
rise to power thwarted many Western predictions: Putin may not have
respected the spirit of the constitution, but he complied with the letter of it by
rejecting many proposals to change it that would have allowed him to serve
a third consecutive presidential term. Although Medvedev had been a part of
Putin's inner circle since the 1990s, his election was not a pure political fic-
tion. By becoming prime minister, Putin risked losing control of his protégé
and finding himself unable to return to power in the next election. He was
careful, however, to transfer the essential functions previously exercised by
the president (supervision of the Ministries of the Interior and Defense, the
FSB, etc.) to his new role as head of the government.

For four years, the Medvedev–Putin diarchy affected the general political
system.[31] With Putin positioned as head of both the government and the presidential party, those two institutions suddenly gained increased media visibility and policy credibility. Members of the government more clearly emerged
in the public eye as figures with their own personalities, and the presidential
party, which had until then essentially functioned as an electoral machine,
became more structured. Ideological trends emerged, from "liberals" to
"conservative patriots," representing a wide range of interests and deploying

openly contradictory discourses.[32] Previously hidden conflicts of interest also went on public display—for instance, that between Igor Sechin, head of the oil company Rosneft, known for his conservative and *siloviki* views; and Yuri Trutnev, the minister of natural resources and ecology, who supported greater openness to foreign and private capital.

Medvedev created an autonomous space for the revival of liberal thought, symbolized by the Institute for Contemporary Development (INSOR), Igor Yurgens's think tank, which addressed sensitive issues such as the sustainability of the political regime, the need to reform inefficient post-Soviet regional institutions, and even the possibility of Russia's NATO membership.[33] At the same time, new liberal figures stopped getting elected to the Duma and those who remained moved into the opposition, such as former chess world champion Gary Kasparov, former prime minister Mikhail Kasyanov, former deputy prime minister Boris Nemtsov, and representatives of Yeltsin-era liberalism such as Grigori Yavlinsky of the Yabloko party.

Medvedev's presidential term was marked by the theme of "modernization"—mainly economic in nature (see chapter 5) but also social and political. Although Putin and Medvedev maintained their popular legitimacy, polls showed the progressive disengagement of the middle and upper classes, who believed less and less in the regime's ability to point out the path to modernization.[34] This was reflected in local and municipal elections in Moscow and St. Petersburg, where the ruling United Russia party struggled to win a majority. The party was no longer seen as an instrument of progress but as a bureaucratic machine that represented the interests of a privileged caste.

Although greater ideological diversity was noticeable among the Russian elite, Medvedev's interlude was also when some elements of the future "conservative turn" began to take shape. The Moscow Patriarchate was gaining power: having already established a presence in the penitentiary system and the military, it strived to influence the education system and social legislation more generally. Several Church figures managed to obtain various positions within the working groups of the Duma Committee on the Family, Women, and Children, spearheading the passage of more restrictive laws on protecting children from online content and championed pro-life slogans. The president's wife, Svetlana Medvedeva, positioned herself as a mediator between certain religious figures who served as "confessors" for the president and his inner circle—such as Father Tikhon, Father Vladimir Volgin, and Father Kiprian.

In 2010, Medvedev approved the introduction of a new subject into the school curriculum: Fundamentals of Spiritual and Moral Culture of the Peoples of Russia, later renamed Fundamentals of Religious Cultures and Secular Ethics. After trial runs in some parts of Russia, the course became mandatory across the country in 2012. Several versions were made available, allowing parents to pick and choose course content. The results did not meet the expectations of the Moscow Patriarchate, which had hoped to see the beginning of formalized Orthodox education in public schools. Parents' choices demonstrated the deep roots of secular values within the population and the educational realm. In 2018, more than 40 percent of them chose the Ethical Values option for their children, only 34 percent chose Orthodox Values, and more than 20 percent selected the more neutral Introduction to World Religions.[35] There were many criticisms of the implementation, as a lack of trained teachers sometimes resulted in Orthodox priests teaching catechism disguised as ethics courses, while in several Muslim republics such as Chechnya, this course became an invitation to adopt Islamic rules.

Globally, the "liberal temptation" noticeable during the Medvedev presidency remained weak and was unable to drive a radical transformation of the political system. The security services continued to practice political assassinations when needed, mostly of journalists and human rights lawyers such as Stanislav Markelov, Anastasia Baburova, and Natalia Estemirova. Nor did modernization succeed economically. However, the Medvedev interlude did produce the largest popular protest movement yet experienced in post-Soviet Russia, further accentuating the association the regime sought to cultivate in people's minds between democratization, instability, and foreign influence.

## THE 2010s: SECURITIZING THE REGIME

### Putin III: The Conservative Turn

Putin's third term (2012–2018) promised to be difficult. It started with the biggest protests the country had seen in twenty years. When Putin and Medvedev revealed, in September 2011, that they were about to exchange their respective offices again and had decided to do so as early as 2008, the actively-engaged segment of public opinion became incensed. Critics denounced the contempt for voters displayed by the presidential "couple," the sham of elections with predetermined outcomes, and the widespread corruption of the system. Between the December 2011 parliamentary elections and the March 2012 presidential elections, tens of thousands of people took to the streets almost every week in Moscow as well as other major cities. At the height of the protests, in late February, over a hundred thousand people were on the streets chanting anti-Putin slogans, demanding the resignation of the Electoral Commission and members of the government, and calling for transparent elections.[36]

The protesters belonged mainly to the urban middle class. They were employed in the service industry and/or the private sector that had emerged in the 2000s and communicated using social media channels such as Facebook and its Russian equivalent, Vkontakte. These new middle classes rarely thought of themselves as politicized and did not identify with any party. However, they shared a number of values and commitment mechanisms, as well as mutual-aid communities that were ready to take to the streets to defend ethical slogans. During the huge forest fires of summer 2010, which threatened several cities and semirural areas around Moscow, volunteer groups were formed to help the firefighters and overcome the obvious disruption of public services. These often-spontaneous voluntary actions were publicized via Facebook and LiveJournal. Surveys of anti-Putin protesters showed that many who took to the streets in 2011–2012 were involved in social networks that dated back to the forest fires of the previous year.[37] The same pattern was noted with the Khimki movement, named for a forest near Moscow that was going to be destroyed by the construction of a highway. Many involved in the environmental movement found themselves protesting against the regime a few months later.[38]

The demonstrators mostly presented themselves as unaffiliated with any party but wanting to live in a freer and less corrupt society in which the authorities did not so obviously violate citizens' rights. Dignity, respect, honesty, and transparency were their key slogans, and the color white came to symbolize the movement. Alexey Navalny, the lawyer and blogger who emerged as the charismatic leader of the movement, coined the anti-Putin "party of crooks and thieves" slogan used to denounce United Russia. In his heyday, his blogs—among the most widely read in Russia at that time—punctuated the protests.[39] Other personalities also emerged, as the old liberals were joined by a new generation, including economist Vladimir Milov, and gathered together in a new liberal party, the Russian People's Party (PARNAS). Even the oligarch Mikhail Prokhorov ventured to become involved in liberal politics, a path that had been closed to the superrich since the beginning of the Khodorkovsky case, and temporarily received support from Navalny.

The liberals were not the only ones in the streets. They shared the pavement with some nationalist circles that linked the corruption of state bodies to the migration issue and the threat migrants supposedly posed to the Russian nation. Navalny himself embodied this ambivalence, espousing a liberal discourse that invites Russia to move closer to the European model while clearly sympathizing with the positions of the French National Front and other European national-populist parties.[40] In September 2013, after a complicated judicial drama, Navalny was allowed to run in the Moscow mayoral election against the official United Russia candidate, Sergey Sobyanin, and won 27 percent of the vote, confirming the mistrust of ruling elites felt by part of the capital city's middle class.

Another outcome of the protests was the emergence of a "new Left." In Russia, the term refers to all those who claim progressive leftist values and refuse to recognize the two embodiments of the post-Soviet nationalist Left: the Communist Party, led by Gennady Zyuganov, and Eduard Limonov's National-Bolshevik Party, which combines Soviet nostalgia with Russian nationalism. This new countercultural Left shares values with the European and American Left and seeks the intellectual rehabilitation of Marxism. Some read Noam Chomsky and Slavoj Žižek; others revive Bolshevik art or engage alongside the "Left Front" of Sergey Uldaltsov, who was very visible during the 2011 demonstrations and was subsequently placed under house arrest (he served a three-year sentence in a penal colony from 2014 to 2017).

The scale of the demonstrations took the Kremlin by surprise, but the response was fairly swift. The main leaders of the protests were placed under house arrest to await what the press called "Bolotnaya trials," after the public square not far from the Kremlin where the protesters gathered. The authorities' main response was to quickly tighten the legal apparatus, including introducing new legislation on "foreign agents"—institutions, and then individuals, suspected of receiving foreign money. The most famous case is probably that of Memorial, a leading Russian NGO active since perestroika, which focused on rehabilitating the victims of Soviet repression. Higher education institutions (the Higher School of Economics in Moscow and the European University at St. Petersburg) and independent research centers (the Independent Sociological Research Center in St. Petersburg) that were seen as too liberal were subjected to more red tape and threats and placed under the supervision of meddlesome judicial bodies. Several professors with liberal views were pushed to resign or were dismissed from the country's leading universities; others preferred to emigrate.[41]

The online realm, hitherto largely left alone, also saw the imposition of greater restrictions. Since 2012, new laws have been passed that require the most popular bloggers to declare themselves to be "independent media" and thus subject to a range of procedures related to that status. Internet services such as Google have being pressured to store information on Russian territory rather than abroad, and to agree to provide user information upon request from judicial entities. Officially, the purpose of these measures was to protect the Russian digital system, Runet, from cyberattacks or information leaks that would benefit foreign powers, but they were also intended to control the flow of ideas.[42]

As a more comprehensive response to the ideological challenges of 2011–2012, the Kremlin undertook to marginalize the middle classes and their liberal convictions by turning its attention to the silent and more conservative majority of the population, which still formed the backbone of the regime's electoral support. This "conservative turn" was signaled by the trial of Pussy Riot, the feminist performance group responsible for staging an anti-Putin "punk prayer" in the Moscow Cathedral of Christ the Savior in 2012. The authorities hyped this news story to denounce "hooliganism," the immorality of liberal thought, and the need to protect authentic values and the Church. The conservative turn has also been notable in several other areas. The terms "morality" (*nravstvennost'*) and "spiritual" (*dukhovnyi*) became pervasive in Putin's discourse.[43] The president began blatantly championing the defense of Christian values, accusing the West of forgetting its moral roots, and state propaganda began stressing LGBTQ+ rights as a "civilizational" line of divide between a decadent West, labeled "gayropa," and a healthy heterosexual Russia.

The authorities, led by Minister of Culture Vladimir Medinsky, have further sought to sanctify everything identified as a symbol of Russian culture. On an annual basis, Putin meets with descendants of Pushkin, Tolstoy, Dostoevsky, Sholokhov, Pasternak, and Solzhenitsyn to celebrate Russia's contribution to world culture. Conversely, any attempts to treat religious symbols with irreverence—such as the *Icons* exhibition organized by gallery owner Marat Gelman, a staging of Wagner's opera *Tannhäuser* in Novosibirsk, or Uchitel's film *Matilda*, which portrays the love relationship between the late Tsar Nicholas II and a young dancer—were quickly labeled blasphemous and incited hostile activity by nationalists and ultra-Orthodox activists.[44]

The second turning point of Putin's third mandate was obviously the Euromaidan revolution in Kyiv and the subsequent annexation of Crimea, coupled with covert support for secessionist movements in the Donbas backed by Moscow. The new "color revolution" was once again interpreted as a direct threat to Russia's national security, as explicitly formulated in the 2015 Russian National Security Strategy:

> The West's stance aimed at countering integration processes and creating seats of tension in the Eurasian region is exerting a negative influence on the realization of Russian national interests. The support of the United States and the European Union for the anti-constitutional coup d'état in Ukraine led to a deep split in Ukrainian society and the emergence of an armed conflict. The strengthening of far-right nationalist ideology, the deliberate shaping in the Ukrainian population of an image of Russia as an enemy, the undisguised gamble on the forcible resolution of intrastate contradictions, and the deep socioeconomic crisis are turning Ukraine into a chronic seat of instability in Europe and in the immediate vicinity of Russia's borders. The practice of overthrowing legitimate political regimes and provoking intrastate instability and conflicts is becoming increasingly widespread.[45]

Thanks to Crimea's annexation—a quite unique moment of huge unanimity and enthusiasm in Russia, with Putin's ratings reaching their highest, at over 80 percent[46]—the regime was able to secure a rally-around-the-flag effect that calmed the dissatisfaction expressed in 2011–2012 and offered a few more years in favor of the status quo. The Western sanctions imposed in 2014 in response to this did not make the state–society consensus more fragile; on the contrary, even in the face of declining living standards, Russian public opinion stood by its president and showed a high level of resilience to changes in everyday life.[47] Citizens set aside their dissatisfaction with the lack of reforms and the malfunctioning of the Russian state. Even anti-immigrant xenophobia eased in the face of conflict with the West.

The regime took advantage of this rally-around-the-flag effect to consolidate its repressive legislative apparatus, marginalize what remained of public dissident voices and spaces, and recentralize its security apparatus. The creation, in 2016, of a Russian National Guard aimed to group the different security agencies—all interior troops, including OMON (Special Purpose Mobility Unit) and SOBR (Special Rapid Response Unit)—into a giant force numbering around 340,000.[48] Institutions that formerly depended on the regional branches of the Ministry of the Interior now find themselves answering directly to the president and to the guard's director, Putin's former bodyguard Viktor Zolotov. The creation of this new federal institution points to the ongoing restructuring of the power ministries and circles around Putin, with the implicit mission of protecting the regime and potentially suppressing internal dissidents.[49] Political assassination continued, with former deputy-prime-minister-turned-opposition-figure Boris Nemtsov killed in February 2015 almost right in front of the Kremlin, and Mikhail Lesin, who founded the English-language television network Russia Today (RT), found mysteriously dead in Washington, DC, in 2016.

The Russian political system has also continued to sustain particularly infamous "subregimes," such as the one of Ramzan Kadyrov in Chechnya, known for its violations of human rights and its caricatural antigay stance.[50] For years, Kadyrov has worked at integrating Chechnya nation building as a crucial *matrioshka* (nesting dolls) component of a pan-Russian nationalism.[51] Chechen national pride is presented as a key component of a statecentric nationalism that embraces the cult of ethnic and religious diversity at home and an imperial agenda abroad. Kadyrovism had built a hard-line, puritanical version of Islam inspired by the Gulf States and its interbreeding with traditional Chechen Islam, creating what has been called Islamic Putinism, that is, a version of Russian pro-regime narratives adapted to Muslim contexts.[52]

More importantly to understand the resilience of the regime is the fact that the Kremlin has remained a highly adaptive body able to improvise and adjust to new contexts. This was evidenced by the reintegration, in 2016, of some figures with a more liberal economic agenda, such as former finance minister Alexei Kudrin, whom Putin named deputy head of the president's economic council and asked to draw up a new economic strategy for Russia, and Sergei Kirienko, who, after ten years as the head of Rosatom (the State

Atomic Energy Corporation), became deputy head of the presidential admin-istration. With Kirienko's arrival, the pendulum shifted somewhat away from the most conservative/reactionary positions toward more centrist positions. In 2017, the presidential administration decided to give grants to associations registered as foreign agents, halted direct funding of Putin's Night Wolves patriotic motorcycle club, and repressed Orthodox fundamentalists who crossed the line with their anti-*Matilda* demonstrations.

Once the "Crimea effect" faded, intrasocietal polarization increased: after the release in spring 2017 of the investigative film *He Is Not Dimon to You* by Navalny's Anti-Corruption Foundation, denouncing Dmitri Medvedev's sus-pected role in corrupt practices, mass protests erupted, mostly by the younger parts of the population in big urban centers. While the protests were smaller than the ones in 2011–2012, they were the first of such scale since the rally-around-the-flag moment of Crimea's annexation. Dissatisfaction was also motivated by the planned demolition of apartment buildings from the 1960s, the *khrushchevki*, in what the population saw as a way to create a new, more expensive, housing market.[53]

## Putin IV: The Turning Point

The 2018 presidential elections proved the regime's success at managing pub-lic opinion. Putin was able to obtain his highest score ever, with 76.6 percent of the vote in the first round. Even if there were obvious cases of electoral fraud, this feat was made possible by securing the voters of Russia's big cit-ies: usually with a low voter turnout, they massively turned out to vote, and they voted for him this time. There are several explanations for this, but it is probable that the feeling of a lack of choice and the notion that, aside from its flaws, only the current regime could attempt to reform the country, played a critical role.[54]

The regime became increasingly static, with no new faces emerging close to the president. Putin's entourage was gradually reduced to the most hawk-ish figures, especially Nikolai Patrushev, the FSB director and secretary of Russia's Security Council and a fervent supporter of anti-Western conspiracy theories.[55] Yet several big names were removed from their roles: Sergey Ivanov, former chief of staff of the presidential executive office; Vladimir Yakunin, head of Russian Railways; and Anatoly Serdyukov, minister of defense from 2007 to 2012, were all dismissed from their posts but not charged with any wrongdoing. Moscow mayor Yuri Luzhkov was offered a golden parachute.

The Russian political system also became increasingly punitive for second-tier elites, with about 1.5 percent to 2 percent of regional elites facing prosecution annually.[56] At the same time, a new generation of technocrats in their thirties and forties were promoted: well trained in managing a modern and neoliberal state, totally unknown to the public, and not directly connected to Putin, they were loyal to the system as a whole and embodied the beginning of a possible "Putinism after Putin." Indeed, the regime seemed to arrive at a point where its natural death by inertia appeared a plausible scenario at the time, symbolized by what some saw as Putin's likely last term in office. The mismanagement of the pension reforms, which provoked mass protests in June 2018, sent a signal that welfare policies had to remain a central element of the population's acquiescence to the regime.

What seems like a slow, smooth decay of the political system was shaken by several external factors, both domestic and international. The COVID-19 pandemic totally isolated Putin—literally: afraid of contracting the coronavirus, the president worked for almost two years isolated from his staff and government members, with limited travels at home, and with reduced physical interactions. Mikhail Zygar, a Russian journalist who has closely studied the president's "court," stated that one of the few who was able to spend time with the president was Yuri Kovachuk, a billionaire reputed to be Putin's banker and a fervent supporter of mystical Orthodoxy and Russian imperialism.[57] This physical isolation is likely to have accentuated the bias of information delivered to Putin by the FSB through classified documents—now his only window into society and the world.

During the two years of the pandemic, the Russian regime accentuated its control over society. First in July 2020, in the midst of a coronavirus lockdown, the authorities organized a referendum to ratify amendments to the constitution. Beyond the main goal of allowing the president to run for several new consecutive terms, letting him potentially remain in power until 2036, they mandated that the state take charge of several social provisions. This included regularly indexing pensions and social benefits to inflation and guaranteeing a minimum wage at or above the poverty line—measures that were widely publicized to ensure popular support for constitutional reform. The widely approved constitutional changes also enshrined conservative and patriotic values in the constitutional text: marriage can only be heterosexual, any action in favor of the "separation of a territory" (*otchuzhdenie territorii*), including calls for separatism, are forbidden (Crimea was in the drafters' minds, as well as the Kuril Islands between the Kamchatka Peninsula and northern Japan), dual citizenship is forbidden for those seeking elective office, and the memory of the Great Patriotic War is sacred and cannot be challenged without legal consequences, among other changes.[58]

Repression toward political opposition hardened, and the remaining spaces for free expression faded. In August 2020, Navalny was poisoned with a Novichok nerve agent and hospitalized in serious condition in Germany, with multiple investigative teams confirming the role of the FSB in the poisoning.[59]

Navalny returned to Russia in January 2021 only to be arrested and jailed, first for parole violations and then sent for nine years to a maximum-security penal colony after being charged and found guilty of large-scale fraud and contempt of a court.[60] Pressures on memory and history issues became aggravated, symbolized by the closure of Memorial, the most respected Russian NGO working on Soviet crimes and contemporary human rights.

On the international scene, tensions with the West became heightened, and Ukraine became an even bigger focal point. The Kremlin vehemently denounced Western military support (mostly US, Canadian, and British) given to the Ukrainian Army, seeing it as an attempt by the West to bypass Kyiv's non-NATO status and directly threaten Russia's 2014 gains—that is, Crimea and the not-so-frozen conflict in the Donbas. The failed attempt at making Ukrainian president Volodymyr Zelenskyy into a pliant partner of Russia ready to implement the Minsk II agreement (which would have more or less federalized Ukraine in reintegrating the so-called people's republics of Donetsk and Luhansk) triggered the Kremlin's ideological hardening. In March and April 2021, Russia began amassing thousands of personnel and huge amounts of military equipment near its border with Ukraine but partially withdrew them later. In June, Putin published his infamous article on the unity between Russians and Ukrainians, which was seen as the ideological justification for a possible war. Yet he continued throughout the year to send mixed signals to the West about Moscow's level of interest in an armed conflict and insisted on opening negotiations with the United States about the European security architecture.

## Wartime Regime

With the full-scale invasion of Ukraine on February 24, 2022, the Russian regime had to address its biggest crisis since the collapse of the Soviet Union. This "power vertical," which had gradually been constructed over two decades, had annihilated any intermediary institutions that could have challenged the decision to go to war. The Security Council held on February 21 and broadcasted on television showed an immobilized, if not terrified, membership listening to the president's decision and acquiescing out of fear. Unprepared and uninformed, Russian elites seemed at first to panic, but they rapidly stabilized and reconsolidated around the Kremlin.

One year and a half after the beginning of the war, we have seen almost no defection from elite members, with some minor exceptions, such as already marginalized figures (for example, Anatoly Chubais or the two oligarchs, Mikhail Fridman and Pyotr Aven, owners of Alfa Bank). The wide-ranging sanctions launched by the West against Russian elites have had the unintended consequence of pushing them closer to depending on the regime, rather than away from it. But the war has also relaunched intraelite fights: several high-level businessmen or CEOs of big firms have been killed, have "committed suicide," or have died by strange accidents at home and abroad—likely a sign of property rights readjustments between different vested interests groups.[61]

The so-called systemic liberals (that is, the technocratic elites in charge of managing finances and the economy) have remained loyal to Putin and have excelled at adapting state spending and the budget to the war context. Political parties, both United Russia and the so-called systemic opposition (the Communist Party, the LDPR, and A Just Russia—For Truth), now seek more creative ways to signal their loyalty and utility, and they compete even more to incubate new repressive legislation.

The regime's political equilibrium has moved toward the more hawkish side, with an increasingly vocal "party of war" that encompasses the security services, myriad ideological and media entrepreneurs, and the new phenomenon of "war correspondents" (*voenkory*)—that is, journalists embedded with the Russian Army and paramilitary groups on the front lines. Many of them consider today's war as the long-awaited continuation of unfinished business from 2014: that is, the annexation of Donbas.[62] With hundreds of thousands of followers on the social media platform Telegram, these war correspondents have, paradoxically, become new opinion leaders in an increasingly repressive political system and have the capacity to criticize the regime for its lack of effectiveness at organizing the army, preparing troops, and mobilizing society for war.

Closely interconnected to the rise of pro-war opinion leaders is the consolidation of warlord-like political-military figures, in particular the infamous Yevgeny Prigozhin, who uses the war and the successes of his Wagner mercenary group on the front to promote himself on the domestic scene and to try to win a place among the established elites. As Julian Waller states, "The rise of political-military barons—that is, these political figures with personal control over real military resources and favored, clientelist connections to the apex executive—is an important change"[63] in the history of Russian politics. The failed attempted coup by Prigozhin in June 2023 has confirmed the new uncertainties brought by these new political actors.

The regime also moved to repress society even further. The implicit social contract that was made with private citizens in exchange for their noninvolvement in politics has been broken. This was not caused by the war itself but by the September 2022 mobilization, which due to its disorganization gave the impression that every family could be touched and had to send its men to the front.

To address these challenges, the Duma passed the highest number of laws ever, more than six hundred over the course of the year.[64] Among the highlights, the March 5 law treats any fake information on the "special military operation" and the Russian military as treason against the nation.[65] It was followed by a series of laws that increased the list of conditions that could lead one to be labeled as a foreign agent (with the dubious notion of "being under foreign influence" as a criteria), restricted internet freedom (about four hundred thousand more websites have been blocked by Roskomnadzor between the beginning of the war and January 2023)[66] as well as criminalized the use of VPN to bypass digital walls, and placed the Russian economy on a war footing, with government orders given priority.

Repression has grown in scale: during the first year of the war, about twenty thousand people protesting against it were at least temporarily detained (four-fifths of them in the war's first month),[67] more than five thousand people were fined for "discrediting of the Russian forces,"[68] opposition figures such as Ilya Yashin and Vladimir Kara-Murza received exemplarily harsh punishments of nine years and twenty-five years in prison, respectively, and an older human rights NGO, the Helsinki Group, was closed down. Ideological indoctrination was accentuated with the launch of new classes on patriotism for school-age children and university students and coercive techniques to force youth to demonstrate solidarity with the war.

The mandatory military service age has been extended to those thirty years old, which will allow the army to enroll students once they have finished higher education. In preparation for a potential second mobilization, the Duma passed a new law in March 2023 announcing that men will be called for service via simple email—a way to avoid them hiding as during the first mobilization—and those failing to report for duty will be forbidden to leave the country and may see their assets seized. The more radical voices, among them Duma chairman Vyacheslav Volodin, also advocated for harsh measures such as punishing those who left Russia (seizure of their assets, loss of their citizenship), while Kremlin spokesperson Dmitri Peskov hoped for these "resettlers" (*relokanty*) to come back to Russia once the most active part of the war has ended and therefore called for forgiveness, so the brain drain would not be too damaging to the country's future.

## WHAT IS PUTINISM?

### Putinism as a Regime

Much has been written to try to pin down the Russian regime's ideological characteristics. The first feature to note is its flexibility, its ad hoc capacity to adapt: since Putin came to power in 2000, the regime's "nature" has dramatically changed to meet new conditions.[69] One can then question the legitimacy of envisioning the regime under one unifying term over more than two decades. And yet, the components of continuity are there too. At a human level, Putin and key members of his entourage have formed a relatively stable group since their formation in the 1990s–early 2000s.[70] The human continuity aspect of the regime goes even deeper, as about 60 percent of Putin-regime elites have a Soviet nomenklatura background.[71]

At an ideological level, continuity is also visible, as at least four deep-seated beliefs have shaped Putin elites since the beginning: (1) first, that Russia could not survive a new state collapse, such as the Soviet Union's in 1991; (2) second, that the state embodies Russia as a nation and should therefore be given priority over its citizens' well-being; (3) third, that Russia is a civilization-state in itself, with a "natural" Eurasian regional identity/sphere of influence; and (4) fourth, that the West has an essentially anti-Russian "cultural code."

Beyond this core human and ideological continuity, Putinism has been an evolving reality. First, in its vision of Russia's ability to be heard on the international scene, and especially by the West and the United States, "early Putinism" was much more optimistic about Russia's prospects for success in integrating into the Western political and economic community and having its strategic interests considered against those of the neighboring states. That hope failed on several occasions, and turning points have been numerous since Putin's Munich speech in 2007, in which he expressed a very disillusioned view of the West liberal order, up to today's war narrative, which emphasizes that, in essence, Russia's and the West's "civilizational codes" are antithetical to each other.

Just as important, Putinism as a public policy and a policy toolkit has also significantly evolved: the level of consensus with the majority of the population, the shared values and hopes that the Russian government represented, and the level of repression needed to keep society united have dramatically evolved from a genuine "honeymoon" between Putin and society in the early 2000s to a repressive regime today.[72] While for long the state was supportive of a multiplicity of voices as long as they were not too directly oppositional, that room for expressing divergent views has since shrunk into the production of a much more uniform and rigid framing of domestic and international affairs.

The important point here is not so much that the narrative has evolved but that what was said before to generate genuine support is now said to generate fear. And as we saw in chapter 2, fears of the arbitrariness of the state and of state repressions have increased again in the population. To this should be added the many silences of Russian public opinion, its self-censorship, and the "hidden scripts" of dissatisfaction that are not easily visible to outside observers—even if we can guess that a plurality of the population is still supportive of the regime.[73]

Depending on whether one looks at Putinism as a historical phenomenon over two decades or at wartime Putinism, one can use different terminologies to define it. For a long time, the regime was presented in political science works as electoral authoritarianism,[74] a kleptocracy,[75] and/or a neopatrimonial system[76] (these terms may often overlap). With the Russo-Ukrainian War, debates about the Russian political system being a full autocracy,[77] a personalistic dictatorship,[78] or a totalitarian regime[79] have increased. Yet Putin's Russia is still far from the omniscient, repressive toolkit of Xi Jinping's China; and contrary to the situation seen in a totalitarian regime, the Russian authorities push for the population to be demobilized, not mobilized. While the level of repression is rapidly increasing, it remains targeted and not massive, and parallels being drawn with Stalinism are therefore misguided.[80]

## Putinism as an Ideology

The place of ideology in the regime's construction has been the subject of heated debate too. Some have denounced Putin's "fascism"[81]; others identify two other pillars as the structures of his thoughts: "the idea of empire and the glorification of war"[82]; and some others argue that the regime only instrumentally uses ideology. These disagreements in interpretation are often due to the lack of a clear definition for what is meant by "ideology." The regime's main figures have their own beliefs and worldviews, shaped by their own personal experiences and the cultural environment in which they operate. Conspiracy theories about the West's supposed permanent struggle with Russia are dominant in Russia's international affairs culture.[83] This is articulated with the need to defend the Russian state at any cost and to secure popular support and national unity around patriotic values (now with the conservative touch added). These core elements have shaped the regime's key figures' decision-making. Putin's speeches since the invasion of Ukraine, particularly those of February 21, February 24 (during the lead-up to and onset of the war), and September 30, 2022 (on the annexation of four Ukrainian regions), are a testimony of the significance of this worldview.

In terms of what the regime has pushed out toward the population, Russia's political ideology has a dual objective: to be sufficiently offensive tactically in order to marginalize and delegitimize all those who question the regime, in particular the liberals, while remaining sufficiently vague or broad so that the majority of the population can adhere to it. There is a common core to this worldview, a minimum set of requirements for everyone: (1) publicly express patriotism and support for its great-power identity (with different visions of what constitutes being a great power); (2) demonstrate pride in the country's recovery since the fall of the Soviet Union and criticize the unbridled liberalism of the Yeltsin years that led the country to the brink of civil war; and (3) cultivate a certain Soviet nostalgia and share in at least some conservative values, even if symbolically. One should also support the idea that Russia cannot afford another revolution or shock and should be reformed gradually, at its own pace, and reject all those who still advocate for the outright adoption of a Western model. One must consider Russia's view of its "near abroad" to be legitimate and to welcome the reemergence of a Russian voice in the world, with a cynical view of the international community as being manipulated by the interests of the strongest under the guise of great idealistic principles, and share in a culture of conspiratorial thinking.[84]

Once this baseline is accepted, several ideological products are offered for collective consumption, especially in the memory field. One could choose between nostalgia for the Soviet Union or for the Tsarist Empire. One could consider Ivan the Terrible, Nicholas II, Pyotr Stolypin, Vladimir Lenin, Josef Stalin, Yuri Gagarin, or Vladimir Putin himself as the most important hero of national history. The regime, for instance, decided not to commemorate the one-hundredth-anniversary of the 1917 revolutions, with Putin remaining silent on all key dates for both the February and October revolutions. Indeed, as its authority is based on a firm counterrevolutionary ideology, the Kremlin considers any kind of revolution, whatever its "color," harmful. Yet it let other political actors take the stage: the Communist Party celebrated the Bolshevik Revolution, while the Orthodox Church mourned the collapse of Tsarism.[85]

Within the ideological framework authorized, one might just as freely hope that Orthodoxy becomes the state religion as take pride in Russia's religious diversity or even uphold the Soviet secular tradition. One may see Russia as a country of ethnic Russians in permanent struggle for survival against minorities, or celebrate the country's multicultural harmony—the latter narrative being the official one promoted by the Kremlin, even more so since the 2022 onset of Putin's newfound insistence on Russia's multi-ethnicity and anticolonial culture One can advocate for complete isolationism or exalt Russia's commitment to re-creating a multipolar world with its allies. One may express the wish to update pan-Slavism to embrace brother Orthodox Slavs, to reunify the divided Russian nation with its compatriots abroad, to re-create the Russian Empire and its Eastern Slavic unity with Ukrainians and Belarusians, to promote Eurasianism with reference to the Turkic-Mongol world, or to look for a model to the Byzantine Empire . . . or present-day China.

The new Russian Foreign Policy Concept, released in March 2023, attempts to blend several of these repertoires into a coherent language. It presents Russia "as a vast Eurasian and Euro-Pacific power that brings together the Russian people and other peoples belonging to the cultural and civilizational community of the Russian world."[86] As we can see from this quote, the text conflates Eurasia with a post-Soviet sphere of influence, and

Eurasia with a turn toward Asia and the Russian world. It also uses the notion of "near abroad," describing "the CIS and other neighboring countries, linked with Russia by centuries of common statehood, profound interdependency in various spheres, shared language, and proximate cultures" as part of the "cultural-civilizational unity."[87]

Over the years, the elasticity of ideological production has faded, and some bedrock notions have emerged as the regime's newspeak. Four key notions dominate: (1) Russia as a separate civilization, (2) the need to reassert Ukraine's "Russianness," (3) the West as the center of conspiracy against Russia, and (4) the renewal of the "fight against fascism" to justify the war.

"Civilization" has become a catchall term in Russia, used and abused by the media as well as the government. Putin and Medvedev have spoken repeatedly of Russia's "civilizational codes," of Russia as a separate civilization with its own cultural and moral foundations, but the terminology is deliberately blurry. References to Russia—whether as a European civilization, a distinct Orthodox civilization, or a Eurasian civilization oriented toward a Euro-Asian equilibrium—can be found scattered throughout Russian official discourse as both context and reference point.[88] Allusions to Europe predominated for a long time: namely, the theme of Russia as the authentic, Christian Europe charged with remembering the continent's genuine identity, in contrast to a Western Europe that has forgotten its roots.[89] Yet after 2014, the state language has gradually shifted to defend Russia's "unique path" (*osobyi put'*) and specific "state-civilization," with rapidly declining reference to its sense of European belonging.

Parallel to this change in definition of the essence of Russia's civilizational identity has been the gradual emphasis put on Ukraine as the crux of both strategic and normative challenges posed by the West and the re-creation of a mythified Russia in which historical junctures and territorial discontinuities would be erased or repaired. Ukraine finds itself the centerpiece of both components of this blend: it embodies the failure of Russia to be attractive enough to keep Kyiv in its orbit against Western competition, and it symbolizes the historical and territorial disjunctures that have broken the mythified East Slavic unity.

In such a context, memory has become the leading ideological weapon used by the regime both to justify its attack on Ukraine and to indoctrinate its citizens. The abuse of references to the memory of the Great Patriotic War has become the regime's main ideological monopoly, the sole source of symbolic legitimization. While the Great Patriotic War has long been the driving element of consensus surrounding the national identity, its highly instrumental use since 2014—and even more since 2022—is now eroding this major uniting symbol and emptying it of any substance.[90] The argument of the need to fight against "the renewal of fascism" was used to justify the annexation of Crimea and the subsequent war in the Donbas, with Ukrainians presented as neo-Nazis and Russian insurgents as *opolcheny*, or popular militia formed for wartime resistance.[91] With the full-scale invasion of 2022, this narrative reached its preposterous peak with Moscow's calling for "denazifying" Ukraine, and using other dehumanizing semantic tools such as "Ukrofascists."

The West itself is portrayed as the origin of this evil: the CIA would foment neo-Nazism in Ukraine, the EU would represent the "Fourth Reich," marked by decadent values forcing people to become gay to avoid having children, and on and on. Russia's wartime ideological production appears as a schizo-phrenic combination of narratives where everything is framed as a war except the real war in Ukraine, which is called a "special military operation." This extreme Manichean vision of the world has also been filled out in religious tones—Russia's mission would be to "de-Satanize" Ukraine—bringing the war to a metaphysical level.[92]

For over two decades, Putin's regime has managed to reconstruct a political language that the population has widely accepted and internalized, through mutual agreements on what to remember from the past and what to obscure, state media propaganda and repressive tools, as well as horizontal pressures from within society itself against those who generate cognitive dissonance. Over the years, the regime has become progressively more explicit in its ide-ology and offered increasingly normative frameworks, all while broadening coercive mechanisms.

The final objective has largely been attained: the population protects itself from the regime by returning to private life, tending to the affairs of every-day life and supporting the authorities in a passive way. This is visible in the ambiguous level of support for the war as well as support for a ceasefire scenario, meaning the majority of the population sides with whatever the Kremlin considers good for the country. The regime still enjoys the public support of the plurality/majority, even if it is difficult to know how much this is exactly, given the lack of reliability of wartime sociology, and Putin continues to be seen as the symbol of the nation and state, despite criticisms of the government or the military.

Yet the war has stretched the regime to the extreme, and signs of tension and exhaustion of its internal dynamics are becoming gradually more visible. The 2024 presidential election is on the horizon, and the question of whether Russia will find itself on the battlefield or in a peacetime scenario may dra-matically impact the ability of the regime to renew itself. To these challenges should be added the difficulties of managing a strained but resilient economy.

## NOTES

1. Alexei Yurchak, *Everything Was Forever, Until It Was No More: The Last Soviet Generation* (Princeton, NJ: Princeton University Press, 2005).

2. See Eliot Borenstein, *Plots against Russia: Conspiracy and Fantasy after Socialism* (Ithaca, NY: Cornell University Press, 2019); and Ilya Yablokov, *Fortress Russia: Conspiracy Theories in the Post-Soviet World* (New York: Polity Press, 2018).

3. See, for example, Louis Sell, "Embassy under Siege: An Eyewitness Account of Yeltsin's 1993 Attack on Parliament," *Problems of Post-Communism* 50, no. 4 (2003): 43–64.

4. See Dmitry Gorenburg, "Regional Separatism in Russia: Ethnic Mobilization or Power Grab?" *Europe-Asia Studies* 51, no. 2 (1999): 245–74; Dmitry Gorenburg, *Minority Ethnic Mobilization* (Cambridge: Cambridge University Press, 2009); Elise Giuliano, *Constructing Grievance: Ethnic Nationalism in Russia's Republics* (Ithaca, NY: Cornell University Press, 2011).

5. Jean Radvanyi, *La Russie face à ses régions: Problèmes politiques et sociaux* (Paris: La Documentation française, December 1994).

6. Richat Sabitov, *Le fédéralisme russe contemporain et la République du Tatarstan* (Paris: Fondation Varenne, 2013). See also Gulnaz Sharafutdinova, "Paradiplomacy in the Russian Regions: Tatarstan's Search for Statehood," *Europe-Asia Studies* 55, no. 4 (2003): 613–29.

7. Anatol Lieven, *Chechnya: Tombstone of Russian Power* (New Haven, CT: Yale University Press, 1999).

8. Nina Tumarkin, *The Living and the Dead: The Rise and Fall of the Cult of World War II in Russia* (New York: Perseus Books, 1994).

9. "Yeltsin o natsional'noi idee," *Nezavisimaia gazeta*, July 13, 1996.

10. More in Laruelle, *In the Name of the Nation. Nationalism and Politics in Contemporary Russia* (New York: Palgrave MacMillan, 2009), 122–24.

11. Lev D. Gudkov, "Ethnic Phobias in the Structure of National Identification," *Russian Social Science Review* 39, no. 1 (1998): 89–103.

12. Mikhail Gorshkov, ed., *Mass Consciousness of the Russians during the Period of Social Transformations: Realities versus Myths* (Moscow: Russian Independent Institute of Social and Nationalities Problems, 1996), cited in Fiona Hill, "In Search of Great Russia: Elites, Ideas, Power, the State, and the Pre-Revolutionary Past in the New Russia, 1991–1996" (PhD diss., Harvard University, 1998).

13. See more in Hill, "In Search of Great Russia."

14. Vladimir Putin, "Rossiia za rubezhe tysiatseletii," *Rossiiskaia gazeta,* December 31, 1999; see the English translation at https://pages.uoregon.edu/kimball/Putin.htm.

15. "Gosudarstvennaia programma 'Patrioticheskoe vospitanie grazhdan Rossiiskoi Federatsii na 2001–2005 gg,'" Gosudarstvennaia sistema pravovoi informatsii, https://docs.cntd.ru/document/901781482.

16. Alexander Agadjanian, "Religious Pluralism and National Identity in *Russia,*" *International Journal on Multicultural Societies* 2, no. 2 (2000): 97–124.

17. On the role of the Federation Council at that time, see Nikolai Petrov and Darrell Slider, "Putin and the Regions," in *Putin's Russia: Past Imperfect, Future Uncertain,* 2nd ed., ed. Dale Herspring (Lanham, MD: Rowman & Littlefield, 2005), 75–98.

18. Beat Kernen, "Putin and the Parliamentary Election in Russia: The Confluence (Slijanie) of Russian Political Culture and Leadership," *East European Quarterly* 38, no. 1 (2004): 85–107.

19. "Vladimir Putin's Big Government and the 'Politburo 2.0,'" Minchenko Consulting, http://minchenko.ru/netcat_files/File/Big Government and the Politburo 2_0. pdf; see also Ievgenii Minchenko, "Sistemnye riski komandy Putina," *Nezavisimaia gazeta,* December 2, 2014, http://www.ng.ru/ng_politics/2014-12-02/9_risks.html.

20. "Ikh dom—Rossiia," in "Korporatsiia Rossiia: Putin s druz'iami podelili stranu," *Novoe vremia,* October 31, 2011, https://newtimes.ru/articles/detail/45648.

21. Vladimir Pribylovskii, *Kooperativ Ozero i drugie proekty Putina* (Moscow: Algoritm, 2012).

22. On the situation of the children and spouses of the Russian political elite, see Aleksandr Limanov, "Vsio luchshee–detiam," *Novoe vremia,* no. 21, June 18, 2011, https://newtimes.ru/articles/detail/40588.

23. See Karen Dawisha, "Vladislav Surkov, 1964–," in *Russia's People of Empire: Life Stories from Eurasia, 1500 to the Present,* ed. Stephen Norris and Willard Sunderland (Bloomington: Indiana University Press, 2012), 339–49; and Richard Sakwa, "Surkov: Dark Prince of the Kremlin," *openDemocracy,* April 7, 2011, https://www .opendemocracy.net/en/odr/surkov-dark-prince-of-kremlin.

24. "Gosudarstvennaia programma 'Patrioticheskoe vospitanie grazhdan RF na 2006–2010 gody,'" Gosudarstvennaia sistema pravovoi informatsii, https://docs.cntd .ru/document/901781482.

25. See Stephen White, "Soviet Nostalgia and Russian Politics," *Journal of Eurasian Studies* 1, no. 1 (2010): 1–9; and Charles Sullivan, "Motherland: Soviet Nostalgia in Post-Soviet Russia" (PhD diss., George Washington University, 2014).

26. The Second World War is one of the major historical contexts of these patriotic television series, but so are the years of the Soviet "Golden Age"—the Brezhnev decades. The Tsarist past is exalted by series that depict the great Russian novels of the nineteenth century or major figureheads such as Admiral Alexander Kolchak.

27. Lev Gudkov, "Pamiat' o voine i massovaia identichnost' rossiian," *Neprikosnovennyi zapas,* no. 40–41 (2005), http://magazines.russ.ru/nz/2005/2/gu5.html.

28. "President Restores Name 'Stalingrad' to Moscow War Memorial," RFE/RL *Newsline,* July 23, 2004, http://www.hri.org/cgi-bin/brief?/news/balkans/rferl/2004 /04-07-23.rferl.html#11.

29. "Stalin Monument to Be Erected by V-Day," RFE/RL *Newsline,* April 1, 2005, http://www.hri.org/cgi-bin/brief?/news/balkans/rferl/2005/05-05-10.rferl.html#15.

30. Kathy Rousselet, "Butovo: La création d'un lieu de pèlerinage sur une terre de massacres," *Politix* 20, no. 77 (2007): 55–78.

31. Richard Sakwa, "Putin's Leadership: Character and Consequences," *Europe-Asia Studies* 60, no. 6 (2008): 879–97.

32. Marlene Laruelle, "Inside and around the Kremlin's Black Box: The New Nationalist Think Tanks in Russia," *Stockholm Papers* (October 2009), http://isdp.eu

/content/uploads/images/stories/isdp-main-pdf/2009_laruelle_inside-and-around-the
-kremlins-black-box.pdf.

33. See, for instance, Igor Yurgens, ed., *Obretenie budushchego: Strategiia 2012* (Moscow: INSOR, 2011), https://novayagazeta.ru/articles/2011/03/16/6510-obretenie
-buduschego-strategiya-2012.

34. "Elektoral'nyi reiting politicheskikh partii," VTsIOM, https://wciom.ru/news/ratings/elektoralnyj_rejting_politicheskix_partij.

35. "Rossiiskie shkol'niki chashche vybiraiut izuchenie etiki, chem osnov pravoslaviia," TASS, July 12, 2019, https://tass.ru/obschestvo/6659493.

36. See Samuel Greene, *Moscow in Movement: Power and Opposition in Putin's Russia* (Stanford, CA: Stanford University Press, 2014); and Graeme Robertson, "The Election Protests of 2011–2012 in Broader Perspective," *Problems of Post-Communism* 60, no. 2 (2013): 11–23.

37. Eva Bertrand, "Pouvoir, catastrophe et représentation: Mise(s) en scène politique(s) des incendies de l'été 2010 en Russie occidentale" (PhD diss., Sciences Po, Paris, 2016).

38. Alfred B. Evans, "Protests and Civil Society in Russia: The Struggle for the Khimki Forest," *Communist and Post-Communist Studies* 45, no. 3–4 (2012): 233–42.

39. See Pål Kolstø, "Marriage of Convenience? Collaboration between Nationalists and Liberals in the Russian Opposition 2011–12," *Russian Review* 75, no. 4 (2016): 645–63.

40. Marlene Laruelle, "Alexei Navalny and Challenges in Reconciling 'Nationalism' and 'Liberalism,'" *Post-Soviet Affairs* 30, no. 4 (2014): 276–97.

41. See Maria Lipman, "How Putin Silences Dissent," *Foreign Affairs*, April 18, 2016, https://www.foreignaffairs.com/articles/russia-fsu/2016-04-18/how-putin
-silences-dissent.

42. Andrei Soldatov and Irina Borogan, *The Red Web: The Kremlin's Wars on the Internet* (New York: Public Affairs, 2017).

43. Gulnaz Sharafutdinova, "The Pussy Riot Affair and Putin's Demarche from Sovereign Democracy to Sovereign Morality," *Nationalities Papers: Journal of Nationalism & Ethnicity* 42, no. 4 (2014): 615–21.

44. On Russia's policy in the cultural realm, see the special issue of *Kontrapunkt/Counterpoint*, no. 4 (2016), http://www.counter-point.org.

45. See the English translation of the 2015 Russian National Security here: https://www.russiamatters.org/node/21421.

46. Julie Ray and Neli Esipova, "Russian Approval of Putin Soars to Highest Level in Years," *Gallup*, July 18, 2014, http://www.gallup.com/poll/173597/russian
-approval-putin-soars-highest-level-years.aspx.

47. Timothy Frye, "Are Sanctions Pushing Russians to 'Rally around the Flag'? Not Exactly," *Washington Post's Monkey Cage*, June 15, 2017, https://www.washingtonpost.com/news/monkey-cage/wp/2017/06/15/are-sanctions-pushing
-russians-to-rally-around-the-flag-not-exactly.

48. "Lichnyi sostav voisk Rosgvardii sostavil 340 tys. chelovek," *Interfax*, November 25, 2016, https://www.interfax.ru/world/538542.

49. The reform represented a challenge to the Ministry of Defense, which saw itself excluded from internal security and, now, managing only the defense of Russia against external enemies; it also weakened the FSB, the citadel of Putin's power. Alexander Bortnikov, director of the FSB, who also heads the National Anti-Terrorism Committee, had to cede some of his power to the National Guard. In addition, two flagship institutions of the 2000s, the Federal Migration Service and the Federal Drug Control Service, lost their status as independent agencies and became branches of the Ministry of the Interior. See Pavel Baev, "Newly Formed National Guard Cannot Dispel Putin's Multiple Insecurities," *Eurasia Daily Monitor* 13, no. 70 (2016), https://jamestown.org/program/newly-formed-national-guard-cannot-dispel-putins-multiple-insecurities; Anna Baidakova, "Gennadii Gudkov: 'Natsional'nuiu gvardiiu gotoviat k podavleniiu sotsialnogo protesta," *Novaia gazeta*, April 6, 2016, https://www.novayagazeta.ru/articles/2016/04/06/68105-gennadiy-gudkov-171-natsionalnuyu-gvardiyu-gotovyat-k-podavleniyu-sotsialnogo-protesta-187.

50. Dominic Scicchitano, "The 'Real' Chechen Man: Conceptions of Religion, Nature, and Gender and the Persecution of Sexual Minorities in Postwar Chechnya," *Journal of Homosexuality* 68, no. 9 (2021): 1545–62.

51. Nikolai Silaev, "Chechen Nation-Building under Kadyrov: A Belated 'Korenizatsiya'?" *Problems of Post-Communism* (July 2022).

52. Marlene Laruelle, "Kadyrovism: Hardline Islam as a Tool of the Kremlin?" *Russie.Nei.Visions*, no. 99, Ifri, March 2017, https://www.ifri.org/sites/default/files/atoms/files/rnv99_m._laruelle_kadyrovism_en_2017.pdf.

53. Regina Smyth, "How the Kremlin Is Using the Moscow Renovation Project to Reward and Punish Voters," PONARS Policy Memo no. 513, March 6, 2018, https://www.ponarseurasia.org/how-the-kremlin-is-using-the-moscow-renovation-project-to-reward-and-punish-voters.

54. Kirill Rogov, "Putin's Reelection: Capturing Russia's Electoral Patterns," PONARS Eurasia, June 7, 2018, https://www.ponarseurasia.org/putin-s-reelection-capturing-russia-s-electoral-patterns-a-discussion-with-kirill-rogov.

55. Filip Kovacevic, "The Second Most Powerful Man in Russia," *New Lines Magazine*, March 10, 2022, https://newlinesmag.com/reportage/the-second-most-powerful-man-in-russia.

56. Nikolai Petrov, "The Repressions Spiral," PONARS Eurasia Commentary, March 11, 2019, https://www.ponarseurasia.org/the-repressions-spiral.

57. Mikhail Zygar, "How Vladimir Putin Lost Interest in the Present," *New York Times*, March 10, 2022, https://www.nytimes.com/2022/03/10/opinion/putin-russia-ukraine.html.

58. Marlene Laruelle, "Russia's Constitutional Amendments Keep Several Futures Open for Putin," *Russia Matters*, June 25, 2020, https://www.russiamatters.org/analysis/russias-constitutional-amendments-keep-several-futures-open-putin.

59. See, for instance, Bellingcat, "FSB Team of Chemical Weapon Experts Implicated in Alexey Navalny Novichok Poisoning," Bellingcat, December 14, 2020, https://www.bellingcat.com/news/uk-and-europe/2020/12/14/fsb-team-of-chemical-weapon-experts-implicated-in-alexey-navalny-novichok-poisoning.

60. Jan Matti Dollbaum, Marvan Lallouet, and Ben Noble, *Navalny: Putin's Nemesis, Russia's Future?* 2nd ed. (London: Hurst Publishers, 2021).

61. "Sem' sluchaev smertei rossiiskikh top-menedzherov za etot god," *holod*, September 1, 2022, https://holod.media/2022/09/01/deaths-2022.

62. Agnes Wenger, "Return of the *Voenkor*: The Military as a New Opinion Leader in Russia?" *Russia.Post*, August 15, 2022, https://russiapost.info/politics/voenkor.

63. Julian Waller, "Public Politics in the Wartime Russian Dictatorship," War on the Rocks, January 17, 2023, https://warontherocks.com/2023/01/public-politics-in-the-wartime-russian-dictatorship.

64. "Gosduma prinyala v 2022 godu rekordnoe chislo zakonov—653," *Kommersant*, December 22, 2022, https://www.kommersant.ru/doc/5736100.

65. Federalnyi zakon ot 4 marta 2022 g. N 32-FZ, "O vnesenii izmenenii v Ugolovnyi kodeks Rossiiskoi Federatsii i stati 31 i 151 Ugolovno-protsessualnogo kodeksa Rossiiskoi Federatsii."

66. "Monitoring of Registry," *Roskomsvoboda*, February 24, 2022, through December 31, 2023, https://reestr.rublacklist.net/en/?status=all&gov=all&date_start=24-02-2022&date_end=31-12-2023.

67. "Svodka antivoennykh repressii. Odinnadtsat' mesiatsev voiny," OVD-Info, January 2023, https://ovdinfo.org/node/45937.

68. "Chislo del o diskreditatsii rossiiskoi armii priblizilos'k 5 tysiacham," RBK, October 25, 2022, https://www.rbc.ru/politics/25/10/2022/635272fd9a7947da7737e7e1.

69. Henry Hale, Maria Lipman, and Nikolay Petrov, "Russia's Regime-on-the-Move," *Russian Politics* 4, no. 2 (2019): 168–95.

70. Bryan Taylor, *The Code of Putinism* (Oxford: Oxford University Press, 2018).

71. Maria Snegovaya and Kirill Petrov, "Long Soviet Shadow: The Nomenklatura Ties of Putin Elites," *Post-Soviet Affairs* 38, no. 4 (2022): 329–48.

72. Gulnaz Sharafutdinova, *The Red Mirror: Putin's Leadership and Russia's Insecure Identity* (Oxford: Oxford University Press, 2020).

73. Marlene Laruelle, "Which Popular Support for a New State Ideology?" *Russia. Post*, January 18, 2023, https://russiapost.info/society/state_ideology.

74. Vladimir Gel'man, "The Rise and Decline of Electoral Authoritarianism in Russia," *Demokratizatsiya* 22, no. 4 (2014): 503–22.

75. Karen Dawisha, *Putin's Kleptocracy: Who Owns Russia?* (New York City: Simon & Schuster, 2014).

76. Allen C. Lynch, "Russia's 'Neopatrimonial' Political System, 1992–2004," in *How Russia Is Not Ruled: Reflections on Russian Political Development* (Cambridge: Cambridge University Press, 2005): 128–65.

77. Ido Vock, "How Russia Descended into Authoritarianism," *New Statesman*, March 9, 2022, https://www.newstatesman.com/international-politics/2022/03/how-russia-descended-into-authoritarianism.

78. Waller, "Public Politics in the Wartime Russian Dictatorship."

79. Andrei Kolesnikov, "Putin's War Has Moved Russia from Authoritarianism to Hybrid Totalitarianism," Carnegie Center for International Peace, April 19, 2022, https://carnegieendowment.org/2022/04/19/putin-s-war-has-moved-russia-from-authoritarianism-to-hybrid-totalitarianism-pub-86921.

80. Vladimir Gel'man, interview, January 9, 2023, https://meduza.io/feature/2023/01/09/kak-voyna-izmenila-putinskiy-rezhim-kakuyu-tsenu-zaplatit-rossiya-posle-smeny-vlasti-i-est-li-voobsche-nadezhda-chto-putin-ne-navsegda.

81. See, for instance, Alexander Motyl, "Putin's Russia as a Fascist Political System," *Communist & Post-Communist Studies* 49, no. 1 (2016): 25–36.

82. Michel Eltchaninoff, *Inside the Mind of Vladimir Putin* (New York: Hurst, 2018).

83. Martin Kragh, "Conspiracy Theories in Russian Security Thinking," *Journal of Strategic Studies* 45, no. 3 (2022): 334–68.

84. More in Yablokov, *Fortress Russia.*

85. Olga Malinova, "The Embarrassing Centenary: Reinterpretation of the 1917 Revolution in the Official Historical Narrative of Post-Soviet Russia," *Nationalities Papers* 46, no. 2 (2018): 272–89; Marlene Laruelle, "Commemorating 1917 in Russia: Ambivalent State History Policy and the Church's Conquest of the History Market," *Europe-Asia Studies* 71, no. 2 (2019): 249–67.

86. https://mid.ru/en/foreign_policy/fundamental_documents/1860586.

87. https://mid.ru/en/foreign_policy/fundamental_documents/1860586.

88. Henry Hale and Marlene Laruelle, "Civilizational Discourse in Russia" (forthcoming).

89. More in Marlene Laruelle, "Russia as an Anti-Liberal European Civilization," in *The New Russian Nationalism: Between Imperial and Ethnic*, ed. Pål Kolstø and Helge Blakkisrud (Edinburgh: Edinburgh University Press, 2016), 275–97.

90. Ivan Kurilla, "How is the Kremlin Eroding Russia's Major Uniting Symbol?" *Russia.Post*, November 22, 2022, https://russiapost.info/politics/uniting_symbol.

91. Marlene Laruelle, *Is Russia Fascist? Unraveling Propaganda East and West* (Ithaca, NY: Cornell University Press, 2021).

92. Lisa Gaufman, "Bandera, Bats, and Birds: Change and Continuity in the Pro-Kremlin Ukraine Discourse," *Russia.Post*, January 25, 2023, https://russiapost.info/page33512308.html.

## 5

# The Economy

## *From the Quest for Sovereignty to War Economy*

Russia's mineral raw materials complex plays an important role in all spheres of the life of the state. . . . In the near term, this strategic factor in Russia's economic growth must be restructuring the national economy on the basis of the available mineral raw materials resources with the goal of significantly increasing its effectiveness. . . . Regardless of whose property the natural resources and in particular the mineral resources might be, the state has the right to regulate the process of their development and use.

—V. V. Putin, doctoral thesis, 1997[1]

We were naive to think that international economic rules would not be eroded by politics. This must encourage us to increase our sovereignty in the economic sphere while remaining of course a natural, organic part of the world economy.

—V. V. Putin, 2015[2]

Russia and its economy are passing through a new period of major turbulence. Since 2014, the country has been targeted by a series of sanctions imposed by the United States, the EU, and their allies. Initially aimed at Crimean or Russian officials involved in this operation, they were expanded in the summer of 2014 after the start of the fighting in the Donbas. They then radically changed in nature after Russia's full-scale invasion of Ukraine in 2022. Over more than ten waves, the new US and EU sanctions have had the explicit aim of isolating Russia economically and politically from the rest of the world

115

and provoking a major economic recession likely to push the Russian Armed Forces out of Ukraine or even topple Putin's regime.

These sanctions cover different layers. First, there is a list of personalities close to Putin (initially about twenty, then a few hundred) who became banned from traveling to the European Union and North America, and whose bank assets or properties (houses, yachts) have been frozen or confiscated. These measures are complemented by sanctions targeting companies close to the government and linked to the war; they started by restricting or banning access to credit and foreign investments, as well as on the purchase of dual technologies (that is, which can be used for either civilian or military purposes) by energy sector firms (Rosneft, Novatek, Gazprom) and industries linked to the military-industrial complex.

The Russian banking sector was also sanctioned, with the decoupling of the main banks from the Western SWIFT financial transactions network and the freezing of certain deposits in Western banks, including those of the Russian Central Bank. One of the side effects of these measures and the pressure exerted by Western governments and public opinion was the withdrawal of many Western firms engaged in investments or partnerships in Russia, in a striking break from more than thirty years of cooperation.

These measures, unprecedented in recent history, are taking place in a Russian economic context that has already been stressed by the global recession in trade and industrial activities linked to the COVID-19 crisis of 2020–2021. As with each of the recent crises—1998, 2008, 2014—pessimistic comments have multiplied, both in the Russian press, which is prone to dramatic interpretations, and in the Western media, where there has been some schadenfreude over the Russia's difficulties and excessively optimistic comments about the sanctions' capacity to impact decision-making in the Kremlin. While the effects of these massive sanctions have been real, the resilience of the Russian economy holds strong, and, at least initially, the sanctions have not diminished the Kremlin's desire to carve up Ukraine and overthrow its government. On the contrary, Russian leaders have made the sanctions a major propaganda instrument to reinforce public support for their president's actions.

## TENSE DEBATES ON RUSSIA'S ECONOMIC DIRECTION UNDER SANCTIONS

While the war wages on, debates on the short- and medium-term evolution of the Russian economy have been exacerbated, and positions have become more clear-cut, as indicated by the title of the report presented at Yale University in August 2022, "Business Retreats and Sanctions Are Crippling the Russian Economy," with the subtitle "Measures of Current Economic Activity and Economic Outlook Point to Devastating Impact on Russia."[3] The report's conclusions seem to be irrefutable:

> Russia's strategic positioning as a commodities exporter has irrevocably deteriorated; . . . Russian imports have largely collapsed, and the country faces stark challenges securing crucial inputs, parts, and technology from hesitant trade partners, leading to widespread supply shortages within its domestic economy; . . . Despite Putin's delusions of self-sufficiency and import substitution, Russian domestic production has come to a complete standstill with no capacity to replace lost businesses, products and talent; . . . As a result of the business retreat, Russia has lost companies representing ~40% of its GDP. . . . Putin is resorting to patently unsustainable, dramatic fiscal and monetary intervention to smooth over these structural economic weaknesses. . . . Looking ahead, there is no path out of economic oblivion for Russia as long as the allied countries remain unified in maintaining and increasing sanctions pressure against Russia.[4]

Yet without denying the relevance of many of the remarks made by the report's authors, it is clear that the Russian economy has not collapsed as so many Western politicians and media had imprudently predicted. And despite strong fluctuations, the exchange rate of the ruble and the primary Russian macroeconomic indicators remain under control.

Russia's recent history has been punctuated by incessant debates on macroeconomic policy and budgetary authority—often between members of the presidential administration, the government, and the central bank—over the need for more rigor in the state budget, the relaxation of exchange controls, and guidelines for investment and social spending.[5] Since the early 2000s, the presidency has dictated that increasing military spending and developing significant social programs remain the top priorities. The 2014 crisis exacerbated these policies: the sharp fall in the value of the national currency and the prospect of lasting stagflation (sustained growth and inflation exceeding 10 percent) forced the government to develop a crisis plan and slow down projects in many areas. Since the full-scale invasion of Ukraine, the authorities have multiplied policies to stabilize the national economy and transform it into a war economy.

Several nagging issues have resurfaced in these debates. The first, already discussed in the context of the Soviet era, took the form of a paradox. Russia's notorious natural resource wealth makes it one of the few states in the world to consider itself nearly self-sufficient in primary-sector goods (as the Soviet Union did). The question was whether this wealth would become a curse. The significance of the fiscal and commercial revenues gained from that real income had negative effects on several occasions during the twentieth century in that the situation allowed Soviet leaders to postpone necessary reforms.

Several authors have mentioned the notorious "Dutch disease," a financial phenomenon, observed for the first time in the Netherlands in the 1960s, that consists of an influx of foreign currency to primary industries, followed by a crisis in other industrial sectors subject to inflationary pressure.[6] Yet scholars are far from unanimous about the presence of such a phenomenon in Russia, and several authors prefer to speak of a "Russian disease" due to the specificities of the governance model built by the Putin regime.[7]

Diversifying industrial output and increasing productivity to an internationally competitive level have been two of the main challenges facing the Russian leadership since the collapse of the Soviet Union. The raw materials extractive sectors, though they represent a limited share of the total value added to the economy and employment (12.9 percent and 1.6 percent, respectively, in 2019, the last pre-COVID year, according to official data), they account for 56.2 percent of total exports (table 5.1),[8] as well as about 60 percent of budget revenues (more than 45 percent for hydrocarbons alone in 2022).[9]

The volatile nature of oil prices and the sudden changes in the hydrocarbon market associated with the decoupling of the European Union from its former Russian supplier generate tension and inspire pessimism. Western observers are happy to forecast Russia's collapse, stalemate, and unavoidable decline, but caution should remain the watchword. Russia successfully overcame the effects of the global economic crises in 1998 and 2008, but it is still too early, at the time of the writing of this book, one year and a half after the launch of the full-scale war on Ukraine, to draw conclusions on the current crisis's long-term impact on Russia's economy.

Since the end of the Soviet Union, foreign capital has found its way to Russia, encouraged by the conclusion of a limited agreement on the infamous "Russian loans,"[10] the legacy of another period of intense investment

Table 5.1.    Structure of Russian foreign trade by product (%), 1995 and 2021

| Products | Import | | Export | |
|---|---|---|---|---|
| | *1995* | *2021* | *1995* | *2021* |
| Minerals | 6.4 | 1.9 | 42.5 | 56.2 |
| Woods | 2.4 | 1.4 | 5.6 | 3.4 |
| Metals and precious stones | 8.5 | 7.2 | 26.7 | 16.8 |
| Chemicals | 10.9 | 18.3 | 10.0 | 7.7 |
| Machinery, equipment, and transport | 33.6 | 49.3 | 10.2 | 6.6 |
| Textiles, leather, and fur | 6.0 | 5.8 | 1.9 | 0.4 |
| Agriculture and food | 28.1 | 11.6 | 1.8 | 7.3 |
| Miscellaneous | 4.1 | 4.0 | 1.3 | 1.6 |
| Total, in billions of dollars | 60.9 | 293.5 | 81.1 | 493.1 |

*Sources:* Goskomstat, *Statist. Ezhegodnik* 1996 and 2022.

in infrastructure and industry in the country at the end of the nineteenth century. The liberal reforms under Yeltsin and expanding privatization, including the ability to create 100 percent foreign-capital-controlled companies in various sectors, appeared to be encouraging signs of a Russia on its way to finally becoming a "normal country," as the president himself put it in a 1992 speech.[11] Thousands of companies from all over the world have since found their way to Russia.

Under the new sanctions imposed by the main Western states, some of these foreign players are now leaving the country or scaling back their activities. Is this really a sign of a definitive break, and will the Russian economy collapse? This is not the first time that particularly pessimistic predictions have been made about the Russian (or Soviet) economy, and in order to understand the difficulties in correctly assessing its trajectory, we need to dig deep into its recent history, its structural weaknesses, and the extreme singularity of its operational mechanisms.

## LESSONS FROM THE 1990s–2000s: CRISIS, GROWTH, AND IMBALANCE

Russia has in no way been a model student. It did not fit easily into the analytical models offered to it, as evidenced by the eighteen years of negotiations it took for Moscow to enter the World Trade Organization (WTO).[12] While most analysts, Russian and Western alike, thought in terms of deepening market reforms, integration into the global market, technological cooperation, and the interlinking of financial systems, Putin's leadership had a different priority: defending national sovereignty and security, particularly in light of the threat that the country was losing control of strategic economic sectors. Most deviations from the Western model were then interpreted as warning signs of the weakness of an economy where some Soviet practices never disappeared. Some authors indicated that changes had brought about a new mafia state, a kleptocracy,[13] the sole purpose of which was the enrichment of the president's inner circle, whether his name was Yeltsin or Putin.

As in the political and social spheres, challenges and fears became inextricably mixed. The main challenge was clearly stated by candidate Putin in the earliest declarations of his first election campaign: it would take fifteen years of 8 percent average annual growth to reach the level of Portugal and Spain, or fifteen years at a 10 percent growth rate to reach the level of France and Great Britain.[14] This would also require remobilizing the whole country—its elite and its human and financial resources—while accepting the infusion of foreign capital, technology, and experience.

Since then, however, Putin has changed course, expressing fear about what he sees as the imposition of external models unsuited to Russia's specific characteristics: "The modernization of our country cannot be achieved only by the simple transfer to Russian soil of abstract models and diagrams drawn in foreign textbooks."[15] This is in line with longstanding Russian fears regarding the hoarding of natural resources and the takeover of strategic sectors or decisions for the benefit of foreign actors (corporate or state) in a new context where a liberalized Russia is subject to legal frameworks and international standards over which local leaders have no influence.

It is the intermingling of the desire for modernization and fears about loss of control that has shaped Russia's new economic policy. Lying at the crossroads of financial and industrial strategies, Russia is deeply marked by a desire for finding the right economic balance, the main aim of which is to strengthen national sovereignty. It is certainly in this context that one should interpret Putin's turn toward the state's takeover of a range of strategic sectors when he came to power in 2000. The main question then becomes to what extent such practices contribute to Russia's initial goal of becoming a modern industrial nation and restoring its decisive and autonomous position.

There is something contradictory about the Russian economy. This huge state, with its wealth of natural resources, has always drawn fascination, attracting travelers, traders, and entrepreneurs. In the nineteenth century, Russia lay on the periphery of industrial Europe. The country started to make up for some of its infrastructural deficiencies and began its own industrialization process, which intensified under the Soviet regime. After recovering from the damages incurred during the Second World War, the Soviet Union took its place as the world's second-largest economy, and a large part of its industrial strength was found in Russia.

Although the last Soviet leaders praised this achievement as a success of the political system, it was based on precarious grounds. The Soviet economy functioned largely outside global markets; hence it developed excess autarky, considered as a guarantee of national security. Soviet industry could operate within a protected economy, organized on a closed circuit, and enjoy this monopoly on a continent-sized state of 250 million people plus some socialist partners. The shortcomings of this economic model were revealed as soon as Gorbachev and Yeltsin introduced market mechanisms and opened the country to global trade.

## An Unprecedented Crisis and Russia's Rebound

The crisis in Russia in the 1990s has been described as more dramatic than the West's 1929 Depression.[16] Industrial production value fell by over 60 percent as a consequence of the Soviet breakup of extensive technical cooperation within integrated enterprises, and due to political and monetary disorder. Combined with the sudden application of new economic practices, the beginnings of privatization, and the careless opening of the country to the global market, whole industrial sectors disappeared, precipitating a crisis with social consequences in cities and entire regions, as described chapter 2. Incomplete reforms created uncertainty that led to the collapse of agriculture as an investment, and state aid dried up (the law on the privatization of agricultural land was only enacted in 2002).

This profound crisis also affected other economic sectors, chiefly light industries that produced household and electronic consumer goods. Products made in Soviet factories did not compare well at all, in quality or appearance, to the goods from Asian or European producers. The variety of imported household appliances, textiles, and leather goods created such brutal and overwhelming competition that domestic production collapsed within a few years, and in some cases only a few months. Consumers were stunned to discover the variety of packaged products offered by the large distribution networks that had begun to appear in the country, from fast-food restaurants to supermarkets and clothing and furniture brands.

Conversely, the extractive industries and those processing raw materials—oil, ferrous and nonferrous metals, and basic chemicals—found more profitable export promotion in different countries when deprived of part of their tumbling domestic market, leading to a period of sustained growth from the late 1990s onward. This success was by no means immediate, however: though gas production remained virtually unchanged, oil, coal, and iron all saw significant drops in production before slowly regaining their output levels from the late Soviet period (see table 5.2). As in many developed countries, production sectors tended to lag simultaneously. In current prices, industry fell from 38 percent of GDP in 1990 to 30.5 percent in 2011, while agriculture saw its share drop from 16.5 percent to 4.3 percent. An impressive drop occurred in industrial employment during the same period, from 22.8 million workers to 13.3 million; its share of the labor force fell from 30.3 percent to 19.5 percent. Manufacturing industries saw the deepest erosion, declining from 14.8 million workers to 7.7 million.[17]

Those dark years were ones of profound and accelerating transformation of the country's economic fabric. While some sectors disappeared, others emerged from almost nothing—for example: banking, insurance, differentiated commercial networks, and services of all kinds. The share of services reached 60 percent of GDP in 2011, and the number of jobs in the sector rose from 33 million in 1990 to 42 million, or 62.3 percent of total employment, by 2011. This major transformation of the Russian economy had a commensurate effect on society and urban landscapes, with service enterprises taking over ground floors or whole buildings and large commercial

**Table 5.2.   Evolution of Russian output between 1990 and 2021**

|  | *1990* | *1997* | *2021* | *2022* |
|---|---|---|---|---|
| Oil (million tons) | 516 | 306 | 523 | 535 |
| Gas (billion m3) | 641 | 571 | 763 | 673 |
| Electricity (10.9 kWh) | 1,082 | 834 | 1,159 | 1,167 |
| Coal (*million tons*) | 395 | 244.4 | 432 | 442 |
| Copper (*thousand tons*) | 692 | 600 | 990 | 1,000 |
| Steel (million tons) | 89.6 | 48.5 | 77.7 | 71.5 |
| Fertilizers (million tons) | 16 | 9.5 | 26.4 | 23.5 |
| Synthetic fibers (thousand tons) | 673.5 | 128.9 | 204 | 188 |
| Plastics (thousand tons) | 3,258 | 1,578 | 11,138 | 10,325 |
| Cement (million tons) | 83 | 26.7 | 60 | 60.5 |
| Turbines (million kWh) | 12.5 | 3.6 | 7.8 | —** |
| Metal-cutting machines (thousands) | 74.2 | 9.4 | 7.2 | 7.2 |
| Tractors (thousands) | 214 | 12.4 | 7.8 | 6.2 |
| Combine harvesters (thousands) | 65.7 | 2.3 | 6.8 | 4.7 |
| Bulldozers (thousands) | 14.1 | 2.4 | 1.1 | 1.07 |
| Trucks (thousands) | 665 | 146 | 186 | 141 |
| Cars (thousands) | 1,103 | 840 | 1,365 | 608 |
| Freight wagons (thousands) | 25.1 | 5 | 63.1 | 48.9 |
| Washing machines (thousands) | 5,419 | 800 | 5,600 | — |
| Refrigerators (thousands) | 3,774 | 1,186 | 4,100 | 2,380 |
| Televisions (thousands) | 4,717 | 327 | 6,400 | — |
| Shoes (millions of pairs) | 385 | 33 | 107 | 115 |
| Textiles (million square meters) | 8,449 | 1,565 | 1,949 | — |
| Cereals (all grains) (million tons) | 105* | 73.7* | 125.4* | 153.8 |
| Potatoes (million tons) | 35.9* | 38.5* | 20* | 22 |
| Milk (million tons) | 54.2* | 36.3* | 31.9* | 32.3 |

\* Average production of the last three years.

\*\* Rosstat did not publish all its data for 2022.

*Sources:* Goskomstat, *Statist. Ezhegodnik* 2017; *Promyslennost'*, 1998 and 2016; *Sel'skoe khoziaistvo*, 2004; Russian press 2023.

complexes mushrooming on the outskirts of all cities. Millions of Russians of all backgrounds left their previous, often state-paid positions to try their luck in tertiary services.

When commodity prices rose in the 2000s, the growth of these new service jobs allowed the country to bounce back from its 1998 monetary crisis and launch a strong recovery (over 6 percent annual GDP growth on average between 1999 and 2008) that more than made up for the losses of the Soviet collapse and the degree to which the gap between Russia and the rest of Europe had widened during the early post-Soviet period.

Multiple factors contributed to this rebound. Adaptation to new economic rules was facilitated by the high level of education among managers, the implementation of sound monetary and fiscal policies that enabled Russia as early as 2006 to repay Soviet debts to the Paris Club group of international creditors ahead of schedule, and high returns on foreign investments. However, this would not have been possible without a long period of rising commodities prices, particularly for oil, which ensured Russia saw a dramatic increase in its trade surplus and budget revenues (see figure 5.1).

In some sense, the proportion of extractive and raw materials primary-processing industries in Russia's economy, which is unusually high for an industrialized country, should actually be regarded as normal given the size of Russia's territory and its vast natural-resource wealth. That said, if the country aspires to play a leading role among major economies, it must also patch up a number of gaps in its industrial fabric, which still shows many tears from the end of the Soviet system.

Without covering all sectors, it is notable that among intermediate goods (machine tools, heavy electrical equipment, and transport), particular situations remain highly variable. The most frequently cited factors for this variability are the level of obsolete equipment still in place (it is officially estimated at between 35 percent and 65 percent, depending on the sector), privatization terms, whether government controls were maintained (such as for some military hardware), and leaders' capacity to maintain some market share. Acclaimed industries from the Soviet era, such as shipbuilding and civil aviation, have practically ceased to exist and remain in critical condition today. Others, such as parts of the military-industrial complex, civilian and military nuclear activities, the space industry, and railway equipment production have

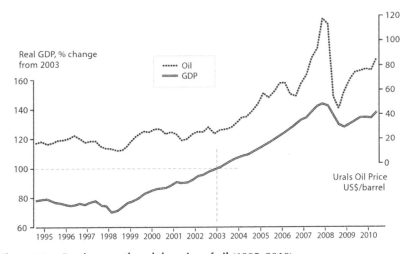

**Figure 5.1.   Russian growth and the price of oil (1995–2010)**

been buoyed by a combination of state subsidies, foreign technology purchases, and protectionist measures preventing severe local crises. The next
section delves more deeply into the automotive and aviation industries, two
crucially strategic sectors to Russian society given the country's size.

## Planes and Automobiles: The Fragility of
## Russian Industry

Before the war in Ukraine, the automotive sector was a good example of
Russian industry's capacity to rebound in a key area of domestic consumption.
Households were faced with a significant car shortage at the end of the Soviet
period. The sudden opening of the domestic market to foreign models (including a considerable influx of used vehicles) placed Russian manufacturers in
a difficult position. National production had collapsed, while annual sales
figures exploded, to the benefit of imported cars. The rescue of this at-risk
sector, fully privatized in the early 1990s, was achieved only after the adoption
of radical measures that mixed protectionism (the application of more onerous
import tariffs and technical standards to limit the influx of used vehicles) with
incentives to encourage foreign direct investment (FDI) in Russia.

Specifically, from 2002, foreign automakers that wished to sell their models in Russia were invited to invest a minimum of US $250 million in the
country, either in existing plants or in building new ones, and had to ensure
that within five years, more than 50 percent of the parts used in their manufacturing processes would be produced in Russia.[18] Given their great interest
in this growing market, Western manufacturers agreed to these new rules,
which entailed a transfer of investment, technology, and know-how.

One historical example is Italian automaker Fiat's collaboration with the
Soviet government in establishing the VAZ/Volga factory in Togliatti (in
Samara oblast) in 1966. Forty years later Russian manufacturers took advantage of the momentum to introduce new practices in management and quality
control, as well as reforming sales channels to adapt to changing consumer
expectations regarding postpurchase services (all of which were sorely lacking). The impact of the 2022 sanctions on that sector will be important, but
over twenty years, the adoption of new production methods has played a critical role in explaining the sustainability of that sector amid Russia's decoupling with the West. Significantly, in the 2000s, similar rebounds occurred in
consumer goods (refrigerators, washing machines, and televisions), also due
to a major opening to large foreign firms, which were allowed to produce
under license in various parts of the country.

Conversely, civil aviation exemplifies a leading Soviet industry that has not
yet found the path to growth, due to inertia. This sector, which according to
official figures still accounted for some 500,000 jobs in 2002, was one of the

highlights of the Soviet system. However, the fully closed-circuit manufacturers took no account of international standards for noise or fuel consumption, such that after 1991, many foreign countries threatened to ban the entire Russian fleet. This was compounded by the dispersion of production among multiple competing firms (Ilyushin, Tupolev, Antonov, and Yakovlev for civil aviation, MiG and Sukhoi for the military, and Mil and Kamov for helicopters) spread over more than 20 sites from Moscow to Komsomolsk-on-Amur, near the northeasternmost part of the border with China. Production fell from around 150 short- and long-haul aircraft and 300 civilian helicopters per year during the Soviet era, to three planes and one civilian helicopter in 2000.[19]

Several explanations have been provided for this industrial disaster, which led Russian companies to buy dozens of Airbus and Boeing aircraft, including for domestic flights as passenger demand resumed after 1998. Revealing an obsessive Russian fear, one of the country's first responses was to blame the decline on the US firm Pratt & Whitney, which, at the height of the industrial crisis in 1992, had acquired 25 percent of the shares of the engine factory in the city of Perm, just west of the central Urals, a leading supplier of civilian and military aircraft engines. The press stirred up suspicions that the Americans had purchased the firm to recover some patents and prevent the development of a new generation of engines adapted to international standards.[20] More fundamentally, under pressure from major manufacturers and regional leaders who wanted to save all of "their" factories, the authorities soon began to weigh in on decisions.

In 2006, Russia's Unified Aircraft Corporation (UAC), a consortium of general aviation companies, was formed in close cooperation with Rosoboronexport (the state holding company for the military-industrial complex) and all major civil and military aviation manufacturers. In a sign of the times, Russian aviation finally ended its isolation and started to cooperate. Although the government maintained strict control over the military part of the sector, even that area opened slightly. While civil aviation has seen the most evolution, it has been without any real positive outcomes. The only major completed project has been the manufacture of the 98-seat Superjet 100 (SSJ100) regional aircraft, available since 2010, which was the fruit of cooperation between Sukhoi and several foreign manufacturers.

The planes were assembled in Komsomolsk-on-Amur, but more than 70 percent of the parts (including the engines) were imported, and the ultramodern factory in Komsomolsk was entirely equipped with French, German, and Japanese computer-assisted design and manufacturing systems.[21] With 230 units produced between 2007 and 2022, the initial model never took hold due to the excessively elevated cost of maintenance, and on March 14, 2022, the European Union Aviation Safety Agency (EASA) withdrew the SSJ100's flight certificate. UAC was more successful with Sukhoi Superjet NEW, launched in 2018 ahead of schedule and in which most of the imported components were replaced by Russian-made parts, including a new engine—the PD8 from the Perm plant.

At the same time, another axis has been engaged to save this ailing sector. In 2014, during a visit to Beijing, Putin announced the formation of a consortium between UAC and the Commercial Aircraft Corporation of China (COMAC) to manufacture a long-haul aircraft (named the CR929: *C* for China and *R* for Russia) capable of competing with Boeing and Airbus. The engine would be Russian, and the final assembly would be done near Shanghai.[22] However, in 2022, while the first aircraft was being assembled, the UAC announced that it was modifying its participation in the project due to a disagreement on sharing the production market with China, and would limit its role in supplying certain elements, including engine parts. The announcement is a tangible sign of the difficulties of the industrial partnership between the two countries.[23]

## Persistent Imbalances in Foreign Trade

The return to growth during Putin's first terms was not enough to reverse one of the most commonly cited shortcomings of the Russian economy: its foreign trade imbalance. The country was not in a deficit—quite the contrary. During these years, the foreign trade balance remained positive, which was fundamental to resuming overall economic growth. However, the dominance of low-value-added products, raw materials (especially oil), and basic products (metals and chemicals) among Russia's exports means the balance is highly dependent on world price fluctuations. Yet to catch up its technological delays, Moscow needs to continue buying equipment and consumer goods on a massive scale, while the range of exported products remains limited. Outside of commodities, Russia is among the world's top three weapons exporters and also exports some large industrial and power station equipment (see table 5.2).

The notable recovery in the production of many industrial products during the 2000s, including those in table 5.1, had little impact on the nature of exports since these sectors, oriented toward the domestic market, struggled to find external buyers. This is crucial, however, because it counters the theory of Dutch disease, which is typically accompanied by lasting weakness in processing sectors. In the Russian case, several authors insist they observe a complementarity in this period between the growth in income generated by oil exports and the growth and diversification of domestic industry.[24]

It is in light of these trends, and in an assessment of the portion of imported capital goods, that some observers were optimistic about Russia's future in the manufacturing sector, which had benefited from foreign capital and technology despite insufficient levels of investment.[25] However, real productivity progress should not mask the continued existence of structural obstacles that were already present during Soviet times: the lack of transport infrastructure in many regions, as mentioned; the partitioning between military and civilian industries; the weakness of small and medium enterprises (SMEs), which are known to play a key role in innovation; and low interest in innovation among large commodities groups with majority state ownership.

Considering the significant foreign direct investment flows into Russia in the early 2000s, it is notable that only one-quarter went to the manufacturing sector. Coming largely from places such as Cyprus and Barbados, FDI flows often reflected the return of Russian capital from offshore centers. The flows were mainly directed toward the services sector (commerce and communications) and, to a lesser degree, to the industrial sector (particularly mining) and construction.

The first Western sanctions of 2014 led to contradictory effects. On the one hand, the government reacted by systematizing its development aid to Russian manufacturers for import substitution; agribusiness is a good example of these successes. On the other hand, innovation and productivity gains from technology imports suffered.[26] Even many companies that were not directly affected by the sanctions had to restrict imports because the fall in the ruble's value made such purchases too expensive. Moreover, the foreign trade imbalance between sectors widened further (see table 5.2), increasing the fragility of the whole economy when commodity prices suddenly dropped. This trend may be related to the fundamental changes seen in the organization of large Russian businesses, the evolution of which is guided by the highest-level political authorities.

## Shock Therapy: Crisis and Reorganization

For over two decades, the Russian economy's organizational structure was deeply disrupted. In early 1992, the first Yeltsin government decided to throw open the domestic market to the global economy and accelerate the application of market rules that had begun under Gorbachev. Following the precepts of Western advisers on "shock therapy," the government made the controversial decision to liberalize prices on January 1, 1992, a first step in substantially changing the country's economic mechanisms.

Privatization made most Russian citizens homeowners almost overnight. Yet the government-launched movement was far broader, the details of which have been described in other works.[27] In general, the first step carried out privatization through vouchers given to each citizen and auction sales for most small businesses, shops, services, and small factories, which were usually scooped up by local leaders, former party officials, managers, or chief engineers. In the second step, in 1995–1996, the government released the crown jewels of Russian industry (oil and metallurgy, along with chemical, civil, and mechanical engineering) under the so-called loans-for-shares system, whereby, as collateral for loans, the state gave a dozen major Muscovite banks shares in the largest national companies for a period of three years. Everyone knew that the state would not be able to repay the loans, making the initiative a concerted redistribution of some of Russia's most successful companies to oligarch-controlled financial groups on the understanding that they, in turn, would support Yeltsin in the 1996 presidential election.[28] Some key strategic sectors (the core of the military-industrial complex, nuclear, space, electricity, gas, and parts of the transportation infrastructure) remained totally or partially under state control.

## The Choice of the Oligarchy

The oligarchs of the Yeltsin era were often former Komsomol (Communist Youth) or Communist Party leaders who benefited from relationships that allowed them to accumulate initial capital in import–export. By creating their own banks, they could buy vouchers from the population and use them to diversify their activities in industry, services, insurance, and communications. In 1995, the most powerful already had a solid footing in finance, industry, and media, as many of them had purchased publishing and broadcasting groups. This was the heart of their agreement with Yeltsin, the first version of the new bargain that bound together the highest echelons of political power and the new masters of the economy. In exchange for financial assistance and favorable media coverage to ensure the re-election of a weakened president, the oligarchs bought for a bargain the highlight of the Russian economy— sectors with the best export opportunities.

Thanks to this agreement, groups such as Oleg Deripaska's Bazovy Element or Vladimir Potanin (Interros) and Mikhail Prokhorov's Onexim-Bank specialized in nonferrous metallurgy, aluminum, nickel, and rare metals; Alexei Mordashov's Severstal focused on the steel industry; and Mikhail Khodorkovsky's Yukos or Roman Abramovich's and Boris Berezovsky's Sibneft centered on oil. The oligarchs also pushed for the adoption of favorable administrative and fiscal rules that allowed them to locate much of their business outside Russia in order to minimize their taxes while better protecting their capital and profits.

In this respect, as in many others, Russian financial and industrial operations fully embraced the rules of Western multinationals in applying a practice euphemistically called "tax optimization." Their systematic offshore investments explain, in part, what the press has described as capital flight. However, unlike Western multinationals, the desire to avoid taxes was not their only motivation. The country remained extremely chaotic and new laws were increasingly uncertain. Supported by competing groups, state or regional administrations and law enforcement agencies (police, security forces, and courts) often challenged a thriving business's ownership.

Besides their assets in Russia, most of these oligarchs invested part of their capital abroad, acquiring properties in various countries and inserting themselves into the economic and cultural life of those places by buying football clubs or publishing houses. The most advanced started to list their companies on Western stock exchanges (London's in particular), both to protect their assets from the rough-and-tumble of Russian political life and to more easily obtain loans from Western partners. The Western media may have criticized Yeltsin's management of the Chechen crisis and various failures to uphold democratic standards, but they never failed to congratulate the Russian authorities for their accelerated integration into the global system, which seemed to confirm the continuation of Russia's "transition" to adopt the main rules and mechanisms of the Western liberal system, as propounded by large international financial institutions such as the World Bank, the International Monetary Fund (IMF), and the Organization for Economic Cooperation and Development (OECD).

However, the prospect of rapid internationalization raised serious concerns among some of the country's elite, who saw in this transition the risk of permanently weakening Russia by abandoning entire segments of the economy in favor of large foreign groups. A few symbolic examples of privatization, such as the sale of a famous porcelain factory in St. Petersburg, had already made headlines under Yeltsin, mobilizing public opinion.[29] Putin's election as president in March 2000 significantly changed the country's economic strategy. His systemic choice to reorganize Russia's main economic sectors reflects what Anders Åslund has described as "crony capitalism."[30]

## PUTIN'S REASSERTION OF NATIONAL SOVEREIGNTY

One of the first signals the new president sent to the economic elite was in a speech he gave on July 28, 2000, to a group of twenty-one major oligarchs he had invited to the Kremlin. Reportedly, he spoke bluntly to them: the authorities knew that the oligarchs had become rich by taking advantage of the previous regime's weaknesses.[31] The regime would grant forgiveness on two conditions: that they now use their economic power to support the country's recovery, and that they end any interference in politics, whether directly or through the media they controlled. Some complied. Others, realizing that the tide was turning, gave up parts of their empires and settled elsewhere—such as Vladimir Gusinsky (who went to Israel) and Boris Berezovsky (who went to the UK).

One oligarch, Mikhail Khodorkovsky, believed he could defy the new president; he announced his intention to sell a large part of his oil group to ExxonMobil, openly challenging the new president's economic strategy, and to use his resources to support an opposition group in which he would take an active role. In 2003, the authorities broke his resistance and made an example of him by imprisoning him for more than a decade. In 2004, the bulk of Yukos's oil assets were acquired in a scandalous sale to Rosneft, headed by Igor Sechin, the longtime chief of staff to the man who had started out as St. Petersburg's first deputy mayor: Putin.[32]

In addition to the return to an authoritarian phase, the Kremlin wanted to regain control of the real levers of economic sovereignty, which it perceived as being under serious threat. The intense strengthening of state control closely combined economic and political measures. This critical phase (recall the simultaneous reform of relations between the center and periphery, with the new regional policy) first involved ensuring control of the political public image as disseminated by mainstream media. The fact that the major oligarchs were also owners of large media groups was not without consequence as the new president decided whom and what to target first.[33] Second, the authorities decided what could and could not be privatized. The cap on foreign ownership was lowered in forty-two sectors deemed sensitive to foreign interference. Putin also did not hesitate to resort to pure intimidation, increasing the number of arrests and show trials of those who resisted his new injunctions. Public opinion believed that no oligarch's fortune could have been legally built, and therefore people tended to support these discretionary measures.

Quickly, foreign investors came to understand that the proposed measures were not just about Russian stakeholders. Aside from the hit to Khodorkovsky's projects, two other cases demonstrated Russian authorities' desire to regain control of the hydrocarbons sector, considered one of the keys to sovereignty, to the point of breaking contracts. In 2005, the government undermined the conditions under which one of the emblematic examples of Western involvement had developed. The Sakhalin-2 oil and gas field, initially controlled by a consortium composed entirely of foreign companies— Royal Dutch Shell (55 percent), Japan's Mitsui (25 percent), and Mitsubishi (20 percent)—became subject to various pressures. In late 2006, the consortium had to sell half of its stake (50 percent plus one share) to a subsidiary of Gazprom, which became the majority shareholder.[34] This example was followed by TNK–BP, which began in 2003 as a 50–50 joint venture between the British oil company and a private Russian oil major (Company Tyumen). In 2008, TNK-BP came under political pressure that culminated in the 2012 sale of its exploration rights to Sechin's oil giant Rosneft.[35]

Within this policy of state control of key strategic sectors, Putin generalized a new type of organization by forming a series of integrated state holding companies to cover all research and development institutes or firms in a sector. These "national champions," created to revive the sectors considered vital to sovereignty, were placed in the care of individuals close to the president—almost all *siloviki* linked to the FSB. Besides the examples already mentioned in aviation (UAC) and machine tools, this approach was also applied to the space sector (Roskosmos, established in 1992 to take over for the Soviet-era Glavkosmos) and extended in 2007 to nuclear power (Rosatom), nanotechnology (Rosnano), and shipbuilding (OSK). Some of these state holdings are entirely national, especially in the military field (Rosoboronexport); others are mixed or trying to attract some foreign investors (Rostekhnologii). Most Western experts, as well as former finance minister Alexei Kudrin, have criticized these large administrative machines as inflexible and overly opaque. However, they bear a resemblance to some great French postwar entities, such as the Atomic Energy Commission (CEA/AEC) and Aerospatiale and may indeed be effective.

## Sharing and Controlling Rent

As discussed in chapter 4, an analysis of Putin's inner circle, the so-called Russia, Inc., reveals that it covers virtually all the strategic sectors of the economy. It is not a question of simple nationalization, as pointed out in the small excerpt from Putin's thesis highlighted at the beginning of this chapter. Many of the undertakings concerned are private (petroleum, metallurgy, and construction) or mixed, with varying proportions of public and private ownership. In fact, the expectations of this system are more complex, because it is responding to a mobilization of resources meant to consolidate a certain approach to national development. This practice is based on a singular system of managing the cash distribution from the commodities sector.[36]

Schematically, rent is divided into four portions to meet specific needs. The first is intended, as in any capitalist enterprise, to cover production costs, wages, fixed assets, and depreciation, as well as investments needed to continue and develop the business. The second part is to pay taxes and levies, which have substantially increased in the commodities sector since Putin came to power. In addition to the normal taxes on business revenue, there are now special taxes on raw materials extraction and the export of petroleum products; these two new taxes have helped fill the coffers of the reserve fund, which was established in 2008 following the model of Norway's petroleum fund. In his memoirs, then prime minister Mikhail Kasyanov described oil barons' (including Khodorkovsky's) opposition to these new taxes that deducted profits on a sliding scale that increased as oil prices exceeded certain levels.[37]

The third, and most opaque, part concerns what Clifford Gaddy and Barry Ickes call "informal taxes," which they believe to be more sizable than the legally required taxes. Informal taxes include corruption, often in the form of kickbacks (*otkaty*). In the Russian case, Gaddy and Ickes also mention other forms of hidden subsidies, which are significant to the operation of many companies. Two main subsidies consist of the share of the production that large businesses (oil companies and metallurgy firms) sell on the domestic market, often at the behest of the state and at prices well below market value. According to Shinichiro Tabata, the domestic price of gas was set at one-fifth of the world price in 2000 and, after initial adjustments, remained at less than one-third of the world price in 2007, a practice that was regularly denounced during the negotiations for Russia's accession to the WTO.[38]

Big companies are also directed to purchase goods and services (equipment, transport, etc.) at inflated rates, constituting a hidden subsidy to other companies whose low productivity or quality would make them uncompetitive in a truly open and transparent market. This kind of indirect support is especially vital for the many subsidiaries, or subcontractors of large companies, created in the Soviet era. They are an important part of the urban and industrial fabric, particularly in *monogorody*, single-industry towns with fragile social situations.

Another variant of these informal taxes can be defined as "obliged patronage," whereby oligarchs use part of their wealth to fund various social activities, museums, and cultural endeavors, building on the established Soviet-era practice of giving aid to the municipalities where their businesses are located in order to finance various public facilities. Under Putin, these actions took a slightly different turn, with industrial magnates practically obligated to cosponsor various major events, such as the Sochi Olympics, or to invest in a particularly disadvantaged region, as when oligarch Roman Abramovich was appointed the governor of Chukotka, Russia's northeasternmost and one of its most deprived regions, from 2000 to 2008.[39]

Finally, the fourth part is constituted by the legitimate profits expected of a thriving business. In the current Russian context, these profits are indeed extensive. The Russian press has given detailed accounts of the rise of those close to Putin in the *Forbes* ranking of the richest men in Russia. Many of these are first-generation oligarchs, who are often spoken about with regard to their expenses—purchases of yachts, lavish residences on the French Riviera, and English football clubs. The beneficiaries of the Putin "consortium" have, like their predecessors, invested heavily abroad, which explains the sanctions that Americans and Europeans have targeted against them since 2014, such as denial of visas and the freezing of assets deemed illegitimate.[40] The new 2022 sanction lists directly target many of Putin's close oligarchs in forbidding any commercial activities with them.

It is challenging to assess the impact of these indirect subsidies, but according to various authors, it is substantial. In fact, the economy's growth sectors directly contribute to the state budget and, therefore, to any social policy, defense effort, or infrastructure project. At the same time, these practices help a market system constrained by noncompetitive businesses keep many firms afloat throughout the country. Several authors have attempted to assess these indirect subsidies in different sectors. The Russian press has sought to explain the oft-cited anomaly of the country's roads and the cost of construction or repairing the road network. Comparing the cost of roadworks in the Moscow region with those in Canada, which have similar climates, analysts from *Argumenty i fakty* concluded that the cost in Russia is thirty-eight times higher.[41] This is the direct result of an opaque procurement system, high levels of corruption, and retro-commissions that enable an entire sector and its agents at various levels to squeeze out any economic rationality. The proliferation of articles on this topic led Putin to criticize these abuses, though not actually end them. We will return to the issue of the economic efficiency of such a system later in this chapter.

## A Power Vertical of Uncertain Efficacy

Economic actors and the government are pitted against one another in a veritable battle over the level of taxes, legal and informal, that cannot be reduced to a simple accounting calculation. To take the example of oil, the leaders of Russia's major companies constantly complain that the government's tax system is too burdensome, excessively reduces their profit margins, and keeps them from properly funding exploration research and drilling for new deposits that will ensure sustained production levels the next five or ten years. Several US researchers have insisted on this investment weakness, believing that it is a strategic dead end for the system.[42]

At the same time, it is clear that the importance of these informal flows imposes a heavy cost in terms of the efficiency of officially announced investments. Some of the funding allocated in the budgets at different levels of government—for example, for infrastructure spending—never reaches the intended recipients. Instead, it is captured at different levels, whether in financial form (offshore investments and money laundering to facilitate corruption) or in kind (diversion of materials and equipment for private construction or parallel companies).

Another fundamental point is that the entire informal tax system is based on the trust between the true principal actors, government officials who ensure that this complex rent-sharing is actually observed at different levels. Several researchers point out that this is a critical element of Putin's political consensus. Securing systematic participation of the state and the companies it directly controls (such as Gazprom and the major banks) in the shareholding of many companies across all strategic sectors has resulted in the multiplication of consortium officials in the leadership of each group or subsidiary. These trusted individuals are responsible for enforcing the presidency's policy decisions. In exchange, they receive legal compensation ("attendance fees" and allocated dividend shares); they also have ample opportunity to take a share of the kickbacks in place.

Note that this phase of reorganization and takeover by Putin's inner circles is not, as has often been written, renationalization or a return to Soviet management. This is a mistaken view of the actual operation of Russia's economic system. Undoubtedly, the campaign to reaffirm sovereignty coincided with the state's acquisition of shares in many companies.[43] However, the objective is not a general renationalization of companies. According to official data provided by the state statistics agency, Rosstat, the share of private- or mixed-ownership companies increased from less than 10 percent of fixed assets in 1991 to 70 percent in 2000, 77 percent in 2006, and 82 percent in 2013. As Sergey Guriev pointed out at that time, Putin has repeatedly affirmed his commitment to the preponderance of private property and neoliberal management.[44] The system he has in place is an original mixture of statism (direct control of strategic sectors and pervasive state intervention in all major economic decisions) and neoliberalism (private management in many sectors, with "US-style" liberalization of the health sector and education).

## NECESSARY MODERNIZATION AND STRUCTURAL BOTTLENECKS

Although they express it in different ways, the highest-ranking Russian authorities are acutely aware of the economy's weaknesses. Yeltsin, who probably had a sincere belief in the educational effect of the rapid adoption of liberal practices, referred to the need to finally join the "normal" path of Western markets. His successor very quickly demonstrated his misgivings about the adoption of foreign models. In developing his sovereignty strategy for strategic sectors, Putin appeared to trust Russia's internal capacity to gradually make its economy a world leader. The brief tenure of Dmitry Medvedev—to the extent that he ever had actual autonomous agency—was marked by a more flexible discourse, which offered a closer link between modernization (a term that Putin uses infrequently) and several necessary conditions for its implementation: greater transparency, reinforced institutional mechanisms, a more independent judiciary, and an increased role for civil society and external resources (foreign investment, expertise sharing, and technology purchases).

The major element to focus on is how Russian leadership planned to execute modernization, and its associated structural upgrades, regardless of what it was called. One key issue in this regard certainly comprises the level, nature, and evolution of the investments introduced into the economy. According to most experts, these were notoriously weak at the end of the Soviet period and during the 1990s; then they gradually increased as the country saw progress in its hard currency earnings. According to the World Bank, in 2021, gross capital formation stood at about 20 percent of GDP in Russia—not far from levels in Germany (22 percent) or the United States (21 percent), but much lower than in India (29 percent) or in China (42 percent)—yet this is not enough to catch up economically in line with Putin's initial announcement. In his March 2018 address to the nation, Putin promised to bring investments to a level of 25 and then 27 percent of the country's GDP,[45] but he was far from achieving these optimistic objectives, even before launching the war in Ukraine. Despite the diversification of public and private actors and the creation of management arrangements for major state investments, the heart of the modernization-diversification policy debate remained unresolved.

## State Programs, Megaprojects, and Incubators: Modernization by Decree?

Whatever the country, it is impossible to sufficiently account for the influence of inertia on the structures and attitudes at play in the development of management systems. Since the early 1990s, one of the main ways that Russian state resources are engaged has been through the launch of major federal programs. The last large and symptomatic example of this was the Order on National Goals and Strategic Objectives of the Russian Federation through to 2024, announced after Putin's last election in May 2018.[46] Some of the Order's goals were social ("ensure natural population growth, increase life expectancy to 78 years, ensure growth of wages and pensions above inflation, cut poverty in half, improve housing conditions"), while others were regionally focused on the reinforcement of strategic infrastructure ("increasing the capacity of the seaports of the Pacific and Azov-Black Sea basin, increasing the throughput capacity of the Baikal-Amur, the Trans-Siberian, and the Northern Sea Route") or on sectoral growth ("support high-productivity export-oriented businesses in the basic sectors of the economy").

Each of the main strategic sectors—machine tools, aviation, shipbuilding, and pharmaceuticals—has a set of decrees, programs, and committees designed to promote its development. These were standard procedures of Soviet planning, intended to coordinate different ministries, regional party committees, and *soviets*. While central planning may be gone, the desire to coordinate the actions of new players is not, given the proliferation of the powerful presidential administration's departments, interdepartmental committees, and holdings of a particular sector. The systematic use of these programs is an unmistakable sign that administrative decisions still largely outweigh market-based economic mechanisms.

However, this form of management is also related to the distribution mode discussed above, which involves constant trade-offs by the real decision-makers: the president and those in the trusted inner circle in charge of the various "national champions" of all strategic sectors. According to Philip Hanson, the cost of the twelve national priority areas, consisting of sixty-nine federal-level projects, was estimated at 4.3 trillion Russian rubles (US $65 billion) annually, equivalent to approximately 4 percent of 2018's GDP. Some 70 percent of funding is supposed to come from the state budget. The priority given to state investment implies that privatization and reform of the private-sector ecosystem have been neglected.[47]

In the 2010s, authorities established new forms of support for modernization, including wider use of foreign cooperation. In 2010, President Medvedev launched the Skolkovo Innovation Center, a kind of scientific and applied innovation mega-incubator meant to emulate Silicon Valley. The initial focus areas (telecommunications, biomedical and information technologies, new forms of energy, and nuclear technologies) are all sectors where Russians felt they had the theoretical skills but lacked the technology transfer and applications, which they hoped to increase through cooperation with large foreign firms and laboratories. This innovative initiative was followed by the creation of several technology parks, such as the Kazan IT Park and the Innopolis special economic zone in Tatarstan, and scientific clusters in Tomsk and Novosibirsk, both in southwestern Siberia.[48]

Another example of Russia's modernization strategy has been that of the TOR (a Russian acronym for "accelerated development territories") projects, which are archetypal free economic zones. For three decades, the Russian press praised the Chinese version of these zones as a successful model that could close some of the structural gaps affecting the country. Created by law in 2014, these areas offer tax and customs breaks to attract foreign investors and diversify exports. Yet this new initiative, initially proposed for the Far East, was met with skepticism in the Russian press.

Outside of the Kaliningrad "amber zone" (the region produces 90 percent of the world's extractable amber) federal authorities questioned the initial promises of relief. While we have already mentioned the example of Sochi as a success with regard to building infrastructure and attracting various investors, the president had a personal stake in that exceptional project, which enjoyed virtually unlimited access to credit, as well as other special attention related to the Olympics.[49] By contrast, the North Caucasus ski development

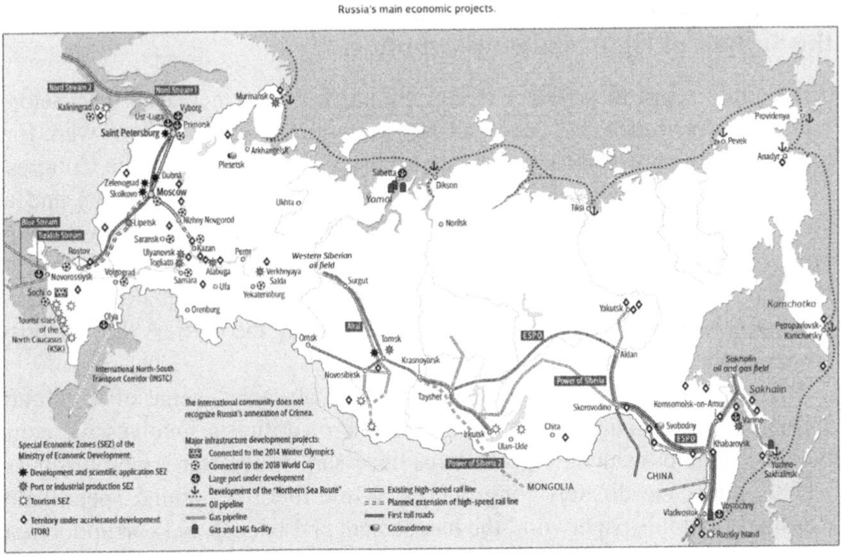

Russia's main economic projects.

Map 5.1: **Russia's main economic projects.** *Source:* Authors' selections from the Russian business press, such as *Kommersant* and *Expert.*

project (*Kurorty Severnogo Kavkaza*, or KSK), which has not received the same attention, has been delayed.

Regional budgets and investments outside Moscow are also crucial and complex for regions that do not benefit from priority federal programs. In the growth period of the 2000s, many cities and regions borrowed heavily to improve their infrastructure and to attract investors. Although there are a few success stories—Kaluga, Ulyanovsk, and Voronezh, all in Central European Russia—many regions have found themselves with significant amounts of dollar-denominated debt and "toxic" credits and become reliant on federal government assistance to rescue them.

The exceptional procedures that created these federal programs all present the same paradox: they are based on tax and regulatory exceptions that seek to bypass various bureaucratic obstacles, which are clearly identified as possibly linked to corruption and as roadblocks for "normal" companies, and to introduce mechanisms that run parallel to the sectors' ministerial bodies. As such, they underscore the same criticism they seek to address: if the government can identify these roadblocks and unnecessary administrative measures, why not eliminate them across the entire economy? This circles back to an old debate on the business climate in the country.

## The Serpentine Nature of the "Business Climate" and the Supposed Fight against Corruption

Since Putin came to power, Russian authorities have increased discussions with business circles, both national and foreign. These interactions were formalized by the president's and prime minister's appearances at the Congress of the Union of Industrialists and Entrepreneurs of Russia (RSPP) and at annual forums in St. Petersburg and Sochi in the presence of many foreign guests. This was both to promote investment opportunities available to Russian and foreign actors and to discuss the investment climate with them. These exchanges are often somewhat surreal, since the barriers they identify are endemic.

For years, actors have denounced the same obstacles, some of which are similar to those found in the West. One line of criticism involves the complexity of the bureaucratic procedures necessary to register a new business, which entails inordinately long delays. While there is nothing specifically Russian about this paperwork, the harassment and widespread corruption that surrounds acquiring the proper paperwork is persistent and constantly weighs on companies.

Although all countries suffer from some amount of corruption, Russia does so to a greater degree than most. The country occupies an unenviable position in the international corruption indexes. In 2022, Transparency International ranked Russia 137th (tied with Paraguay and Mali) in its annual Corruption Perceptions Index; despite political elites' regular promises to fight corruption, this indicator has only deteriorated since the early 2000s.[50] Corruption presents itself in different forms in various situations. In everyday life, any citizen may pay a bribe during a routine traffic stop or for simple administrative paperwork; in some regions, bribes have even been assessed on the payment of "maternal benefits" (bonuses for having a second child) to families.

All businesses, large and small, have faced paying a "commission" to obtain an authorization or to avoid an excessive fine during an inspection. The Swedish head of IKEA Russia once created a scandal by denouncing the kickbacks that the Moscow authorities demanded to obtain land and connect the store to the regional road network.[51] At the same time, the case of Sergei Magnitsky shed light on another aspect of these abuses: the hostile takeover of businesses from competitors with the covert support of the judiciary, the Ministry of the Interior, or the FSB.[52] This case had an international dimension, as US investors held some shares in the firm that Magnitsky, a lawyer, had been defending. The Russian government's refusal to clarify the reasons for Magnitsky's imprisonment or the circumstances of his death in jail drove a wave of sanctions passed by the US Congress.

In Russia itself, the denunciation of these abuses saw the formation of various critical initiatives. In several explicitly titled brochures[53] that mixed historical facts with unverifiable rumors, former deputy prime minister Boris Nemtsov denounced what he saw as President Putin's direct responsibility for the perpetuation of this system. But the most effective attack was Anti-Corruption Foundation founder Alexey Navalny's decision to launch an anti-corruption initiative. In 2010, he and some associates created a dedicated website, RosPil, where citizens were invited to read about the corruption they face. The site has highlighted some regions notable for the personal enrichment of their governors—for instance, Krasnodar krai, where then governor Alexander Tkachev's family took advantage of the concentration of significant public investments in the run-up to the Sochi Olympics as well as major agriculture and infrastructure development projects (the port of Novorossiysk and new oil and gas terminals on the Black Sea). The authorities' reaction was swift: they compiled a series of criminal charges against Navalny and his family and then built several cases against him and his team.

To all observers, the eradication of these abuses is key to cleansing Russia's notorious business climate. While both Russian and foreign investors are used to corruption and informal economies, the extent of these practices in Russia has become a real obstacle to progress. Uncertainty over business sustainability, benefits, property rights, and patents, as well as raids (*raiderstvo*), are a leading cause of capital flight and reluctance to invest in certain sensitive areas. Russia has leapt from 124th place in the World Bank's Ease of Doing Business Index in 2010 to 36th place in 2015 and 28th in 2019, but that same year was ranked only 72nd out of 190 countries for its protection of minority investors.[54]

It is difficult to imagine that a genuine fight against these scourges can be undertaken without reforming other crucial segments of society—the judiciary, the media, the role of NGOs, and public opinion. The judiciary is probably the central piece of the puzzle, as it has been tightly controlled by the regime: in 2011, Putin put the Investigation Committee (the office of the inspector general in charge of investigations, including all corruption cases) under his direct supervision and named one of his former classmates from their time at the Pushkin Leningrad State University School of Law, Alexander Bastrykin, as its head, while in 2014 he merged the relatively independent Supreme Court of Arbitration with the Supreme Court.[55]

One of the few high-ranking figures to voice outright criticism against the system, former minister and then chairman of the Accounts Chamber Alexei Kudrin publicly stated that it is the lack of political competition that has slowed Russia's economic growth and caused it to sink into a "deep stagnant hole."[56] In 2017, his Center for Strategic Research proposed a thoroughgoing reform of the judicial system in order to make justice more independent and restore the confidence of both Russian and foreign entrepreneurs.[57]

## The 2022 Sanctions: Crisis and Resilience

More than a year after the start of the full-scale invasion of Ukraine, it remains difficult to forecast the medium- and long-term effects of massive Western sanctions. On a daily basis, Russian citizens are given the impression that everything is in order. Transportation, services, and shops function almost normally, and while about one-third of Russians regret the disappearance of stores selling their favorite foreign brands (Adidas, Zara, H&M, or Nike), the absence of these previously imported products from now-declared "unfriendly states" is a widely accepted inconvenience, a gap that new networks are trying to fill.[58] The situation is certainly different for families who have lost a member or who have seen a son or husband go into exile to escape mobilization, but the majority of the population seems to resignedly accept the reality even when it does not adhere to the official "special military operation" narrative.

The first sanctions of 2014 prompted authorities to change some of the rules. After some banks and members of Putin's inner circle had their assets frozen, the government introduced a requirement for officials to declare their holdings abroad and encouraged the repatriation of all offshore assets.[59] Yet at the same time, the government provided various forms of assistance to Russian companies to compensate them for sanctions-related losses and the unavailability of credit. The sanctions imposed in 2022, however, are on a completely different scale, and their effects will certainly be far more profound. Should we expect a major crisis? The question remains disputed.

Eager to demonstrate the effectiveness of the February 2022 sanctions, Western media have regularly highlighted their first effects, which are not negligible. Beyond the disappearance of certain previously imported goods, the Russian press has reported the closure of many brand-name stores in the large US-style malls that sprang up around all major Russian cities, to the point of calling into question the very existence of the weakest.[60] The retail sector, which, as with all economic activity during the COVID-19 crisis, had to deal with the pandemic-related disruption of business, saw a new decline in 2022 (see table 5.3).

## Russia's Macroeconomic and Targeted Answers

The Russian banking and financial sectors were among the sanctions' first targets. The majority of banks and those close to the government had their assets in the West frozen; these banks were cut off from the SWIFT system,

Table 5.3. Main indicators of Russian economic growth (% on previous year), 2015–2022

| | 2015 | 2016 | 2017 | 2018 | 2019 | 2020 | 2021 | 2022 |
|---|---|---|---|---|---|---|---|---|
| Population | 100.2 | 100.2 | 100.05 | 99.9 | 99.98 | 99.6 | 99.6 | 99.8 |
| Natural increase, decrease of population per 1,000 | 0.3 | −0.01 | | −1.6 | −2.2 | −4.8 | −8 | −0.7 |
| Annual average number of employed | 99.5 | 99.5 | 99.7 | 99.6 | 99.3 | 97.9 | 101.8 | |
| GDP, in billions of rubles | 97.2 | 99.8 | 101.8 | 102.8 | 102.0 | 97.0 | 104.7 | 96.5 |
| Investments in fixed capital, in billions of rubles | 103.1 | 103.8 | 104.8 | 105.4 | 102.1 | 98.6 | 103.7 | |
| Industrial production, in billions of rubles | 96.6 | 101.1 | 103.7 | 103.5 | 103.4 | 97.9 | 106.4 | 99.7 |
| Agricultural production, in billions of rubles | 102.6 | 104.8 | 102.9 | 99.8 | 104.3 | 101.3 | 99.6 | 103.5* |
| Real money income of population, in billions of rubles | 95.9 | 94.4 | 99.8 | 101.1 | 101.9 | 98.6 | 103.8 | 97.8** |
| Retail trade turnover | 90.0 | 95.4 | 101.3 | 102.8 | 101.9 | 96.8 | 107.3 | 90*** |
| Foreign trade turnover | 66.4 | 88.6 | 125.0 | 117.2 | 97.2 | 85.2 | 139.2 | |
| Year inflation rate | 12.9 | 5.4 | 2.5 | 4.3 | 3.0 | 4.9 | 8.4 | 11.9 |

Sources: Rosstat, *Ezhegodnik*, different years (except other sources [starred])

* Minselkhoz

**RIA Novosti

***Retail.ru

and those with government ties had their lending ability reduced. However, due to concern over the public's possible negative reaction to the war's social consequences, the government took care to support the pensions or salaries of many categories of workers (including all *siloviki*, army and police members) to avoid any financial panic. Although there were some fluctuations in the ruble's exchange rate, no massive money withdrawal from the population has been observed beyond a general reduction of all operations.

Internally, the Russian banking system was already decoupled from SWIFT and, apart from very brief periods of tension, the Central Bank of

Russia was able to preserve its major financial balances. The most affected categories are in fact the many Russians who fled the country in March after the "special military operation" was launched or in September after the mobilization decree. Many of them were cut off from their Russian assets with unusable credit cards, and alternatives such as the Chinese Cross-Border Interbank Payment System (CIPS) proved unaffordable due to US pressure on Chinese banks.

Quickly affected by the withdrawal of many Western firms and the embargoes on the delivery of spare parts and all materials, several industrial sectors have faced the most pressing problems. There are reports of cars being produced without airbags or other safety features and of "cannibalism" in aviation (the dismemberment of certain Boeing or Airbus aircraft to salvage parts for repairing others) and in certain weapons systems as well. For example, American sources have claimed that certain Russian weapons were fitted with electronic chips taken from household appliances.[61] And yet, if Russian industrial production has stagnated in 2022 (down 0.6 percent, according to the figures released by Rosstat), the situation remains highly variable: some sectors are indeed in difficulty, such as the automotive industry and mining production or the equipment suppliers that serve it, while others are announced to be on the rise, such as the pharmaceutical industry, textiles, aerospace, or metal constructions.[62]

There are many reasons why the Russian economy has resisted a wave of unprecedented sanctions. The first is undoubtably due to the specific characteristics of the country's economy and society. We have noted the very particular structure of Russian industry and exports, marked by the unusual importance of the raw material and manufacturing sectors. Although these generate less added value, they are also less dependent on imported technological inputs, especially since Russia has faced embargoes on drilling equipment for many years and has always managed to adapt. Over the past three decades, Russian consumers have welcomed the diversification of products made available through new distribution networks, but their ability to adapt to new partial shortages outweighs their discontent with the loss of Western suppliers.

A second group of factors in this resistance is how Russian authorities prepared for these sanctions. In effect, even if their magnitude was underestimated, the experience gained after 2014 and the countermeasures implemented since then have helped mitigate their effects. We can cite, for instance, the incentives to repatriate overseas assets, the accumulation of different reserve funds, the injunctions to avoid the use of Western software in sensitive sectors, the preparation of alternatives to SWIFT, or the rise of Russian internet software and of Glonass (the Russian equivalent of GPS).

Even in a chaotic or imperfect way, this strategy of "sovereignty" is mitigating the sanctions' effects.

All economic experts, whether Western or Russian, question the potential effectiveness of the "substitution" strategy (*importozameshenie*), that is, the replacement of imported products or technological inputs in sectors deemed strategic with Russian equivalents. Launched in 2014, this process is now complicated by the withdrawal of multiple Western actors from partnerships implemented over the past three decades. The authors of the Yale University report on Russian business in 2022 underlined the importance Putin has given this strategy. And, indeed, he did not hesitate to appoint his younger daughter, Katerina Tikhonova, cochair of the Russian Union of Industrialists and Entrepreneurs' Import Substitution Coordination Council. However, the Yale authors claim that this strategy is "not feasible."[63] Yet other authors are more cautious, noting that this process is long-term, and its effects cannot yet be measured.

Here again, the situation varies greatly by sector. The import-substitution strategy's results from one strategic sector, agriculture and agribusiness, have been successful. While this sector has been in near collapse since the Soviet era and has had to import a significant proportion of products in order to be able to feed the Russian people, production levels of key commodities have improved dramatically (see table 5.1). Annual grain production has risen from an average of between 30 million and 50 million metric tons in the late 1990s to more than 130 million in 2020–2021, allowing Russia to become a leading exporter, and overtaking the United States (35 million metric tons versus 28 million metric tons).[64]

The best Russian specialist in this field, Tatiana Nefedova, however, calls for caution. These results were obtained thanks to a complete overhaul of the production system, giving prominence to highly capitalized "agro-holdings," which received substantial government aid under Russia's Food Security Doctrine. But to obtain these rapid results, new investors have largely relied on imported inputs and, according to Nefedova's calculations, Russian agriculture is highly dependent on these for seeds (80 percent for sugar beets, 60 percent for sunflowers) or selected breeds of livestock, as well as for agricultural equipment (the firm John Deere, which had a strong presence in the southern part of the country, stopped delivering machines and spare parts in 2022). The government has relaunched the creation of breeding centers and assistance to producers of agricultural machinery, but it will take years to meet all of the demand.

The two examples previously discussed, of civil aviation and automobiles, reveal this situation's complexity. In aviation, after the inconclusive test of Sukhoi's medium-haul Super Jet, whose new version should limit the use of imported components, and the partial withdrawal of the Russian–Chinese

RC929 project, Moscow is trying to accelerate the production of new models, including the long-haul aircraft MS21. Following the European Union's decision to ban technical maintenance and insurance for all Western aircraft (Airbus and Boeing) in Russia (at the beginning of 2022 they represented 64 percent of civil aircraft and 36 percent of helicopters in the Russian fleet), the Russian government has been allocating 44 billion rubles (about US $537 million) to accelerate the development of Russian engines.[65] According to Sergey Chemezov, the CEO of the defense sector's Rostec Corporation, the first six MS21 jetliners with Russian PD14 engines will be delivered by 2024, despite the sanctions.[66]

The situation is more challenging in car production due to the withdrawal of almost all major Western, Japanese, and South Korean manufacturers from the country. New car sales have fallen to 687,400 (down 59 percent compared to 2021), a negative record explained by the shutdown of most factories linked to foreign manufacturers that have stopped supplying essential parts, and by the drop in purchasing power of Russian consumers who have postponed their purchases. But a market of nearly two million vehicles a year does not remain empty for long. While the large dealerships are trying to work around the embargoes via the parallel importation of cars or spare parts via third countries, new brands, especially Chinese ones such as Aiways, Nio, or JAC, are working to replace the boycotters by taking over their abandoned factories and building on the know-how acquired by Russian manufacturers. Moreover, as in aviation, several Russian players, including Rosatom, are working to create a more autonomous industry, including in the field of electric vehicles.

A last essential element in the relative effectiveness of sanctions is the list of the countries that implemented them. While Russian aggression was overwhelmingly condemned at the UN on March 2, 2022 (by a vote of 141 to 5, with 35 abstentions; see map 5.2), the map of sanctioning countries (see map 5.3) looks quite different. Despite strong pressure from the United States and its allies, most Asian, African, and Latin American countries have not applied sanctions or only partially do so, citing either their own economic interests or their doubts about the sanctions' effectiveness. Many are reluctant to violate some of the sanctions for fear of US retaliation, but this gives Russian decision-makers the opportunity to circumvent the embargoes.

Controversy has also arisen over the number of foreign companies that have left Russia. According to Simon J. Evenett and Niccolò Pisani, as of November 2022, of the 1,404 EU and other G7 companies with commercially active equity investments in Russia before the February 2022 invasion, a total of 120 (8.5 percent) had left. The database maintained by the Kyiv School of Economics announced, as of January 2023, that 1,202 companies have stayed in Russia, 1,652 have scaled down, and 158 have completely withdrawn from

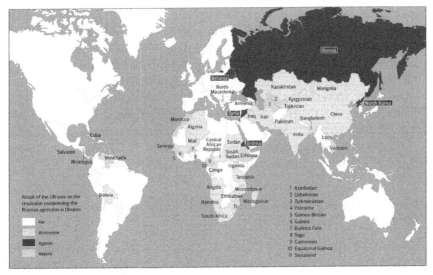

Map 5.2: Russia's condemnation at the UN—March 2, 2022. *Source:* https://news.un .org/en/story/2022/03/1113152.

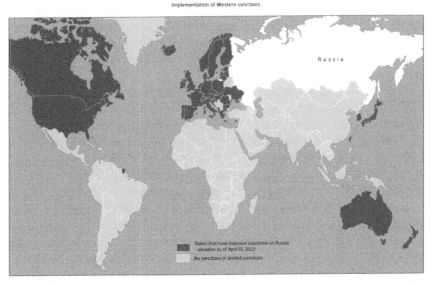

Map 5.3: Implementation of Western sanctions. *Sources:* Peterson Institute for International Economics; Economist Intelligence Unit, 2022.

Russia.[67] These findings contrast with the report published at Yale University, which put the number of Western companies that had left the Russian market by March–April 2022 at 450.[68] This gap can be explained because there are many ways to "leave" Russia, from the complete shutdown of all activities, to partial closure with the maintenance of employees' salaries, and various ways to allow the companies a "temporary" placement in Russian buyers' hands.[69]

The next few years, while as yet full of uncertainties regarding the degree of the Russian economy's resilience, which will necessarily take years to adapt to the sanctions' effects, will be decisive nonetheless. But the key to success will be the battle for the hydrocarbon sector and other mineral resources, a vital element in the country's financial balance.

## Mineral Resources: Between Economic Constrains and Geopolitical Reality

As we have shown (table 5.2), in 2021, mineral products accounted for 56.2 percent of all Russian exports, according to official Rosstat data, with hydrocarbons (crude oil, refined products, and gas) alone accounting for 42.4 percent of Russian total exports. These sales provided around 60 percent of the revenue for the Russian federal budget. Therefore, it is logical that this sector has become the priority target for Western sanctions. In reality, the European Union has long been aware of its own dependence on Russia for energy (more than 50 percent of its gas in 2021 came from this single supplier), and for years it has sought to diversify its sources of supply and, while taking environmental concerns into account, reduce its reliance on fossil fuels more generally.

In an article with a title that is more a political statement than an academic analysis, "The World Economy No Longer Needs Russia,"[70] Sonnenfeld and Tian, two of the lead authors of the report published at Yale University, are sure of one thing: for them, the sanctions and other measures introduced in 2022 have definitively broken Russia's capacity to profit from the country's hydrocarbon wealth, and Russian power has been considerably weakened as a result. Yet one may yet nuance this radical statement.

Since the 1990s, Russia has maintained and developed a system of oil and gas commercialization based on a network of pipelines passing though Ukraine and Belarus, which it recently complemented with underwater pipelines built in the Black and Baltic Seas. The multiyear contracts, which were renewed regularly, forced customers and suppliers into a mutual codependence, ensuring regular income for Russia in exchange for deliveries at reasonable prices compared to the world market. The EU's decision to set a price ceiling for purchases and to boycott Russian hydrocarbons in the long term has now upset this system. European countries are accelerating their strategy to diversify their purchases by increasingly resorting to liquefied natural gas (LNG), a growing share of which is being supplied by the United States.

For its part, Russia has been forced to find new customers for its hydrocarbons, which is difficult for two reasons: it must establish contracts by negotiating rates with new customers who are trying to obtain significant discounts given the current situation, and it must find new ways to deliver its supplies. It should be noted that Russia had begun this customer diversification in the early 2000s by developing pipelines to China and in the Pacific Ocean. This strategy was completed in 2010 by Novatek, an independent competitor of Gazprom, with its attempt to clear Russia's backlog of LNG production with the Sabetta megaproject in the Gulf of Ob, on the Arctic Ocean coast just northeast of the Ural Mountains. But in the new conditions created by Russian aggression in Ukraine, a new "Great Game" (see chapter 6) is now engaged in the redefinition of hydrocarbon markets in the entire Eurasian space and beyond. In this complex battle with its many intertwined factors, Russia has some advantages.

Apart from a residual flow that is still transiting through the Ukrainian network in 2023, Russia has voluntarily cut off its exports to the EU through the existing pipeline networks—the Nordstream 2 Pipeline (created in an agreement signed with Germany after the annexation of Crimea despite US pressure against it) was not put into service, and Nordstream 1 was rendered inoperable at the end of September 2022 by an unidentified (at the time of writing) attacker. But at the same time, Moscow is determined to utilize countries that refuse to apply sanctions against it, starting with Turkey with which Russia has been renewing relations for years (see chapter 6). Thanks to the two gas pipelines built under the Black Sea (Blue Stream and TurkStream), Putin plans to help Turkey supply potential customers in southern Europe with gas not only from Russia but also from the Caspian Sea rim.

Most of Russia's efforts are, however, directed toward Asia, with two privileged clients: India, whose purchases of Russian oil increased spectacularly in 2022 (up 25 percent), and China, a regular client associated with the construction of two oil pipelines to the Pacific, named the Power of Siberia and the Eastern Siberia-Pacific Ocean (ESPO) pipelines, whose capacities will be increased. To complete this arrangement, meetings between Russian leaders and their Central Asian neighbors (Kazakhstan, Uzbekistan, and Turkmenistan) have intensified. One objective has been to reverse the pipeline flows in this region (which have until now delivered gas or oil to Russia) in order to supply China.

Other maneuvers are also underway on Russia's Asia-Pacific coastline, such as the redesign of the Sahkalin 1 project (managed by Rosneft, Igor Sechin's company) following the departure of ExxonMobil, which held 30 percent of the project and was replaced by the Indian company Videsh and the Japanese company Sodeco. For their part, the Chinese are involved in the construction of the Arktik-Sabetta 2 LNG terminal, which should be operational by the end of 2023 with a capacity of seven million tons. The Power of Siberia 2 gas pipeline was relaunched during Xi's visit to Moscow in March 2023. A possible recovery of the Chinese economy after the lifting of restrictions imposed under the country's so-called Zero COVID policy could accelerate these projects by boosting the consumption of oil products, with a likely positive impact on their price.

Against the backdrop of the war in Ukraine, this new oil Great Game has only just begun and will be played out over time. The next few years will be a decisive test of Russia's ability to maintain its activities in this strategic sector, especially as Moscow has had to offer significant discounts on oil. Tellingly, the authors of the Yale University report do not dwell on the dramatic increase in Europe's energy bills, especially Germany's, which will significantly impact the future of global geo-economic balances, reducing several EU countries' industrial productivity.

### Resilience versus Growth?

The Russian economy's resilience has always been underestimated; moreover, the proponents of sanctions certainly could not anticipate all of their consequences. After the 2014 sanctions, the main international financial organizations had to readjust their forecasts for Russia, with a return to GDP growth from 2016 onward (see table 5.3). In the same way, the West's pessimistic forecasts for Russian growth in 2022 (a drop of 10 percent to 20 percent was suggested) had to be revised several times, and the final figure (down 3.5 percent) as well as the inflation rate (11.5 percent year-on-year) have been far from the initial catastrophic predictions. Besides the successful mobilization of Russian public opinion around defending the country against Western actions, President Putin has used these challenges to accelerate what now amounts to a strategic turning point in several critical areas.

The technology embargo will certainly have real effects, but for how long and at what scale? Some projects may become more expensive due to the necessity of producing equipment and developing technology domestically, while others may be delayed while Russian enterprises find new partners to replace the Western firms that left. One illuminating example after the 2014 sanctions was one of the most sensitive Arctic projects: the Sabetta LNG plant on the Yamal Peninsula (forming the left bank of the Ob River), which was spared the impact of sanctions by acquiring Chinese investment, including a loan in yuan.

Russia is pressing ahead with the development of domestic supply chains and technology, directing government funds to projects and attracting Asian and even Middle Eastern investment. The ultimate costs and results of this approach remain uncertain, but success would mean the development of Russian industry and technology, more energy revenues kept at home, and a reinforced autarky.[71] Another aspect of these changes, the extent of which is not yet clear, is the defiance toward the US dollar, which is increasingly being replaced with other currencies in contracts signed by Russia, most often the yuan as well as the dirhan or the Indian rupee but perhaps cryptocurrencies in the future, which presupposes that Moscow will pass a law legalizing them.

Certainly, the strategic turn induced by the new sanctions crisis postpones indefinitely the question of deep reform of the Russian economic system. Hard hit by the sanctions, the oligarchs who are Putin's inner circle of decision-makers have so far preferred to close ranks around the president and avoid any radical criticism of his choices in Ukraine. In this context, the peculiarities of rent-sharing, which Gaddy and Ickes saw as one of the main causes of the "Russian disease," are likely to remain.

Most of the rent from the commodities sectors is picked up by a few large companies and holdings that are directly or indirectly led by entrepreneurs close to the state. The rent is then redistributed under the close supervision of the presidential administration, which seeks to ensure that the funds are directed toward national security and, now, toward defense, as well as major social commitments, federal priority programs, and regional balancing. By giving these areas priority as sectors considered strategic to the country's stability, Putin has promoted these lobbies and implicitly prioritized their connection to Russian sovereignty and resilience against growth and diversification. Because the nature of these sectors' output is such that innovation is of marginal concern, their needs for research and development and qualified professionals are relatively low. In addition, the average size of firms in these industries has strengthened the Soviet-era tendency to favor large organizations to the detriment of SMEs, where the innovative capabilities that are vital to new industry and service fields are concentrated.

Another aspect of this problem is the inertia in the decision-making structures themselves. The priority given to major federal programs is probably necessary in a period of infrastructure catchup and the upgrade of major industrial sectors; this is even more so in wartime. But the lack of real control mechanisms from society (parliament, media, NGOs, and autonomous public opinion) opens the door to abuses that reduce efficiency. Such weak social control has another daunting consequence: innovative entrepreneurs receive no reliable protection and are often sidelined, constituting a particular form of brain drain that damages the economic ecosystem.

This is the set of structural defects at the intersection of economic and political practices that has been called the "Russian disease." It facilitates inefficient investment decisions and the mismanagement of huge profits

generated in growth periods. The current period of policy stiffening accompanied by patriotic rhetoric, with the increasingly vehement denunciation of the
influence of "foreign agents," is certainly not conducive to the questioning
of these aberrations. Instead, it accentuates even more significant defects that
only weigh on already weak growth. In a rare example of Russian frankness
on the impact of breaking links with the West, the Institute of Economic
Forecasting of the Russian Academy of Sciences states that the decline in
Russia's GDP "will contribute to maintain Russia's technological delay and
reduce its competitiveness in the world economy."[72]

Taking full account of the abrupt breakdown in economic and trade relations
with its main Western partners, the Russian government has embarked on a
complete overhaul of its foreign economic and industrial cooperation. At a
BRICS summit held via videoconference in June 2022, Putin emphasized
that Russia was redirecting its foreign trade to "reliable international partners"—mostly the BRICS countries. But apart from the fact that it is practically impossible to replace at a moment's notice Russia's multiple thirty-year
relationships with Western firms, it will also be necessary to take into account
Chinese firms' reluctance to increase their investment in Russia. Albeit dis-
creetly, given the sensitivity of the issues involved, the Russian press regularly echoes these questions by reporting on certain warnings published in the
Chinese press.[73]

   Despite the specifics of economic operations, there are issues that go far
beyond management approaches and structures. Russian authorities are effectively questioning some of the international institutions that govern all global
balances, in monetary and financial terms as well as in the areas of arbitration
rules, ratings, and credit instruments. Reaffirming their strong conception of
national sovereignty and security, Russian leaders are redefining a substantial
part of the balance of their foreign policy. We will explore this subject further
in the next chapter.

## NOTES

   1. Vladimir Putin, "Mineral Natural Resources in the Strategy for Development
of the Russian Economy," trans. Harley Balzer, in "Vladimir Putin's Academic Writings and Russian Natural Resource Policy," *Problems of Post-Communism* 53, no. 1
(2006): 48–54.
   2. "Soveshchanie s chlenami Pravitel'stva," January 21, 2015, http://kremlin.ru/
events/president/news/47497.

3. Jeffrey A. Sonnenfeld et al., "Business Retreats and Sanctions Are Crippling the Russian Economy," Yale University, July 19, 2022, https://papers.ssrn.com/sol3/papers.cfm?abstract_id=4167193.

4. Ibid., 4.

5. These debates can be followed by consulting the economy section of the editions since 2013 of the annual *Insights of the French-Russian Observatory* (Paris), http://obsfr.ru/fr/le-rapport-annuel.html.

6. Shinichiro Tabata, "Observations on Russian Exposure to the Dutch Disease," *Eurasian Geography & Economics* 53, no. 2 (2012): 231–43.

7. Among the first authors to diagnose this "disease," one may cite Julien Vercueil, *Transition et ouverture de l'économie russe: Pour une économie institutionnelle du changement* (Paris: L'Harmattan, 2000); Marshall I. Goldman, "The 'Russian Disease,'" *International Economy* 19, no. 3 (Summer 2005): 27–31; and Clifford G. Gaddy and Barry W. Ickes, "Resource Rents and the Russian Economy," *Eurasian Geography & Economics* 46, no. 8 (2005): 559–83.

8. *Russian Statistical Yearbook 2021* (Moscow: Rosstat, 2021); *Natsionalnye Scheta Rossii 2013–2020* (Moscow: Rosstat, 2021).

9. Sergei Mingazov, "Schetnaia palata otchitalas' o roste neftegazovykh dokhodov biudzheta v 1,7 raza," *Forbes*, August 30, 2022, www.forbes.ru/finansy/475741-scetnaa-palata-otcitalas-o-roste-neftegazovyh-dohodov-budzeta-v-1-7-raza; "Biudzhetnye iskopaemye," *RBK*, March 6, 2018, https://www.rbc.ru/newspaper/2018/03/06/5a9818279a7947614fe7c2a3.

10. Tsarist Russia made some considerable state-guaranteed loans at the beginning of the twentieth century. Their nonreimbursement by the Soviet regime was a cause of conflict until an agreement was reached in 1997. See Eric Toussaint, "Centenary of the Russian Revolution and the Repudiation of Debt," CADTM, October 23, 2017, https://www.cadtm.org/The-Russian-Revolution-Debt.

11. "The first thing we want to do now is re-establish a normal country, with a normal economy and a normal life. Not a super life, but a normal human way of life. Our tragic past has convinced us that one of the highest treasures that any human community can have is a normal way of life." Speech by Boris Yeltsin to Canadian Parliament, June 19, 1992, http://www.lipad.ca/full/1992/06/19/13.

12. These began in 1994 and ended with the Duma's ratification of Russia's admission in July 2012. On this topic, see Richard Connolly and Philip Hanson, "Russia's Accession to the World Trade Organization: Commitments, Processes, and Prospects," *Eurasian Geography & Economics* 53 (2012): 479–501.

13. Thomas Piketty, "La Russie poutinienne se caractérise par une dérive kleptocratique sans limites," *Le Monde*, April 7, 2018, http://www.lemonde.fr/idees/article/2018/04/07/piketty-la-russie-poutinienne-se-caracterise-par-une-derive-kleptocratique-sans-limites_5282016_3232.html.

14. Vladimir Putin, "Rossiia na rubezhe tysiacheletii," *Rossiiskaia gazeta,* December 31, 1999, http://www.ng.ru/politics/1999-12-30/4_millenium.html.

15. Putin, "Rossiia na rubezhe tysiacheletii."

16. Gertrude Schroeder, "Dimensions of Russia's Industrial Transformation, 1992 to 1998: An Overview," *Post-Soviet Geography & Economics* 39, no. 5 (1998): 243–70.

17. Goskomstat, *Trud i zaniatnost'* (Moscow: Goskomstat, 2017).

18. Aleksandr Naumov, "Perspektivy razvitiia rossiiskogo avtoproma," *Mirovoe i natsional'noe khoziaistvo*, no. 2 (2010): 51–59.

19. Aleksey Sinitskiy, "Lobovaia ataka rossiiskoi aviatsii," *Finansovye izvestiia*, May 8, 1999.

20. See "Amerikanskii sled na 'Permskikh motorakh," *War and Peace*, March 16, 2012, http://www.warandpeace.ru/ru/reports/view/67755; Aleksey Kondrashev, "Permskie motory: uroki istorii," *Nezavisimaia gazeta*, December 29, 2000.

21. J. P. Casamayou, "Sukhoï investit en Sibérie pour son Superjet-100," *Air & Cosmos*, May 1, 2007.

22. Andrei Bortsov, "Russko-kitaiskii samolet sotrudnichestva vzletaet vse vyshe," *Politicheskaia Rossiia*, June 27, 2016, http://politrussia.com/world/o-russko -kitayskom-dalnemagistralnom-602.

23. "Kitai reshil zamenit Rossiiu na zapadnye kompanii v proekte sovmestnogo samoleta," *Moscow Times*, July 25, 2022, https://www.moscowtimes.nl/2022/07/25/ kitai-reshil-zamenit-rossiyu-na-zapadnie-kompanii-v-proekte-sovmestnogo-samoleta -a22612.

24. Masaaki Kuboniwa, "Diagnosing the 'Russian Disease': Growth and Structure of the Russian Economy," *Comparative Economic Studies* 54, no. 1 (2012): 121–48; Julien Vercueil, "Russie: la 'stratégie 2020' en question," *Revue d'études compara- tives Est-Ouest* 44, no. 1 (2013): 169–94.

25. See, for example, Jacques Sapir, "Stratégie industrielle russe," *Hypotheses* (blog), May 30, 2015, http://russeurope.hypotheses.org/3879; "La Russie sort de la crise," *Hypotheses* (blog), March 21, 2015, http://russeurope.hypotheses.org/3650.

26. Serguey Tsukhlo, "Importozameshchenie: mify i realnost,'" in *Ezhegodnyi doklad Franko-rossiiskogo tsentra Observatorii Rossiia-2016*, ed. Arnaud Dubien (Paris: Le Cherche-Midi, 2016), 92–103.

27. Wladimir Andreff, *Économie de la transition. La transformation des économies planifiées en économies de marché* (Paris: Bréal, 2007).

28. Myriam Désert and Gilles Favarel-Garrigues, "Les capitalistes russes," *Prob- lèmes politiques et sociaux*, no. 789 (August 1997).

29. This factory became American-owned in 1998 through share purchases, caus- ing a highly publicized scandal. An amicable solution was ultimately found when a Russian oligarch purchased the factory in 2002.

30. See Vladimir Gelman, "Russia's Crony Capitalism: The Swing of the Pen- dulum," openDemocracy, November 14, 2011, https://www.opendemocracy.net/en /odr/russias-crony-capitalism-swing-of-pendulum; Anders Aslund, *Russia's Crony Capitalism: The Path from Market Economy to Kleptocracy* (New Haven, CT: Yale University Press, 2019).

31. "M. Poutine propose aux 'oligarques' russes une forme d'amnistie," *Le Monde*, July 30, 2000.

32. Richard Sakwa, *The Quality of Freedom: Khodorkovsky, Putin, and the Yukos Affair* (Oxford: Oxford University Press, 2009).

33. Boris Berezovsky, owner of ORT Television, and Vladimir Gusinsky, owner of NTV (the only private television channel, which was highly critical of the government during the First Chechen War) and of the radio station Ekho Moskvy, were the first to be pushed out of Russia.

34. "Polozhitel'naia ekologicheskaia ekspertiza proekta 'Sakhalin-2' otmenena," RIA *Novosti*, September 19, 2006, https://ria.ru/20060919/54059888.html; "Britaniia ozabochena resheniem po 'Sakhalinu-2,'" BBC Russia, September 20, 2006, http://news.bbc.co.uk/hi/russian/russia/newsid_5363000/5363114.stm.

35. Terry Macalister, "BP Ups Stakes by Accusing Putin of Failing to Stop Hijack by Oligarchs," *The Guardian*, June 13, 2008, https://www.theguardian.com/business/2008/jun/13/bp.russia; Carola Hoyos, Ed Crooks, and Catherine Belton, "Strained Relations Thaw over TNK-BP," *Financial Times*, September 5, 2008, http://www.ft.com/cms/s/23a1bda6-7ae1-11dd-adbe-000077b07658.html.

36. Gaddy and Ickes, "Resource Rents and the Russian Economy"; Clifford Gaddy and Barry Ickes, "Russia's Declining Oil Production: Managing Price Risk and Rent Addiction," *Eurasian Geography & Economics* 50, no. 1 (2009): 1–13.

37. Mikhail Kasyanov, *Bez Putina. Politicheskie dialogi s Evgeniem Kiselevym* (Moscow: Novaia gazeta, 2009).

38. Tabata, "Observations on Russian Exposure."

39. See "Abramovich, Roman," *Lenta.ru*, https://lenta.ru/lib/14161457.

40. "EU Sanctions against Russia over Ukraine Crisis," European Union Newsroom, March 16, 2017, https://europa.eu/newsroom/highlights/special-coverage/eu-sanctions-against-russia-over-ukraine-crisis_en.

41. Viktoriia Nikitina, "Dorogi RF v 38 raz dorozhe i v 2 raza 'nezhnee' kanadskikh," *Argumenty i fakty*, June 8, 2011, http://www.aif.ru/money/25863.

42. Matthew Sagers, "Russia's Energy Policy: A Divergent View," *Eurasian Geography & Economics* 47, no. 3 (2006): 314–20; Matthew Sagers, "The Regional Dimension of Russian Oil Production: Is a Sustained Recovery in Prospect?" *Eurasian Geography & Economics* 47, no. 5 (2006): 505–45.

43. William Tompson, "Back to the Future? Thoughts on the Political Economy of Expanding State Ownership in Russia," *Les cahiers Russie*, no. 6 (2008).

44. Sergey Guriev, "New Wave of Russian Privatization," *Note of the French-Russian Observatory*, no. 2 (January 2013), http://obsfr.ru/uploads/media/130115_Policy_Paper_2_Gouriev_EN.pdf.

45. "Stenogramma vystupleniia Vladimira Putina pered federal'nym sobraniem," *Rossiiskaia gazeta*, March 1, 2018, https://rg.ru/2018/03/01/stenogramma-vystupleniia-vladimira-putina-pered-federalnym-sobraniem.html.

46. *Order on National Goals and Strategic Objectives of the Russian Federation through to 2024*, May 7, 2018, http://en.kremlin.ru/events/president/news/57425.

47. Philip Hanson, *Russian Economic Policy and the Russian Economic System Stability versus Growth*, Chatham House, December 2019, p. 14. https://www.chathamhouse.org/sites/default/files/CHHJ7799-Russia-Economics-RP-WEB-FINAL.pdf.

48. Ildar Ablaev, "Innovation Clusters in the Russian Economy: Economic Essence, Concepts, Approaches," *Procedia Economics & Finance* 24 (2015): 3–12, http://www.sciencedirect.com/science/article/pii/S221256711500605X.

49. See Ekaterina Gloriozova and Aude Merlin, eds., "Sotchi-2014: La Russie à l'épreuve de ses Jeux, les Jeux à l'épreuve du Caucase," *Connexe, les espaces post-communistes en question(s), no. 2* (special issue, December 2016).

50. Transparency International, "Corruption Perceptions Index," 2022, https://www.transparency.org/en/cpi/2022.

51. Lennart Dal'gren, *Vopreki absurdu, ili kaki ia pokorial Rossiiu, a ona—menia: Vospominaniia byvshego general'nogo direktora* IKEA *v Rossii* (Moscow: Al'pina Biznes Buks, 2010).

52. See, for instance, the documentary film directed by Andrei Nekrasov on the topic: *Magnitsky Act–Behind the Scenes* (Stavanger, Norway: Piraya Film, 2016); and, about it, Mark Landler, "Film about Russian Lawyer's Death Creates an Uproar," *New York Times*, June 9, 2016, https://www.nytimes.com/2016/06/10/world/europe/sergei-magnitsky-russia-vladimir-putin.html.

53. Boris Nemtsov and Vladimir Milov, *Putin. Itogi. 10 let* (Moscow: Solidarsnost,' 2010); Vladimir Milov et al., *Putin. Korruptsiia* (Moscow: Solidarnost,' 2011).

54. "Ease of Doing Business Rankings," World Bank, https://archive.doingbusiness.org/en/rankings.

55. See Isabelle Mandraud, "À Moscou, le Comité d'enquête, bras judiciaire de Poutine," *Le Monde*, February 25, 2015, http://www.lemonde.fr/international/article/2015/02/05/a-moscou-le-bras-arme-de-poutine_4570142_3210.html.

56. Ol'ga Solov'eva, "Vmesto pervoi piaterki Rossiia popala v glubokuiu zastoinuiu iamu," *Nezavisimaia gazeta*, November 27, 2018, https://www.ng.ru/economics/2018-11-27/1_7449_crisis.html.

57. "Dat volnuiu Femide: retsepty reformirovaniia sudebnoi sistemy ot Alekseia Kudrina i Borisa Titova," *Real'noe vremia*, March 24, 2017, https://realnoevremya.ru/articles/60123-recepty-reformirovaniya-sudebnoy-sistemy-ot-kudrina-i-titova.

58. "Zhiteli Rossii skuchaiut po zarubezhnym brendam," Retail, January 1, 2023, https://www.retail.ru/news/zhiteli-rossii-skuchayut-po-zarubezhnym-brendam-18-yanvarya-2023-224753.

59. "Chinovnikam zapretili imet' scheta za rubezhom," *Interfax*, April 24, 2013, http://www.interfax.ru/russia/303553.

60. Mariia Perevoshchikova, "Moll da dorog: v Rossii mozhet zakrytsia kazhdyi vtoroi torgovyi tsentr," *Izvestiia*, November 30, 2022, https://iz.ru/1433209/mariia-perevoshchikova/moll-da-dorog-v-rossii-mozhet-zakrytsia-kazhdyi-vtoroi-torgovyi-tcentr.

61. Alberto Nardelli et al., "Putin Stirs Worry That Russia Is Stripping Home-Appliance Imports for Arms," *Time*, October 29, 2022, https://time.com/6226484/russia-appliance-imports-weapons.

62. "Kakie otrasli proizvodstva v Rossii pokazali rost v 2022 godu. Novye vozmozhnosti dlia rossiiskogo promyshlennogo sektora," *Narodnye novosti*, January 3, 2023, https://dzen.ru/a/Y7SlrBtNdHLyYyBC.

63. Sonnenfeld et al., "Business Retreats," 42 and following.

64. T. Nefedova, "Agrokompleks rossii v usloviiakh sanktsii: regionalnoe izmerenie," *Research of Russia* 2 (2023). See also Susanne Wengle, *Black Earth, White Bread: A Technopolitical History of Russian Agriculture and Food* (Madison: University of Wisconsin Press, 2022).

65. "Rossiiskoi aviatsii slomaiut krylia," *Kommersant*, February 26, 2022, https://www.kommersant.ru/doc/5236969; "Pravitelstvo RF vydelit okolo 44 mlrd rublei na proizvodstvo aviadvigatelei," *Kommersant*, November 14, 2022, https://www.kommersant.ru/doc/5667456.

66. "Aviakompanii poluchat pervye 6 samoletov MS-21 s rossiiskimi dvigateliami v 2024 g.," Interfax, April 13, 2022, https://www.interfax.ru/russia/834714.

67. "SelfSanctions/LeaveRussia," Kyiv School of Economics, https://kse.ua/selfsanctions-kse-institute.

68. Simon Evenett and Niccolò Pisani, "Less than Nine Percent of Western Firms Have Divested from Russia," December 20, 2022, https://ssrn.com/abstract=4322502.

69. See their biweekly reports, *CCI France Russie*, https://www.youtube.com/c/ccifrancerussie.

70. Jeffrey Sonnenfeld and Steven Tian, "The World Economy No Longer Needs Russia," *Foreign Policy*, January 19, 2023, https://foreignpolicy.com/2023/01/19/russia-ukraine-economy-europe-energy.

71. Dmitrii Kozlov, "Minpromtorg zanialsia arkticheskoi inzheneriei," *Kommersant*, January 25, 2017, https://www.kommersant.ru/doc/3200888; Iurii Ban'ko, "Importozameshchenie dlia arkticheskogo shel'fa: gonki ne nada, no i ne rasteriat' by uzhe dostignutogo," *Arktik*–TV, June 2, 2016; "Shel'fovye proekty," Rosneft, n.d. https://www.rosneft.ru/business/Upstream/offshore.

72. Institute of Economic Forecasting of the Russian Academy of Sciences, *Potentsial'nye vozmozhnosti rosta rossiiskoi ekonomiki: analiz prognoz*, ecfor.ru, July 19, 2022 https://ecfor.ru/publication/potentsial-rosta-ekonomiki.

73. Olga Solovieva, "Pekin zaiavil o riskakh sotrudnichestva s Moskvoi," *Nezavisimaya gazeta*, November 24, 2014. Vladimir Nejdanov, "'Preodolet nedoverie.' Chto budet s rossiisko-kitaiskimi otnosheniiami v 2020 godu," *Eurasia Ekspert*, January 21, 2020.

# 6

# From Eurasia to the Whole World

## *The Double-Hedged Eagle Challenges Global Equilibriums*

We know that Russia is a European and Asian country. We respect both European pragmatism and Eastern wisdom. That is why Russia's foreign policy will be balanced.

—Vladimir Putin, interview with Chinese media, June 12, 2000

The West has gone too far in its aggressive anti-Russia policy, making endless threats to our country and people. Some irresponsible Western politicians are doing more than just speak about their plans to organize the delivery of long-range offensive weapons to Ukraine, which could be used to deliver strikes at Crimea and other Russian regions.

—Vladimir Putin, televised speech, September 21, 2022

Eighteen months after annexing Crimea in March 2014, Russia launched an armed intervention in Syria, its first major engagement outside the post-Soviet area since the war in Afghanistan (1979–1989).[1] This action significantly changed the West's perception of Moscow's role in the world, which for a long time saw a weakened Russia intervene only in its immediate post-Soviet vicinity. According to then US president Barack Obama, Russia was simply "a regional power that is threatening some of its immediate neighbors not out of strength, but out of weakness."[2]

Obviously, though, this is not how Russia's leaders conceived of their country's role. The country's status as a global actor was then confirmed by its air raids in Syria and the Kalibr cruise-missile attacks (or SSN30, according to the NATO designation) from ships in the Caspian Sea aimed at Syrian targets, all designed to demonstrate Moscow's support for Bashar al-Assad's regime. If Yeltsin had little time for more than a few statements on the subject, Putin has been determined to reaffirm his country's strength, even if it means turning his back on Europeans, as demonstrated by the world crisis triggered when he launched the full-scale invasion of Ukraine. Another sign of the changes underway is that, far from being confined to its "near abroad," Moscow's foreign policy now extends to the entire world, from the Asia-Pacific to the Middle East, to Africa to Latin America, as shown on the map of Vladimir Putin's official trips (see map 6.1).

## RUSSIA AND THE WEST: MUTUAL MISUNDERSTANDINGS

Following Crimea's annexation, Western foreign policy analysts took note of Russia's "Asian pivot," particularly the spectacular rapprochement between Moscow and Beijing, which was billed as a major strategic change for the Kremlin. But if there was a real break in Russian diplomacy, it occurred with the West, a trend that was confirmed in 2022 with Russia's unprecedented decoupling from the West. During the entire period between the annexation of Crimea in 2014 and the full-scale invasion of Ukraine in February 2022, clashes between Russia and the West multiplied—Russia banning the importation of EU agricultural products in retaliation for Western sanctions, Russian intervention in the US presidential election in 2016, and the coordinated expulsion of 151 Russian diplomats by twenty-seven Western countries in 2018 to protest Russia's poisoning attempt of a former double agent, Sergey Skrypal, in the UK, among others—revealing signs of the high level of tensions that opened the path toward the 2022 war.

Russia's perception is undoubtedly marked by a sense of a threat encroaching on its borders. After the negotiations that led to the reunification of Germany in 1990 and the dissolution of the Warsaw Pact under Gorbachev, Russia witnessed the accession of the three Baltic states to NATO and the EU in 2004 and the "color revolutions" in Georgia and Ukraine, all events seen as products of Western pressure in what Moscow has always considered to be its strategic security zone. From the late 1980s to the mid-2000s, Russia was weak. Its lack of diplomatic weight was demonstrated in March 1999, its only visible response to the Western bombing of Belgrade (without any UN mandate) being Prime Minister Yevgeny Primakov canceling his trip to the United States midflight and rerouting the plane back to Moscow. As Russia dealt with internal issues, it saw NATO's spectacular progress toward its territory as a succession of humiliations made possible by the country's temporary weakness. Since then, however, Russia has regained some of its power and confidence and now challenges the second-tier status that has been attributed to it.

## The East–West Rapprochement and Its Limits

Even before the dissolution of the Soviet Union, Yeltsin made plain his desire for closer ties with key Western countries. This Western connection remained Russia's major foreign policy priority for two decades. In some regards, it was echoed in the support Putin expressed to President George W. Bush following the September 11, 2001 attacks and in Putin's and Medvedev's proposals for a greater EU–Russia strategic partnership. However, it is simplistic to interpret these gestures, symbolic though they are, as evidencing Russia's "return" to the Western path.

The first Russian president and those around him were sincere in their desire and declarations of interest in moving away from the Soviet path of development as quickly as possible. Imbued with European culture (a point that Mikhail Gorbachev had repeatedly stressed), Russian elites naturally thought to draw from various Western practices, whether German, French, or American. Trade exchanges, already broadly initiated under Gorbachev, were reinforced by a full complement of Western advisers ready to offer guidance on writing a new constitution, developing various regulations, and privatizing the banking system. Europeans and Americans saw these reforms, which they cheered, as signs of Russia's "normalization" and its acceptance of the so-called transition, a concept implying that the former socialist states were finally going to adopt elements of the Western system they had previously fought against, and that they would melt into the liberal mold.

But in the minds of Russian leaders, there was no necessary link between the technical and policy practices of a new form of governance borrowed from the West and a reconceptualization of the country's foreign policy. The apparent geopolitical rapprochement actually obscured deep differences and a double misunderstanding. On the Russian side, although the desire for reform was real, the new government had not abandoned the idea of Russia having a major role in what it considered its almost exclusive zone of influence in the so-called near abroad. The creation of the Commonwealth of Independent States (CIS) on December 8, 1991, met this objective, even as the proposal Yeltsin made at the United Nations—that Russia should continue to act as the guarantor of the security of the whole region—was wholly rejected by his Western partners. However, it would take years for the Russian and Western leaders to fully comprehend this difference in perspective.

The West, especially the United States, sought to leverage the Russian leadership's initial goodwill, the opening of the country, and the new opportunities it presented to implement a policy that went beyond simple assistance toward democracy promotion. After their surprise at the sudden collapse of the Soviet system, American and European officials gradually established a strategy of systematic actions on multiple scales, tailored to the different circles that constituted Russia's strategic environment.

No Western propaganda was needed to push the old "people's democracies," which had been part of the Warsaw Pact, to ask to join the EU and NATO. Several decades of subjugation by the Soviet Union and distrust of the new Russian authorities were enough to incite these countries' public opinions to turn toward the models of governance proposed by the West. As early as the spring and summer of 1990, Polish, Czechoslovak, and Hungarian leaders rushed to NATO's headquarters in Brussels to discuss a possible rapprochement.[3] A groundswell of pro-Western public opinion in Eastern European states transformed this part of the continent into one that Moscow could no longer influence. In fact, within a few years, what had been the socialist bloc had become an anti-Russian buffer—and it would be Poland and the Baltic states that led the campaign against the "Russian threat" from within the EU and NATO.[4]

Successive Kremlin leaders tried to preserve some of Russia's economic and geopolitical influence. Issues related to EU accession aside, integration into NATO remained the most controversial subject. Let us note here that some Russian declarations may have given rise to misgivings. In August 1993, while on a memorable trip to Warsaw, Yeltsin said to Polish president Lech Wałęsa that Poland's membership in NATO "was not contrary to the interests of any state, also including Russia,"[5] a declaration that he would later regret. For his part, on his first foreign trip as president in March 2000 (while welcomed in London by Queen Elizabeth II), Putin gave an interview to the BBC. To the question, "Do you see NATO as a potential partner or a rival or an enemy?" he said,

> Russia is part of the European culture. And I cannot imagine my own country in isolation from Europe and what we often call the civilized world. So, it is hard for me to visualize NATO as an enemy. . . . We are open to equitable cooperation, to partnership. We believe we can talk about more profound integration with NATO but only if Russia is regarded as an equal partner. You are aware we have been constantly voicing our opposition to NATO's eastward enlargement.

The journalist asked again, "Is it possible that Russia could join NATO?" To this, Putin responded: "I don't see why not. I would not rule out such a possibility, but I repeat—if and when Russia's views are taken into account as those of an equal partner."[6]

But pitfalls on the way to this possible dialog rapidly emerged, and these words were soon forgotten. Putin quickly adopted the rhetoric of reproaching

Gorbachev for having too easily given in to Westerners on essential points, such as German reunification and the repatriation of Soviet soldiers, without negotiating anything substantial (such as funding for the withdrawal of the Russian military). NATO's expansion into Eastern Europe would become a fundamental and enduring point of contention in East–West relations, with Kremlin leaders accusing the United States of noncompliance with the verbal commitment James Baker had made to Gorbachev that NATO would "not shift one inch eastward from its present position."[7]

After a period of hesitation, Europe put a number of institutional and financial instruments in place for the post-Soviet region, such as Technical Assistance to the Commonwealth of Independent States (TACIS). Initially, these tools were intended to foster the development of democratic and liberal practices and increase cooperation. Under the influence of conservative US advisers, such as former national security advisor Zbigniew Brzezinski, however, a concerted policy relatively quickly took shape with the explicit aim of "decoupling" the new states from their former overlords and decisively "rolling back" Russian influence.[8] It should be noted in passing that this concept of rollback has a much stronger connotation than simple containment, since it is at the heart of one of the most bellicose US documents of the Cold War, the creation in 1950 under State Department director of policy planning Paul Nitze of NSC-68, or "United States Objectives and Programs for National Security," which contained a plan to overthrow the Soviet government.

In all the new capitals, US embassies insisted on the uselessness and even harmfulness of instruments developed within the CIS and offered considerable assistance to government teams that criticized various Kremlin decisions. After NATO launched its Partnership for Peace in 1994, the European Union implemented its Neighborhood Policy (2003) and then the Eastern Partnership (2009), which instituted association agreements for post-Soviet states.

However, the redefinition of relations with the former Soviet republics proved difficult, often garnering the opposition of the pillars of "old Europe"—Germany and France in the lead, anxious to develop political and commercial relations with Moscow in the hope of cementing cooperative patterns between Europeans and Russians—and the hostility of new EU members, particularly Poland and the Baltic states, toward any concessions to Moscow. The Americans became particularly involved in some key post-Soviet countries that Brzezinski called "pivots": Georgia (gateway to the Caucasus); Uzbekistan (the only Central Asian state bordering the four others and claiming its right to play a regional role); and, of course, Ukraine. They promoted pro-Western sentiment in these countries' public opinion, a process that would contribute to the color revolutions of 2003–2005.

Finally, Western action became evident in the heart of Russia itself with the establishment of networks of influence in many realms. These networks' focus areas included the political sphere, with systematic financial and technical support for liberal-democratic organizations, and the religious realm (American Evangelical and other Protestant-funded congregations appeared in even the smallest cities, as discussed earlier). Specific mention must be made of activities in the academic and scientific realms as well, where the Russian government was compelled to withdraw financial support, plunging researchers and engineers into real distress.

Although US government programs did not reach the level of George Soros's activity in Georgia, the proliferation of Western aid and scholarship funds had a double effect: it helped support whole areas of Russia's research and culture at a challenging time, but it also contributed to the region's brain drain.[9] The whole approach was a classic demonstration of the exercise of soft power and indeed contained the elements of a strategy of societal penetration and influence that would eventually elicit strong reactions from the Russian elite. Significantly, it was the Moscow Patriarchate that delivered the first warning: in 1997, it convinced Yeltsin to change the law on religion in order to reduce the influence of "foreign" churches.

Formally, Russia and the West maintained the appearance of a constructive dialog, even developing a range of instruments of cooperation; along with other post-Soviet states, Russia joined the NATO Partnership for Peace (1994) and the Council of Europe (joined in 1996, expelled in 2022). Moscow played an active role within the Organization for Security and Co-Operation in Europe (OSCE, formerly CSCE) even as it became increasingly critical of the organization's mission, since Moscow hoped to make the OSCE the pivot point of a new pan-European security architecture—a plan that would soon be definitively buried. A commitment to enhance the OSCE's role was one of the "nine-point package of 'assurances'" that Baker took with him to Moscow for talks with Gorbachev and his foreign affairs minister Eduard Shevardnadze in May 1990.[10]

Russian relations with the EU were formalized by a partnership agreement signed in 1994. During the 1990s, Moscow and NATO officials discussed cooperation on topics of common interest, such as the fight against terrorism and drugs and arms trafficking. The joint NATO–Russia Council, established in 1997, was reinforced in 2002 under Putin's leadership, although, as leaks at the Lisbon Council later revealed, US officials simultaneously reassured their allies that transatlantic firmness toward Russian policy would remain unchanged. In sum, there were critical topics on all sides, and mutual accusations soon proliferated.

## Pouring Russian Oil and Gas on Already Existing Post-Soviet Fires

One aspect of Russia's foreign policy especially alarmed Western countries and would drive them to intervene more openly among its immediate neighbors. Upon coming to power, Yeltsin interfered in the tensions emerging between some ethnic minorities and governments in the post-Soviet region. Russia was not behind these conflicts; their sources were much older, dating back to Stalin-era geopolitical calculations or even earlier,[11] and they were the natural consequence of the rise of nationalism in the late 1980s. However, the Kremlin exploited these frictions by openly supporting secessionist movements in Transnistria and the South Caucasus to pressure Moldova, Georgia, and Azerbaijan, respectively, to join the CIS and follow Russian directives.[12]

After the first wave of eastward NATO enlargement, Russia's support for secessionist movements became a real strategy to prevent Georgia, Moldova, and Ukraine from joining the alliance, as having an ongoing territorial dispute makes a country ineligible to join NATO. Of a different nature, because the conflict involved took place within Russia's borders, was Yeltsin's decision to reestablish control of Chechnya by force in late 1994; the catastrophic consequences of that intervention marked a turnaround in Western perceptions of the new Russia, even if the West reacted modestly and did not stop Moscow's entry to the Council of Europe.

The OSCE, the UN High Commissioner for Refugees (UNHCR), and various NGOs worked to end the active phases of the conflicts in the region, but they never managed to completely resolve any of them politically. Russian interference in these conflicts mobilized public opinion in the states concerned, a process that eventually weakened the CIS itself. The Kremlin was viewed as being responsible for prolonging the so-called frozen conflicts in order to maintain political pressure on its neighbors. At a summit in the Moldovan capital of Chișinău in 1997, the leaders of several of these states publicly challenged Yeltsin's policy in the CIS.[13] At the time, he agreed to revise his approach but never kept this promise.

The Americans, for their part, stoked the criticism and, in 1997, supported the creation of a new anti-Russian regional front, the GUAM (named for its members: Georgia, Ukraine, Azerbaijan, and Moldova—though Uzbekistan also belonged to it briefly as well). Its member states were all affected by a secessionist movement partly fueled by the Kremlin. GUAM never managed to achieve an influential role in the region, but it served as a convenient platform for its members and US leaders to increase their criticism of Russian policy in one of its sensitive areas.[14]

## Collective Security but Growing Divergences

Another area of dispute arose in the 1990s regarding negotiations over arms control in Europe. In November 1990, the countries of NATO and the Warsaw Pact signed the Conventional Forces in Europe (CFE) treaty, which established ceilings on various types of weapons. Based on the momentum created by Gorbachev, in January 1993 Presidents Yeltsin and George H. W. Bush signed START II (the Strategic Arms Reduction Treaty), which limited the number of nuclear warheads the two major powers could deploy. They undertook to continue negotiations for further reductions, but disputes quickly arose. Western actors pressed Moscow to close its military bases in Georgia and Moldova, which would only partially be carried out; meanwhile, the Kremlin was concerned about successive phases of NATO enlargement that brought the alliance ever closer to Russia's borders.

Yeltsin fought an uphill battle to delay the Baltic states' accession to NATO over the fate of Russian minorities in Estonia and Latvia, who were the objects of discrimination, launching the idea that Russian-speaking populations abroad should be placed under the protection of Russia. Unable to stop the accession, which took effect in 2004, the Russian government tried to carve out specific concessions for Kaliningrad in the form of a permanent transit visa for all residents of the exclave. (The European Commission limited this to an annual transit permit issued on demand.) With each major crisis, Moscow announced the deployment of new missiles to this isolated outpost of Russian territory geographically surrounded by the EU and NATO countries—SS-26 Iskander in 2018 and Kinzhal in August 2022 after the Lithuanian government partly blocked transit between the exclave and the rest of Russia.[15]

The September 11, 2001, attacks seemed to mark a possible change of direction, as Putin proposed engaging with the United States in the battle against the scourge of international terrorism. The Russian president had a vested interest in the proposal, because he wanted to stop criticism of Russia's engagement in Chechnya, which was even more brutal than the one under Yeltsin. The promise of aid had at least one concrete result: the United States was able to use air bases in Uzbekistan and later in Kyrgyzstan to support its attacks on the Taliban in Afghanistan.[16]

But new areas of concern quickly bubbled to the surface. In December 2001, US president George W. Bush declared that the ABM (antiballistic missile) treaty had no further application and announced plans to deploy a missile defense system in several of the new NATO member states. These missiles were supposed to defend against "rogue" states (such as Iran), but the Russians believed they would undermine the credibility of their own nuclear deterrent.

At the same time, the Pentagon arranged for access to bases in Romania and Bulgaria. Putin and George W. Bush signed SORT (the Strategic Offensive Reductions Treaty) in 2002, but as Moscow saw it, US actions had disturbed the balance of power in Europe.[17] The inauguration of Barack Obama in 2008 again seemed to offer the possibility of reducing tensions, as the new US president appeared to question some aspects of his predecessor's antimissile shield. In 2010, in Prague, Presidents Obama and Medvedev signed the New Start Treaty (START III), further reducing the number of warheads and delivery systems in each country. Medvedev even decided to abstain from the UN Security Council vote that allowed a NATO-led coalition to attack Libya in March 2011 and remove its president, Muammar Gaddafi, a decision for which he was publicly reproached by his prime minister, Putin.

During Medvedev's presidency, Russians seemed attentive to new proposals, such as the international Global Zero movement, which advocated for a drastic reduction of nuclear arsenals.[18] But Obama's policy of resetting relations between the two countries soon hit a stumbling block. The Kremlin was adamantly opposed to the United States on the issue of the latter's missile defense policy, and even more so on the possibility of further NATO enlargement, particularly regarding Ukraine. According to the Russians, any new disarmament agreement would have to address the missile defense issue, a ban on deploying weapons in space, and the imbalance in conventional weapons in Europe, in which NATO had a two-to-one advantage, according to US sources.[19] Russian leaders were particularly concerned about American advances in areas such as unmanned aerial vehicles (UAVs, or drones) and nonstrategic nuclear missiles; they believed the Pentagon was prepared to further reduce nuclear arsenals because the United States could now count on these other types of weapons.

Furthermore, although this was never officially stated, the Kremlin was also concerned about the power imbalance with China, whose military budget and armed forces were growing rapidly during this period. This explains the tenet of Russia's military doctrine, published in the 2010 version and maintained in its 2014 successor, that nuclear weapons could be used even in the case of a massive conventional threat ("when the very existence of the state is under threat").[20]

Following this, tensions peaked, and the doors to negotiations closed. In the early 2010s, the White House questioned the "reset" that had characterized US policy toward Russia during the Medvedev years. US Congress's decision to introduce the Magnitsky Act in 2012—named after Sergei Magnitsky, the tax lawyer who died in 2009 while detained in a Russian prison—aroused Moscow's ire.[21] In response, Russian authorities passed a law to prohibit Americans from adopting Russian children. In 2013, Putin managed to thumb his nose at Washington by granting political asylum to Edward Snowden, whose data leaks revealed massive surveillance of both domestic and global communications by the US National Security Agency (NSA).[22]

In March 2015, Moscow announced its definitive withdrawal from the revised Treaty on Conventional Armed Forces in Europe (CFE; it had suspended its participation in 2007, and the United States never ratified the revised version). Russia still wanted to discuss its new security proposals for Europe, but conditions for eventual negotiations were particularly difficult given the security context in Eastern Europe.

The July 2016 NATO summit in Warsaw decided to deter Russia by strengthening the alliance's military presence on its eastern flank. By 2017, there were four NATO battalions in the region, stationed in Poland, Estonia, Latvia, and Lithuania on a rotating basis. Each of these battalions was led by a NATO country—the United States, the United Kingdom, Canada, and Germany, respectively. The 2016 summit also inaugurated NATO's Ballistic Missile Defense, putting a base in Romania; its announced purpose was to counter threats posed by Iran and North Korea, but Russia believes it is also a target. The former Yugoslav republic of Montenegro was invited to become NATO's twenty-ninth member, and discussions were held on the status of Georgia and Ukraine, which angered Moscow.[23] NATO also launched a "Strategic Communication Center" in Latvia and opened a training center in Georgia.[24]

NATO's newly consolidated presence in Russia's western neighborhood and Moscow's responses accelerated a spiral of distrust. Knowing that the gap between the Russian military budget and that of the United States (about US $60 billion against US $700 billion, respectively) could not be bridged, the Kremlin opted for a hybrid strategy to secure its borders. It established an Anti-Access/Area-Denial (A2/AD) strategy, seeking to create territorial "bubbles" that would be almost impossible for NATO countries to access and protect. Moscow deployed various new-generation radar and missile systems, including SS-26 Iskanders (which have nuclear capability) in the Kaliningrad enclave; the only way for NATO to break through was to end Sweden's and Finland's long-standing traditions of military nonalignment, a move that became a legal reality with the outbreak of the 2022 war. The other "bubbles" are along the Baltic–Arctic axis (the Kola Peninsula near northern Finland, the island of Novaya Zemlya extending out to the northeast of there into the Arctic Ocean, and the Franz Josef Land Archipelago north of there), in Crimea, and on the Kamchatka Peninsula.

At the same time, one may notice increasing amounts of blame being leveled by both sides concerning adherence to the Intermediate-Range Nuclear Forces Treaty (INF) regarding the elimination of intermediate- and short-range missiles. US officials have accused Moscow of contravening the treaty's clauses by deploying in its "bastions" new P-800 Oniks and

"9M729" (SSC-8 in NATO's classification) missiles, new-generation S-300 and S-400 missiles, as well as Kalibr-NK rockets, all of which can be either ship-launched (and are thus not subject to the treaty) or made land-mobile, like the Iskander missile.

Russia has made reciprocal accusations that denounce the United States' ability to mount diverse categories of offensive missiles on the MK41 anti-missile complexes at the new American facilities in Romania and Poland or at those that will be built in Japan, as announced in late 2017. On March 1, 2018, during his address to parliament, Putin presented a new generation of missiles, the Kh-47M2 Kinzhal (the NATO reporting name is Killjoy), which are supposedly invulnerable to enemy interception and, therefore, able to keep a strategic balance with the United States even with the immense discrepancy in military budgets—Russia's answer to the Pentagon's 2018 Nuclear Posture Review.

## Pipeline Wars and the New "Great Game"

During all these years, Russia and NATO competed for influence in the post-Soviet space, and quickly, one of the concrete fields of this battle was the redefinition of the transportation networks around Russia, which became referred to as the new "Great Game."[25] Indeed, the post-1991 reorganization of the main communication lines on the margins of Russia's territory became a major issue for all CIS states, with active interference from external actors. As previously observed, the situation resulted from the landlocked status of nine of the fifteen states, as well as Russia's dependence on certain transit states for its exports to Europe. Very quickly, two battlefronts opened. To the east, Moscow tried to preserve its monopoly over the transit of exports from Central Asia. To the west, transit countries (the Baltic states, Belarus, and Ukraine) sought to take advantage of their location in bitter negotiations over the passage of Russian energy resources.

Meanwhile, several external actors quickly stepped in to challenge Moscow's efforts to preserve its influence in this strategic space. In 1993, the European Union, with US support, launched the Europe-Caucasus-Asia Transport Corridor (TRACECA), an ambitious project that aimed to create a major alternative transportation network that would circumvent Russia and Iran; modernize the roads, railways, and ports of the three states of the South Caucasus and the five Central Asian countries; and boost extra-CIS coopera-tion between all the former Soviet states south of Russia. It was open mainly to the non-Russian, non-Iranian midsection of the Caspian Sea, a highly stra-tegic region where the Western oil majors had returned after a seventy-year absence during the Soviet era.

It is precisely within this context of privileged relations that, in 1999, US president Bill Clinton and Azerbaijani president Heydar Aliev managed to launch BTC (Baku-Tbilisi-Ceyhan, the third city being a Turkish port on the Mediterranean Sea), an expensive pipeline to export Azeri oil while avoiding passage through Russia, the Turkish Straits, or Istanbul. It was completed in 2005 and was soon joined by a parallel gas pipeline, Baku-Tbilisi-Erzurum, to export the gas discovered in the early 2000s off of the coast of Baku in the western Caspian. The Europeans, who also wanted to enjoy the benefits of these newly discovered deposits, proposed the Nabucco project, a large pipeline that would import Azeri and Turkmen gas via a pipeline constructed under the Caspian Sea and then routed through Turkey and the Balkans.[26] Ultimately, however, EU hesitation and Russian opposition scuttled the project.

Russian leaders quickly reacted to these initiatives, which reduced the virtual monopoly that had benefited Moscow during the imperial and Soviet periods. At summits in the Caspian states, the Kremlin (with implicit support from Tehran, which challenged the division of the seabed proposed by Azerbaijan and Turkmenistan) managed to block the construction of a trans-Caspian pipeline, preventing Kazakhstan and Turkmenistan from connecting to any Western-funded pipelines in the Caucasus. Simultaneously, and in record time, the Russians built a series of pipelines connecting deposits in northern Kazakhstan to the new oil and gas terminals they had opened between Novorossiysk and Tuapse on Russia's Black Sea coast. Moscow signed special agreements with Kazakhstan to ensure the routing of a large proportion of Caspian crude exports through Russian territory. Finally, to counter Nabucco, in 2003 Moscow completed the Blue Stream underwater gas pipeline between Russia and Turkey, the culmination of Russia's long struggle to maintain its share of gas exports to southern European countries.[27]

Meanwhile, Russian authorities had been active on their western borders. Upon taking office in 2000, Putin began to speed up construction projects at the Vysotsk and Ust-Luga ports, outside St. Petersburg on the Gulf of Finland, in order to reduce transit through the Baltic states and Poland to a minimum—and later, to punish these states for their acquiring NATO membership. The rise of these new facilities, particularly the Vyborg gas terminal and, in 2011, the inauguration of the Nord Stream undersea pipeline to Germany (negotiated with then chancellor Gerhard Schroeder, who would become chairman of the board of Gazprom's subsidiary Nord Stream AG) fulfilled a strategic Kremlin objective: enabling direct Russian gas exports to the core of Europe by avoiding transit states. An agreement to double these exports (Nord Stream 2) was signed in June 2015, despite the already tense situation in Ukraine.[28]

A similar project was planned to the south, with the South Stream natural gas pipeline from Russia to Bulgaria under the Black Sea to supply the southeastern states of the European Union. In the face of Bulgaria's hesitation and under pressure from the European Commission, which sought to break Gazprom's monopoly, Putin finally abandoned the project in December 2014. It was replaced with TurkStream (another Russia–Turkey pipeline, opened in 2020); in the meantime, Ankara and Moscow maintained privileged relations based on their common irritation with EU policy and their partial overlapping interests in the Syrian theater.

The pipeline's completion represented a crucial bargaining chip in the ongoing struggle between the EU and Russia over Ukraine. Given the decline in EU purchases of Russian gas, the pipeline would eventually allow Russians to completely avoid transit through Ukraine.[29] Deprived of this asset, the importance of which was seen during the "gas wars," Kyiv would either have to comply with future tariff conditions imposed by Gazprom or look for other suppliers, which would push the country's weakened economy into an even more critical situation. The onset of war in 2022 dramatically reshaped this strategy, as discussed in the next chapter.

Meanwhile, another actor became involved in this battle of pipelines and export routes: China. Long absent from regional interactions except for some trade with the Central Asian states, Beijing made a notable entrance by negotiating purchases of oil and the construction of the first oil pipeline with Kazakhstan (opened in 2005) and a gas pipeline with Turkmenistan (2009).[30] This was a decisive step for these countries, which were offered an alternative export route that allowed them to overcome Moscow's hitherto near-monopoly. China gradually became Central Asia's main trade partner and gained growing influence even in the South Caucasus. This continental competition will shape the coming decades: in 2013, Beijing launched its own "New Silk Road" project, later renamed the Belt and Road Initiative, which aims to completely reshape the transportation networks between the Asia-Pacific region and Europe. Russia, which has for more than twenty years emphasized its desire to dynamize the Trans-Siberian Railway and revive the Northern Sea Route for shipping via the Arctic Ocean, will have no other choice than to cooperate with China on Beijing's terms.[31]

## A FAILED STRATEGY IN THE NEAR ABROAD

Russia's role in the post-Soviet space has been at the heart of tensions with the West. Since 1991, all Russian leaders have claimed that the states of the so-called near abroad are the most important element of their country's foreign policy, even if, in reality, priority has often been given to relations with the West. This enduring ambiguity reflects a form of myopia among Kremlin leaders, who have acted as if the relationship with the former Soviet states required no special effort. It was seen as obvious that Moscow would retain a natural influence over these countries' futures given their shared history, geographic proximity, and economic and demographic interconnections. But this task of asserting Russia's dominance over its neighbors, now contingent on a multitude of other partners, would prove much more complicated than what Moscow had expected.

## The CIS: An Ambitious Project with Immediate Divergences

The statements signed at the two summits announcing the dissolution of the Soviet Union and the creation of the CIS appeared to fully satisfy Boris Yeltsin.[32] While the Soviet system was officially abolished, Moscow managed to bring together all the former republics into one organization, the CIS—with the exception of Georgia (which postponed its entry until 1993 and would later withdraw its membership following Russia's invasion of Abkhazia and South Ossetia in 2008) and the three Baltic states, which rejected any association with Russia. The signatories undertook to respect each state's independence, the integrity of their territorial boundaries as they were at the end of the Soviet Union, and the inviolability of their borders. The vague and ambitious final declaration allowed advanced cooperation in a visa-free area, with a common currency (the ruble) and common efforts on major economic and trade decisions. A specific statement provided for the denuclearization of the three states—Belarus, Ukraine, and Kazakhstan—where nuclear weapons were deployed during Soviet times; the states concerned committed to dismantling the weapons or transferring them to Russia.

Yet the signatories' perceptions of the agreements varied. Upon his return to Kyiv on December 8, 1991, after participating in the first meeting and signing of agreements in Minsk, Ukrainian president Leonid Kravchuk stated clearly that he had not signed any commitment restricting the sovereignty of his country, which had just voted in favor of independence in a December 1 referendum. Kravchuk's narrative painted the Minsk agreements as "amicable divorce papers," a label that would stick.[33] In fact, although Moscow produced many more agreements and instruments intended to govern this new community, which Russian leadership hoped would be like a European Union for Eastern Europe and Eurasia, virtually none of the successive agreements forged between 1992 and 1996 were signed by all members. The annual presidents' meetings would come and go, a parliament and many government commissions were created,[34] but parts of the initial commitments were cast aside. Gradually, each state created its own currency and military and charted its own course in policy and external trade.

For the most part, the Kremlin's own strategy was responsible for the failures of the CIS. In January 1992, the Russian government liberalized prices and foreign trade in a unilateral decision made without the consultation required by the agreements, thereby backing its partners into a corner and leaving lasting scars. By the mid-1990s, two groupings of countries had formed within the CIS. For various reasons—the economic dependence and landlocked status of Kyrgyzstan and Tajikistan, and near-landlocked status of Kazakhstan (which borders only the Caspian Sea and what is left of the man-unmade Aral Sea); the trade and security interests of Belarus; and Armenia's quest for an ally in its ethnic-territorial conflict with Azerbaijan—some member states adopted virtually all of Moscow's proposals, which then became the basis for future alliances. But another group, composed of Ukraine, Moldova, Georgia, Azerbaijan and, to a lesser extent, Turkmenistan and Uzbekistan, rejected anything that could be seen as interfering with their sovereignty, especially in matters of security and defense; they constituted a sort of rejectionist front that appealed to the United States and its allies for assistance and advice.

Moscow put forward a multitude of proposed treaties in various domains. Among the most important was the Collective Security Treaty, signed in the Uzbek capital of Tashkent in May 1992. Another was the framework agreement for an economic union, which provided for a single economic space, free movement of goods, and the unification of customs procedures; it was signed by nine states in Moscow in 1993 (Ukraine and Turkmenistan were only associated). The framework was followed in 1994 by an agreement for a free trade area and the creation of the union's first supranational structure, an interstate economic committee headquartered in Moscow, in which Russia would hold 50 percent of the votes and Ukraine 14 percent.

But none of these treaties was ratified by all states, especially in the area of defense, which was the most sensitive issue for the Kremlin. Only ten states signed on to the unified air defense system (Azerbaijan and Moldova did not), and only seven accepted the joint defense treaty for external borders. Uzbekistan, Turkmenistan, Azerbaijan, Moldova, and Ukraine were opposed to the presence of Russian guards on their borders. Georgia's decision to join the Collective Security Treaty in 1994 proved to be an ephemeral victory for Yeltsin. In 1999, Azerbaijan, Georgia, and Uzbekistan decided to leave the Collective Security Treaty Organization (CSTO), which has since consisted of just six states: Russia, Belarus, Armenia, Kazakhstan, Kyrgyzstan, and Tajikistan. (Uzbekistan would rejoin a few years later before withdrawing again shortly thereafter.)

## The Rise of Centrifugal Forces

Although the appearance of centrifugal forces within the CIS was entirely predictable, Russia did not anticipate nor consider it for several years. Each state, once it gained independence, sought to affirm the fundamental elements of its sovereignty: defending its borders, raising an army, adopting a national currency, developing a constitution and set of laws, and choosing the symbolic pillars of its identity and history, its national heroes, and so forth. Each state also had to define its strategic direction given its specific geopolitical environment. One of the first challenges that each of the newly independent states faced was redefining its relationship with the former imperial power. Although the Kremlin sought to use the full range of tools at its disposal—economic levers, demographic realities, and various military and geostrategic pressures—the obvious quickly became apparent: Moscow had lost its monopoly and was no longer the only capital city influencing the near abroad.

Added to this was Russia's lack of experience with managing a multilateral organization. The Kremlin has always preferred bilateral relations, where it excels at making the most of its partners' weaknesses; it has not been inclined to make the sort of compromises and concessions involved in the patient construction of an organization that brings together a large number of independent states, such as the EU. As in the case of price liberalization in 1992, the natural tendency of the Russian leadership was always to impose its decisions on its partners, taking advantage of Russia's objective economic, demographic, and military weight. The most difficult issues of the early 1990s were collectively negotiated, including the denuclearization of Ukraine and the leases of the Sevastopol base in Crimea[35] and the Baikonur Cosmodrome in Kazakhstan.

Thus, in December 1994, after bitter negotiations (with Kyiv pushing for maximum compensation from the United States), a memorandum was signed in the Hungarian capital of Budapest regarding the nuclear weapons stationed in Ukraine. In exchange for dismantling these weapons, Kyiv obtained a guarantee, signed by the United States, Russia, and the United Kingdom, of its territorial integrity, a promise that no economic coercion would be exercised against the country, and substantial financial compensation. An important element of the new security balance, this agreement was followed in 1997, during Yeltsin's first official visit to Kyiv, by the signing of a treaty of friendship and an agreement on the sharing of the Sevastopol base, a large part of which was leased to Moscow to house the Russian Black Sea Fleet. But let there be no mistake, the intervention of US president Bill Clinton in the Budapest negotiations marked a decisive turning point, as Russia could not solve the challenge of negotiating with a reluctant Ukraine alone.

Attempts to contain these centrifugal tendencies quickly appeared within the CIS. Fears that they were seeing the assertion of a "Slavic bloc" centered around Russia led several Central Asian leaders to support the creation of a Central Asian Economic Community in 1994[36]; however, due to the strong rivalry between Kazakhstan and Uzbekistan, this never came to fruition. This was to Moscow's benefit. Proposals that relied on external support tended to have a better chance of success. With five newly independent states speaking Turkic languages (Azerbaijan and Central Asian countries with the exception of Tajikistan), Turkey sought to create a federation in the hope of achieving Ankara's dream of pan-Turkism and becoming a regional player. The establishment in Istanbul in June 1992 of the Black Sea Economic Cooperation area (BSEC) symbolized Turkey's vision.

The BSEC brought together eleven states, including, first, the littoral states of Russia, Ukraine, Moldova, Bulgaria, Romania, and Georgia. Turkey insisted on including Azerbaijan even though it did not share a Black Sea border; in exchange, Russia obtained the membership of Armenia and Greece. This cooperative organization was modeled on the Council of Baltic Sea States, which had been established with ten members, including the three Baltic states and Russia, in 1992. For its part, even before launching its neighborhood policy, the EU created a series of Euroregions spanning several states, such as the "Northern Dimension," which included the Scandinavian countries, the Baltic countries, and Russia or the "Dniepr," including regions from Belarus, Ukraine, and Russia.

The United States' role, which grew during the mid-1990s, came to be decisive in this process. As already noted, Washington played a major part in the negotiations with Kyiv and in organizing the "rejectionist front" of GUAM, born in response to Russia's manipulation of local conflicts. The increased US presence was part of the broader decoupling strategy mentioned above. On Russia's southern flank, this action would be formalized in 1999 with the US Congress's adoption of the Silk Road Strategy Act, which offered aid and financial assistance (including for military purposes) to all of the states of the South Caucasus and Central Asia. One aspect of this proactive policy was that it opened up these two regions through the creation of a series of transportation routes that bypassed Russia. The US military made its first appearance in the Caucasus in 2002 when, as part of the Second Chechen War, Putin threatened to intervene in the Pankisi Gorge, a Georgian region populated by Kists (an ethnic group related to the Chechens) that was hosting fighters from the north. To counter this threat, Georgian president Eduard Shevardnadze invited a group of US instructors to advise his army.[37] As an expression of gratitude, in 2003 Georgia became a member of the "coalition of the willing" that supported the US invasion of Iraq.

## Exacerbating Tensions: From the "Color Revolutions" to Crimea's Annexation

The early 2000s saw a rise in tensions throughout the CIS. One primary cause was Putin's much more offensive discourse. Another was the Second Chechen War, which caused a surge of Western criticism over Moscow's policy. Yet another factor was the shock of the September 11 terrorist attacks and their aftermath, including the resurgence of US military activity, which led to a series of swings in the geopolitical orientation of the post-Soviet space. To support their intervention in Afghanistan, the Americans established air bases in Central Asia. In so doing, they relied on the increasing irritation of local leaders toward Moscow, thereby taking advantage of their isolation and these countries' hopes of diversifying their alliances. Initially, Putin reluctantly accepted the opening of US bases in Uzbekistan (Khanabad) and Kyrgyzstan (Manas), but both Moscow and Beijing would later pressure local leaders to renege on those deals.

There was also increased mobilization of pro-Western forces in several states in the region, with the undisguised support of the European Union and the United States. This culminated in the "color revolutions," a generic term given to a series of similar street revolts that began with the overthrowing of Serbian president Slobodan Milošević in 2000. The Rose Revolution in Georgia between November 2003 and January 2004 led to the resignation of Eduard Shevardnadze and the election of Mikheil Saakashvili, a libertarian and pro-Western politician. After several dramatic twists, the Orange Revolution in Kyiv led, in December 2004, to the election of Viktor Yushchenko, the purportedly pro-Western opponent of the Putin-backed candidate Viktor Yanukovych. Finally, the Tulip Revolution in March 2005 led to the resignation of Kyrgyz president Askar Akayev, who fled to Moscow. Extensive literature has already been devoted to these events.[38]

All the popular mobilizations were primarily expressing the population's massive rejection of corrupt elites who had taken advantage of the ongoing liberal reforms to capture much of their respective nations' wealth and manipulate elections to maintain their grip on power. But it would be wrong to underestimate the supporting role played by outside organizations. Within the EU, several governments openly provided assistance: the Baltic states and Poland campaigned for the rapid integration of Georgia and Ukraine into the EU and NATO, for example. On the US side, a series of official and unofficial channels were used to organize and finance networks that were hostile to Russian influence, favorable to the proposals of President George W. Bush, and supportive of these countries' accession to NATO and integration into the European space. For Washington, the decoupling of "sensitive countries" from Moscow was considered key to permanently weakening Russian pretensions.

Nevertheless, it is essential to make several observations. The first concerns the Kremlin's misinterpretation of the nature of these crises. In Moscow's view, color revolutions stemmed primarily from the intervention of outside forces manipulated by Washington—whether indirectly via NGOs such as the Soros-led Open Society Foundations, or directly with the systematic involvement of diplomats and advisers from various US and European entities. Obviously, Putin does not admit that popular majorities can question the powers that be. For him, these revolutions reflect Western will: "One state and, of course, first and foremost the United States, has overstepped its national borders in every way. This is visible in the economic, political, cultural and educational policies it imposes on other nations."[39] Here we observe the significance of conspiracy theories in Russia but also a hollow reading of how Russian leadership perceived the evolution of post-Soviet societies. Moscow largely neglected the genuine democratic aspirations and criticisms of the oligarchic system that had developed in almost all other CIS countries, as well as the profound rejection of various aspects of Russian policy in many of these states.

Second, we need to make note, too, of some misinterpretations made by the West, especially the United States. Indeed, US strategists neglected two points that would later prove decisive: the fragility and complexity of these societies after the collapse of the Soviet Union, particularly due to internal ethnic tensions and regional contradictions, and Moscow's capacity to respond within its sphere of strategic interest.

Russian leadership first reacted by tightening economic relations with states that were trying to escape its grip. With Ukraine, this took the form of what were called the "gas wars." The mechanism is quite simple and based on the real interdependence that binds the two countries. In the 1990s, Ukraine depended almost entirely on Russia for its supply of hydrocarbons. In turn, Russia depended on its neighbor for the transit of about 70 percent of the gas it delivered to various European countries. Early on, trouble emerged between the two forced partners. Moscow deliberately offered Kyiv a permanent discount on gas as compared to global prices (see table 6.1) but made this "friendly" arrangement contingent, in part, on control over Ukraine's policy decisions. Specifically, the Kremlin not only expected that Kyiv would subscribe to the various treaties proposed within the CIS framework but also that Ukrainians would sell Russia some essential elements of their energy infrastructure (pipeline and gas distribution networks, refineries, and power plants), which Kyiv consistently refused to do. In turn, the Ukrainian leadership made the most of their situation by taking a portion of the gas in transit for their own use and exporting a portion of what they received at a discount

Table 6.1.   Price of Russian gas to CIS members (US$ per 1,000 m3)

|          | 2005 | 2008    | 2009      |
|----------|------|---------|-----------|
| Ukraine  | 50   | 179.5   | 201–450** |
| Belarus  | 47   | 119–128*| 140–240** |
| Moldova  | 80   | 188–280*| 160–260** |
| Armenia  | 54   | 110     | 165**     |
| Georgia  | 64   | 280     | 280       |

*Price range over the year
**Price during negotiations
Source: Kommersant Vlast,' January 19, 2009.

to pay off substantial debts. One particularly opaque aspect was that these markets were also a major source of enrichment for Ukrainian oligarchs who were the trading partners of Russian companies.

After the Orange Revolution, relations between Ukraine and Russia soured. The first conflict began in March 2005 and came to a head in January 2006, as Gazprom refused to supply Ukrainian pipelines due to disagreements over the transit price, causing a knock-on energy crisis in several European countries. Similar conflicts arose in the subsequent years, and Kyiv and Moscow each sought to take the other to the European Commission. Moldova and Georgia, two states seeking to move closer to the EU and NATO, would in turn suffer from Russian sanctions when Moscow banned two of their main exports, mineral water and wine.

In addition, Moscow reacted politically. In a famous speech delivered at the annual Munich Security Conference on February 10, 2007, Putin gave his interpretation of these events.[40] He railed against what he called the "unipolar world" that the United States wanted to impose, citing the "unilateral actions" taken by the country, which were "often illegitimate" (that is, when not approved by the UN Security Council). He accused US leaders of breaking the promises given in 1990 by James Baker, then US secretary of state, who promised Gorbachev that "not an inch of NATO's present military jurisdiction will spread in an eastern direction," or in the words of the West German statesman Manfred Wörner, then NATO general secretary, who said more narrowly, "The very fact that we are ready not to deploy NATO troops beyond the territory of the Federal Republic gives the Soviet Union firm security guarantees."[41] Putin went on to discuss the role of NGOs, saying their interference "does not contribute at all to the maturation of genuinely democratic states, but makes them dependent, resulting in economic and political instability."[42]

President George W. Bush's team ignored these warnings. At the NATO summit in the Romanian capital of Bucharest in April 2008, the United States pressured its European allies to endorse Georgia and Ukraine in joining

NATO. The vetoes of France and Germany blocked this process, but the final declaration states very clearly: "NATO welcomes Ukraine's and Georgia's Euro Atlantic aspirations for membership in NATO. We agreed today that these countries will become members of NATO."[43] This was the worst decision: to promise eventual membership without committing any protection. Putin was furious. According to the Russian press, he declared, "Ukraine is even not a state! What is Ukraine? Part of its territory is Central Europe, the other part, the most important part, we gave it!"[44]

From then on, mutual perception deteriorated rapidly on both sides.[45] In Georgia, the West supported Mikheil Saakashvili's ultraliberal reforms and anti-Russian rhetoric without reservation, while ignoring his increasingly frequent meddling in the media and action against opposition forces. Provocations and hostile gestures multiplied on both sides, particularly around the two breakaway regions of Abkhazia and South Ossetia. Although the US State Department warned the Georgian president about the consequences of direct action, other US entities persuaded him that he could retake by force a part of South Ossetia where many Georgians still lived. According to Gerard Toal, on the eve of the Russo-Georgian War, there were 130 American advisers in the Ministry of Defense in Tbilisi.[46]

As one American analyst commented, Saakashvili was not given the green light, but he was not really given a red light either. On the night of August 8, 2008, while Putin was in Beijing for the opening of the Olympics, Saakashvili launched what would become a catastrophic military operation. Long prepared for such a scenario, the Russian Army intervened and effectively occupied the western third of the country.[47] Following EU intervention, the war stopped, but the damage was done. Georgia lost control of the two regions, and Moscow recognized their independence on August 26. For the first time, the Kremlin had called into question a neighbor's territorial integrity, breaking one of the foundations of the 1991 Minsk agreements.

The international community condemned this attack on an independent state's sovereignty, a gesture that was taken as proof of Moscow's neo-imperialist aims. Significantly, none of the other members of the CIS recognized the independence of the two Russian-backed regions. Paradoxically, the EU did not see all the implications of this event, and several of its members, underestimating Putin's determination, led the European Commission toward further integration of Ukraine into the EU in parallel with considering its accession to NATO. As part of the neighborhood policy put forward in 2003, Poland, the Baltic states, and several Scandinavian countries supported the creation of an "Eastern Partnership" in 2009 and then pushed for individual EU association agreements with Ukraine, Georgia, and Moldova.[48] The EU association agreement, which included a comprehensive free trade agreement and also opened the door to potential military cooperation with

European armies, immediately drew objections from Moscow, which pointed out that its adoption would jeopardize economic agreements within the CIS and trigger a thorough review of agreements with Kyiv. Still, the European Commission refused to consider three-way negotiations on the new agreement, saying it was not Russia's concern.

What followed is well known. Facing an impossible choice between two partnerships that were both essential to the Ukrainian economy, in November 2013, President Viktor Yanukovych canceled the signing of Ukraine's EU association agreement in the Lithuanian capital of Vilnius. Massive protests in Kyiv, led by the pro-Western part of the population and the Ukrainian nationalist movement, and supported by many Western leaders, precipitated several bloody clashes and Yanukovych's flight to Russia. Putin capitalized on the crisis to seize Crimea in February 2014, formally annexing it in March, and to support the separatist forces in eastern Donbas, plunging the country and all of Europe into crisis.

For a second time, the Kremlin had changed the borders of a sovereign state while rejecting Western criticism as the manifestation of a double standard in light of the West's recognition of Croatian and Slovenian independence in 1991, which ended Yugoslavia's existence; and the independence of Kosovo from Serbia in 2008.[49] Following Georgia, which had left the CIS in September 2008, Ukraine announced its formal withdrawal from the organization in 2018. An increasing number of voices within Russia itself came to question the value of keeping the organization going, since it was down to nine official members and had never really been effective.

## Disorderly Russian Attempts at Rearranging the Eurasian Space

Aware of the pressures and resistance to reform within their sphere of influence, Russia's leaders tried to respond to the disintegration of the post-Soviet space. But the proliferation of parallel and competing proposals left feelings of hesitation and weakness. As Moscow oscillated between declarations of having a balanced and mutually beneficial partnership, versus the temptation to impose its own vision on its near abroad, it seemed unable to convey a clear strategy in its relations with its neighbors. Russian leaders again tried to use CIS instruments and agreements to their advantage, multiplying technical treatises and trade agreements, lengthening the duration of the "leases" on concession bases, and holding a rotating presidency for the organization, none of which increased the organization's effectiveness.[50] More paradoxically, they proposed, even within the CIS, different types of nested associations, expanding the nature of reciprocal commitments. There is no need to detail each of these associations, some of which never existed except on paper; but the mere mention of them demonstrates the Kremlin's strategic embarrassment at its having to invent a genuine regional policy.

The first example seems circumstantial. In 1996, on the campaign trail for his difficult re-election against a Communist candidate, Yeltsin launched the Union of Sovereign Republics with Belarusian president Alexander Lukashenko. The union's Russian acronym (SSR) brought to mind a draft reconstruction of the Soviet Union (the USSR, in English—or SSSR, in Russian), suggesting that it might be a purely electoral maneuver for the Yeltsin government to capture nostalgic voices. But in 1997, the two presidents signed a Russian–Belarusian Union Treaty that consisted of a political integration program, ultimately providing for a shared parliament, president, currency, borders, and defense strategy. When he came to power, Putin seemed embarrassed by this union with Belarus and its capricious president, but he maintained the association and would later deepen it further. Despite the ups and downs caused by the Belarusian president, the saga of this union has continued under Putin, up to and including the latter's unwavering support for his counterpart in Minsk during the protests following the rigged elections of 2020. But perhaps the Kremlin was already considering the prospect of an operation in Ukraine, in which, as we know, Russian military passage through Belarusian territory would play an important initial role.

Since then, Putin has attempted to create a real customs union. In 2000, the CIS union became the Eurasian Economic Community (EEC). The distribution of voting rights ensured Russia's dominance (40 percent), with the other members sharing the rest (Belarus and Kazakhstan had 20 percent of the votes each, while Kyrgyzstan and Tajikistan received 10 percent each). However, it is clear that, in the Kremlin's view, this type of enhanced economic cooperation—ultimately leading to a single customs and fiscal space and an integrated value-added tax (VAT)—could not succeed without Ukraine, which remained a key partner for Russia in many areas, including the military-industrial complex. Thus, in 2003, a new union of Russia, Ukraine, Belarus, and Kazakhstan—the Common Economic Space—was announced, but it failed. Reflecting on this, in 2010, Putin revived a version of the customs union—with Russia, Kazakhstan, and Belarus—within the Eurasian Economic Community and called it the Eurasian Economic Union. Despite considerable pressure, Ukrainian president Viktor Yanukovych refused to join and, following the 2014 crisis, the issue became moot.

Russia therefore had to constrain its ambitions and return to an old proposal from Kazakh president Nursultan Nazarbayev. On January 1, 2015, it announced the official launch of the Eurasian Economic Union (EEU) between Belarus, Kazakhstan, Kyrgyzstan, and Armenia (Tajikistan has since been a prospective member). This new form of intra-CIS cooperation is certainly the best-planned and most elaborate free-trade project initiated by Russia since 1991.[51] But even setting aside the absence of Ukraine, many Russian experts doubt its effectiveness. Contrary to Moscow's wishes, the union never became political but remained strictly economic, and Russian leadership has never agreed to play by rules of reciprocal and shared interdependence.

The difficulty in constructively organizing the post-Soviet space is one of the major failures of Russia's foreign policy. It indicates a persistent inability to implement a new type of relationship with the independent former Soviet republics and to move away from a colonial mindset. On this point, the Kremlin remains ambivalent. Although Russian leaders say they recognize the former Soviet states' independence, they are obviously setting an essential condition: that these states cannot enter into any coalitions, particularly NATO, that might undermine Russian security.

This policy gives the image, formed over centuries, of an imperial power not interested in equal relations with its periphery. Whatever name one gives to these Eurasian regions—"buffer zone," "security space," "sphere of interest"—Russia can only imagine submissive neighbors, vassals with whom one makes a contract of alliance, or enemies that must submit. However, while conflicts on its borders have multiplied, Russia's vision has only reinforced its partners' distrust and encouraged them to seek actors from outside the CIS to counterbalance the pressures coming from their large neighbor. Moreover, Russia's Eurasian rhetoric is paradoxical for its domestic audience, as Russian society is rife with xenophobic reflexes, and public opinion demands the closing of Russia's eastern and southern borders, or at least a greater control of migration flows (even if the main migrant-sending countries are outside the Eurasian Economic Union, namely, Uzbekistan and Tajikistan).

The series of tensions and crises in the post-Soviet space has generated a great deal of commentary. While one can legitimately be impressed by the peaceful nature of the breakup of the Soviet Union, especially compared to that of Yugoslavia, it is now clear that the aftershocks of this rupture are far from over. Before the 2022 full-scale war, the two main failures, the war in Georgia in 2008 and the first round of the war in Ukraine in 2014, could be seen through the prism of shared responsibility by Russia, the West, and local actors' own agendas.[52] The Western side certainly underestimated the consequences of Russia's temporary weakening, and some states thought they could use this to permanently reduce Moscow's influence. The Western policy of accelerating the democratic transition of several of these countries without truly analyzing their internal complexity or the lessons of history and geography raises questions about the limits of Western interference strategy as a whole. But this series of crises also highlighted Russia's failure to establish constructive relations with its immediate neighbors. The full-scale aggression against Ukraine since February 2022 changes the perspective, confirming Moscow's neo-imperial aspirations and altering the debate on the instruments of power envisaged by the Kremlin.

## RUSSIA'S NEW GLOBAL PRESENCE

If its relationships with the West and with the post-Soviet space have been central in Russia's foreign policy, Moscow has rapidly perceived the importance of new emerging countries and their potential role in redistributing the balance of power on the international scene. By stressing the need for a multipolar world, and by developing networks with what we call today the Global South (see Putin's travels on map 6.1), Russia has tried to take the lead in some of these efforts. Since the mid-2000s, Moscow has developed a genuine global outreach to Asia, Africa, Latin America, and the Middle East,[53] a strategy that is now consolidated with the decoupling from the West, leaving the Global South as Russia's main theater of influence.

### Moscow's Own "Pivot to Asia"

Presented as a by-product of the 2014 Ukrainian crisis, Russia's "Asia pivot" has in fact been one of the strategic pillars of Russian policy since Gorbachev's speech in Vladivostok in 1986 that reengaged the Soviet Union with Asia. The anomaly was the earlier situation, prior to 1986, in which Soviet Russia virtually abandoned any policy on its Pacific coast despite economic and strategic issues in this region. On behalf of the Soviet Union, Gorbachev began talks with Chinese leaders to normalize diplomatic and commercial relations, reopen border crossings for trade, and resume negotiations on the border dispute along the Amur River in the Far East. Yeltsin concluded a new border treaty in 1996, which Putin finalized in 2004 by handing over a dozen islands along the Amur River and half of Bolshoi Ussuriisk Island, near the city of Khabarovsk, thus ending the forty-year dispute. Relations between the two great Asian neighbors were finally significantly expanded, and by 2010, China had become Russia's single largest trading partner.

Although relations with Beijing are now an essential component of the Kremlin's foreign policy, Moscow has been careful not to trap itself in a bilateral relationship that still arouses many fears. While accelerating Russo-Chinese reconciliation, Putin has sought to develop relations with other Asian countries and to involve Russia as much as possible in all Asia-Pacific regional structures. Moscow became a member of the Asia-Pacific Economic Cooperation (APEC) in 1998 and hosted the annual APEC summit in Vladivostok in 2012. Constant efforts have been made to strengthen diplomatic and economic relations with India, whose border disputes in the

Some components of Russia's Presence Abroad.

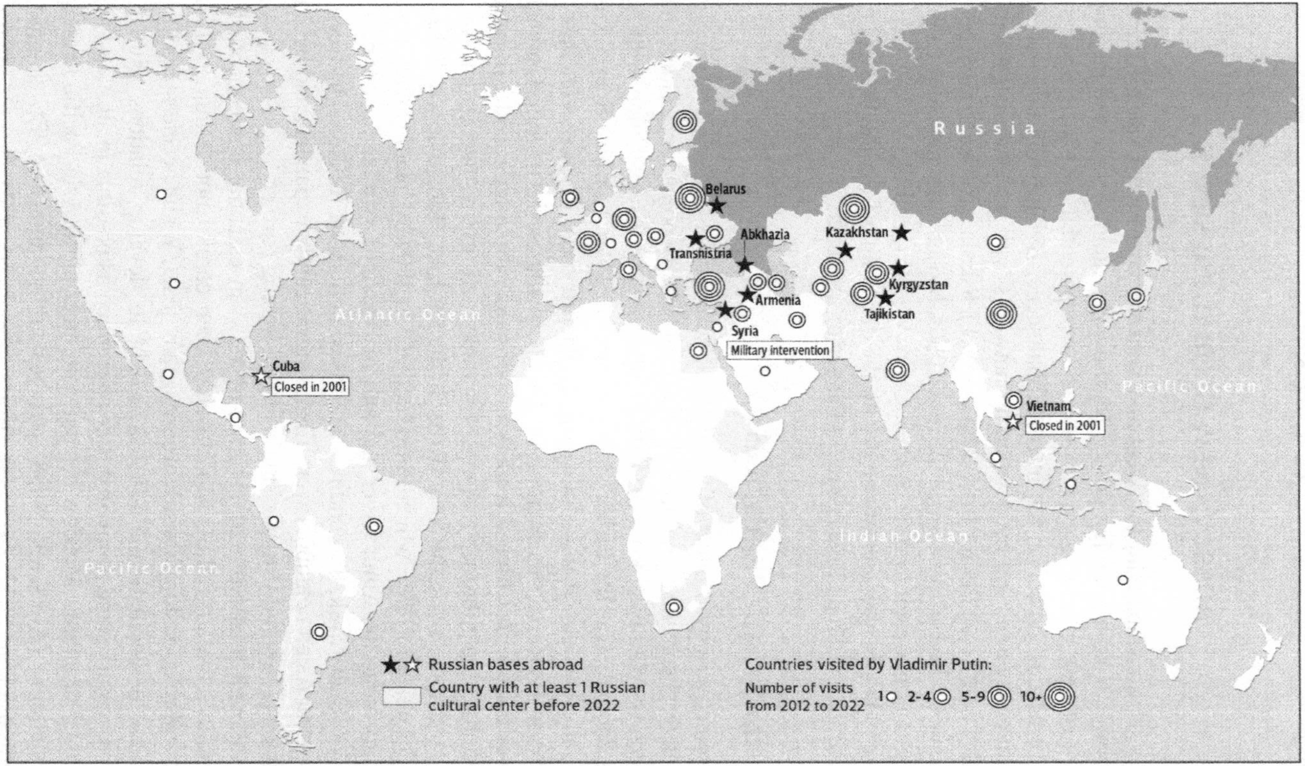

Map 6.1: **Some components of Russia's presence abroad.** *Source:* **http://en.kremlin.ru/events/president/trips.**

western Himalayas with Beijing are well known. In 2000, Putin signed a strategic agreement with New Delhi, and India was invited to participate in the BRIC group at the point of its creation. New relations were also forged with South Korea and the countries of Southeast Asia. From 2000 to 2008, Putin visited China six times and made four visits to India went twice to Japan, South Korea, and Vietnam; and traveled one time each to Australia, Indonesia, Malaysia, and Thailand.

In Asia, the relationship with Japan has remained the most challenging. An end to the conflict over the four southernmost of the Kuril Islands and the signing of a peace treaty with Japan (pending since 1945) would probably prove to be a decisive opening. However, for decades, Japan has insisted on the return of all disputed islands, while Russia—which has at times proposed some form of compromise—has only hardened its position over the last decade, with a 2010 visit from then president Medvedev to the islands and a strengthening of the Russian military presence there.[54] In 2016, however, a joint commission on the economic development and exploitation of the islands was established.[55] The Japanese have been granted visitation rights, but Russia continues to board their fishing vessels, and Japan's implementation of Western sanctions in 2014 and again in 2022 now makes any compromise unlikely.

## From "Yellow Peril" to Strategic Alliance: The Challenges of the Rapprochement with China

Since the conclusion of the first bilateral agreements to open the border, trade relations with China have expanded rapidly. The first to benefit were the "shuttle traders," who carried consumer goods that soon flooded markets in Siberia and the rest of Russia. Chinese merchants appeared in most Siberian cities, as well as in Moscow, and have now spread to every Russian city. This sudden influx of Chinese shoes, leather goods, clothing, and household appliances was one cause of the collapse of Russian light industry. The new presence of the Chinese, the significance of which was exaggerated by the media, also drove the resurgence of the old Russian fear of "yellow peril," the alleged invasion of the country by Asian migrants, an allegation born in the nineteenth century and revived under Khrushchev. Some Siberian leaders invoked this discourse when complaining about the federal center's lack of attention to their concerns. These fears, also found in Moscow, have not prevented bilateral relations from developing in all directions.[56]

The border regions of Siberia and the Far East have become increasingly reliant on Chinese workers and companies, which are given contracts to develop farms, logging, and various other undertakings. Russia has long eyed the Asian market as a destination for its raw materials and hoped to attract

investors to develop mineral deposits in the Far East. Given their desire not
to depend on any single buyer of oil and gas to Russia's east, Russian policy
makers ensured, at least initially, that new pipelines were built not only
toward China but also to the country's Pacific coast, to meet the demands of
other customers, such as South Korea and Japan.

By the late 2000s, the Kremlin had made this a pressure point on Europe,
indicating that if the EU asked for conditions that would limit its purchases
of gas, Russia could replace its European customers with new Asian partners,
a project that the 2022 sanctions have relaunched. But negotiations proved
particularly difficult, with the Chinese seeking to obtain lower prices and
the Russians seeking to impose their usual clauses, long-term delivery contracts, and "take or pay" formula, which requires payment even in the case
of nonpurchase.[57]

Developments in both states have resulted in the rekindling of their relations. Heightened tensions with the EU and NATO have convinced Russian
leaders, now more than ever, to quickly conclude agreements with Beijing.
On the Chinese side, the ambitions of the new leader, Xi Jinping, have facilitated this rapprochement, which has resulted in a record number of bilateral
summits. Putin himself visited China no fewer than eleven times from 2012 to
2022. During his visit to Beijing for the 2022 Winter Olympic Games, just a
few days before the full-scale invasion of Ukraine, the two presidents signed
a long declaration celebrating "the entry into a new era of international relations" and a partnership between them "without limits."[58]

This impressive rapprochement began with an economic aspect. In May
2014, the parties announced their major gas deal, with China pledging to buy
more than thirty-eight billion cubic meters per year over thirty years.[59] And
in 2022, as Western countries were largely disappearing from Russian foreign
trade because of sanctions, its trade with China (as well as with India and
Turkey) reached unprecedented peaks.

It is notable that this cooperation now goes well beyond the simple commercial exchange of commodities for consumer products. This was something Russia wanted; it sought to rebalance its trade with China, one of the
few countries with which it had a trade deficit. Chinese investors have been
invited to intervene in many sectors, including infrastructure (roads, bridges,
and tourism-related infrastructure) in the European part of Russia. In a second
step, the two countries seem to have entered into more in-depth technical
cooperation in the energy, aerospace, automotive, and military-industrial sectors, as in the case of the rescue of the Novatek LNG project on the Arctic,
allowing Russia to partially mitigate the effects of Western sanctions, although
doubts remain about the quality of Chinese technology in these fields.[60]

Many in the West insist on the unequal weight of the two economies and
promise that Russia will be absorbed by its eastern neighbor, which would

only view it as a conveniently placed granary of raw materials. During Xi's visit to Moscow in March 2023, Putin announced an agreement on a new gas pipeline, Power of Siberia 2, going through Mongolia, yet without any precise date for its completion. It seems Beijing is taking full advantage of Russia's weakening to secure its maximum interests. The gap in power with China is indeed growing: whereas China's GDP at purchasing power parity was 58 percent of Russia's in 1991, it has now reached 609 percent, according to the World Bank. Altogether, however, the EU dominated Russian trade until the 2022 decoupling, accounting for 38.2 percent of Russia's exports and 32 percent of its imports in 2021, versus 26.6 percent and 44.7 percent, respectively, for all APEC countries combined (see table 6.2).[61] With the drastic changes in its relations with the EU, Russia will have to rely even more than before on China.

But beyond these economic exchanges, there has been a deepening of political and military cooperation between Moscow and Beijing that is striking in its novelty. Defense experts speculate that the end of Russian military supremacy over China is near, while watching with concern the intensification of technological exchanges between the two national defense industries and the increase in joint maneuvers. The first joint military exercise conducted between the two countries in 2005, Peace Mission, simulated an aerial and naval blockade ending with the amphibious assault on and occupation of a territory. Beijing proposed that it take place in the Taiwan Strait. Moscow declined this suggestion and chose the Shandong Peninsula, which points out into the Yellow Sea toward the Korean Peninsula. Thereafter, these exercises have been held almost every year in one country or the other, and Russia has made clear that it supports China's claims on Taiwan.

Yet China has also refused to fully align itself with Russia in the Ukraine conflict, as can be seen by its abstaining—along with the vast majority of nonmembers of NATO—from voting on UN General Assembly Resolution 68/262, which condemned and declared illegitimate Crimea's independence referendum and subsequent annexation by Russia.[62] Beijing also behaved similarly during the March 3, 2022, vote condemning the full-scale invasion of February 24, 2022, while it has also refused to apply Western sanctions. Although Beijing calls for diplomatic solutions and condemns any possible use of nuclear, chemical, or biological weapons,[63] Xi Jinping still amplifies the majority of Russian arguments about the war and has reaffirmed the "without limits" friendship between the two partners. Not only did bilateral trade between them boom in 2022, with China buying an increased amount of cheap Russian energy, but both countries continue to actively cooperate on many issues—internet control, credit ratings and associated agencies, monetary policy, and some dual-use technologies—where they consider it

Table 6.2. Russia's main trading partners (% of total volume) from 1995 to 2021.

| 1995% total | | 2000% total | | 2010% total | | 2021% Total | |
|---|---|---|---|---|---|---|---|
| Ukraine | 9.5 | Germany | 9.59 | China | 9.49 | China | 17.94 |
| Germany | 8.8 | Belarus | 6.77 | Netherlands | 9.33 | Germany | 7.23 |
| United States | 5.0 | Ukraine | 6.33 | Germany | 8.28 | Netherlands | 5.88 |
| Finland | 3.8 | Italy | 6.18 | Italy | 5.99 | Belarus | 4.91 |
| Kazakhstan | 3.6 | United States | 5.36 | Ukraine | 5.94 | United States | 4.36 |
| Italy | 3.6 | China | 4.52 | Belarus | 4.48 | Turkey | 4.25 |
| Belarus | 3.5 | United Kingdom | 4.04 | Turkey | 4.03 | Italy | 3.95 |
| Netherlands | 3.4 | Poland | 3.77 | United States | 3.76 | South Korea | 3.78 |
| Japan | 3.1 | Netherlands | 3.72 | Japan | 3.70 | United Kingdom | 3.39 |
| China | 3.0 | Kazakhstan | 3.25 | France | 3.60 | Kazakhstan | 3.25 |
| Switzerland | 2.95 | Switzerland | 3.01 | Poland | 3.32 | Poland | 2.85 |
| United Kingdom | 2.9 | Finland | 2.97 | South Korea | 2.83 | France | 2.79 |
| Poland | 2.3 | Turkey | 2.52 | Finland | 2.68 | Japan | 2.51 |
| Ireland | 2.0 | Japan | 2.44 | United Kingdom | 2.54 | India | 1.72 |
| France | 1.8 | France | 2.26 | Kazakhstan | 2.44 | Finland | 1.67 |
| Hungary | 1.8 | Belgium | 2.05 | Switzerland | 1.78 | Ukraine | 1.55 |
| Belgium | 1.6 | Slovakia | 1.63 | India | 1.36 | Belgium | 1.42 |
| Czechia | 1.6 | Sweden | 1.60 | Czechia | 1.35 | Czechia | 0.97 |
| Slovakia | 1.5 | Czechia | 1.54 | Hungary | 1.35 | Brazil | 0.95 |
| Turkey | 1.5 | Cyprus | 1.28 | Belgium | 1.31 | Spain | 0.93 |
| Total Import+Export (billion $) | 142 | | 136.9 | | 625.7 | | 789 |
| among them, EU (% of the total) | 31.1 | | 36.00 | | 49.8 | | 36.2 |
| among them, CIS (% of the total) | 22.7 | | 18.5 | | 14.6 | | 12.2 |

Source: Russian Statistical Yearbook, 2022.

necessary to counterbalance the excessive weight of US and European players, a point that will be revisited in the next chapter.

## Addressing Regional Issues: The Shanghai Cooperation Organization

In 1996, Russia and China created the "Shanghai Group" along with three of the new Central Asian states: Kazakhstan, Kyrgyzstan, and Tajikistan. With the accession of Uzbekistan in 2001, this became the Shanghai Cooperation Organization (SCO; see map 6.2). While the SCO rejects being labeled a military organization, its primary objective has been to ensure the security of all members and protect them from three major risks (the "three evils," in Chinese newspeak): terrorism, separatism, and extremism.

In these years, full of strategic decisions for the Soviet successor states, each of the initial signatories saw advantages in this configuration. All Central Asian states generally wanted to emerge from the burdensome tutelage of their former Russian overlords but were also afraid of falling under the domination of their powerful eastern neighbor. Bringing together these two actors under the banner of a single organization created a reassuring balance. For Russia, this choice allowed Moscow to anticipate the rise of Chinese influence while preserving what it considered essential: maintaining trade and special security relations with Central Asia. For Beijing, which had other priorities in the Pacific region, the SCO allowed it to formally establish high-level relations with its new neighbors while reassuring a suspicious Moscow that, while China would assert a rising economic presence in the region, it would not call into question Russia's role in organizing security as provided for within the Collective Security Treaty Organization (CSTO).[64]

The emphasis on security issues also fits within the logic of a period that saw the rise of secessionist movements in China's northwesternmost province of Xinjiang (Beijing absolutely wants to prevent Uyghur activists from finding refuge with their compatriots in Central Asia) and some incursions into Central Asia of al-Qaeda–influenced groups, such as the Islamic Movement of Uzbekistan. In 2002, these concerns led to the establishment of the SCO's Regional Anti-Terrorism Structure, headquartered in Tashkent, and, since then, some modest joint maneuvers.

At the same time, economic concerns were not absent. The SCO's format has served as a convenient base for the growing presence of Chinese interests in what would, a decade later, become the "New Silk Road." Although Western experts have disparaged the SCO as a mere talk shop, perceptions of the organization have somehow changed as new members have joined, first as observers and then, in the case of India and Pakistan in 2017 or Iran in 2023, as full members.[65] The SCO currently counts nine full member

The Shanghai Cooperation Organization (SCO).

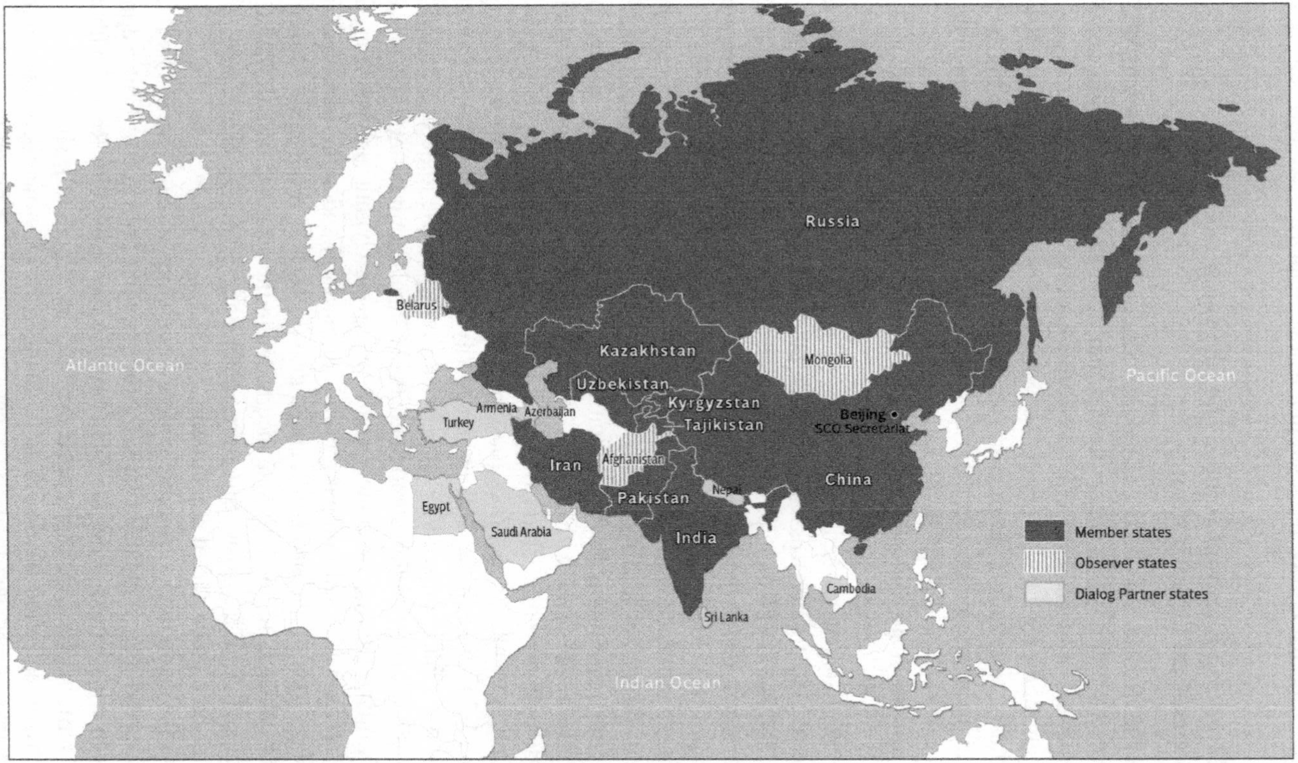

Map 6.2: Shanghai Cooperation Organization (SCO). *Source:* http://eng.sectsco.org.

states, nine "dialog partners" (Sri Lanka, Turkey, Cambodia, Azerbaijan, Nepal, Armenia, Egypt, Qatar, and Saudi Arabia) and four "observer states" (Mongolia, Iran, Afghanistan, and Belarus) in a highly strategic area stretching from the eastern Mediterranean to the western Pacific.

All member states are sensitive to the rise of extremist and terrorist movements, as well as to arms and drug trafficking. Although the Kremlin is broadly satisfied with the actions of the SCO, it shows some signs of concern regarding the slow but noticeable move of China toward increasing military agreements with the Central Asian states. Moreover, the organization has not helped address the tensions that have emerged in recent years between Kyrgyzstan and Tajikistan and between China and India.

## Turkey, Israel, Syria, and Iran: Russia's Complex Game in the Middle East

Russia's direct intervention in the Syrian conflict from September 2015 onward marked a major turning point in the country's foreign policy. As noted, this was the first Russian military action outside the Soviet and post-Soviet space since the war in Afghanistan. Beyond the defense of one of Moscow's most loyal partners in the Middle East and the full-scale testing of new types of weapons, Putin found an opportunity to reaffirm Russia's role as a world power, which he has been claiming for his country since his rise to power. He also saw the chance to make his mark in the complex game that is the Middle East.[66]

In August 2013, a chemical-weapon bombing in Eastern Ghouta, east of the capital city of Damascus, killed hundreds of victims and caused worldwide outrage. The Syrian president, Bashar al-Assad, had crossed the red line set by the United States but, contrary to his stated verbal commitment to take military action against any use of chemical weapons by the Assad regime, President Obama did not intervene. Putin took advantage of this procrastination and proposed a plan to dismantle Syria's chemical arsenal, which was approved by Damascus and Washington. This capitalization on the slightest hesitation on the part of its competitors is typical of Moscow's modus operandi, and it applies to the entire Middle East region, where Russia has in recent decades managed to establish and maintain good relations with practically all the regional players (see map 6.3).

In Syria, the Kremlin primarily defends the only two bases (the Tartus naval base near Lebanon, and the Khmeimim air base, just up the coast toward the border with Turkey) that it enjoys in the Eastern Mediterranean and which constitute fundamental strategic assets. Moscow also defends old half-political, half-trade relations established with Near Eastern countries at the time of decolonization and even during the Tsarist era, especially those

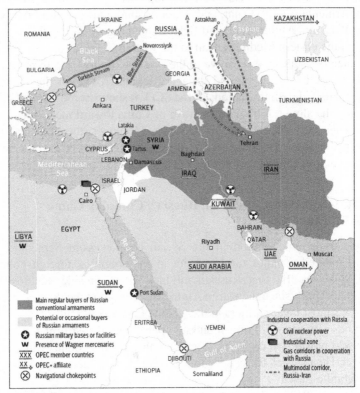

**Map 6.3: Russian presence in the Middle East.** *Sources:* Igor Delanoë, *Russie: Les enjeux du retour au Moyen-Orient; L'inventaire,* 2016; and Russian press.

with a Christian majority or minority. Syria and Egypt are old clients of Russian armaments and civilian equipment. This commercial aspect has only increased with the appearance of new clients, from Turkey and the United Arab Emirates to Iran to Saudi Arabia. Russia also used to be at the heart of the negotiations on Tehran's nuclear policy.

Added to this is Moscow's special role in the great game of hydrocarbons within OPEC+, a grouping that includes all formal Organization of Petroleum Exporting Countries member states plus additional nonmember states in the developing world who often agree to collaborate in boosting global oil prices. This pragmatic alliance between Russia and the Gulf means resisting the expectations of the United States and its allies regarding the volumes of oil put on the market. In this respect, the Kremlin knows exactly how to use the contradictions between the West and its allies in the region. Examples include the criticism leveled by Washington at Saudi crown prince Mohammed bin

Salman in the case of Jamal Khashoggi, the *Washington Post* journalist murdered and dismembered inside the Saudi Consulate in Istanbul, or the authoritarian excesses of Turkish president Recep Tayyip Erdoğan. Finally, there is the religious factor, as Russia presents itself here as an Eastern Christian state, defending Christian communities abused by wars and proposing to restore its protection over the Christians of the East.[67]

In Syria, Russia has succeeded in saving Bashar al-Assad's regime, which is also supported by Iran, from total collapse, while avoiding any direct conflict with Israel, which regularly conducts raids against pro-Iranian forces, or with Turkey, which is trying to reduce the Kurdish territories that have become autonomous on its border with Syria. Russia is thus complicit in the many atrocities that Assad has inflicted on his people. Key cities such as Palmyra, Aleppo, and Deir ez-Zor were taken back by the Assad regime but not without intervention from Russia's air force and special operations troops, including the infamous Wagner private military company. Amnesty International and other observers have accused the Damascus army and its Russian allies of indiscriminately bombing civilian buildings, hospitals, and schools. But unlike the Americans in Iraq or Afghanistan, Russia has been able to disengage relatively easily from this conflict: in late 2017, Russian defense minister Sergei Shoigu announced that most of the troops engaged on Syrian territory had withdrawn, apart from the units needed to operate the Tartus and Khmeimim bases.[68]

Another vector of this Russian search for regional partners is the spectacular renewal of relations with another large neighbor, Turkey. The Russian Empire and the Ottoman Empire fought over the Caucasus and the Black Sea for four centuries. A dozen wars and as many treaties were necessary between 1568 and 1878 to delimit the border between the two empires, and Ankara's admission to NATO in 1952 did not help matters. The rapprochement between the two countries began timidly with the development of commercial relations. In the midst of the Russian–European pipeline wars, in 1997 Yeltsin finalized the agreement that allowed the construction of the first gas pipeline under the Black Sea, Blue Stream (which started operating between Russia and Turkey in 2003), while Ankara favored the construction of the American BTC (Baku-Tbilisi-Ceyhan) oil pipeline project running through the eastern half of its territory and reinforced security measures in the Turkish Straits.[69]

Erdoğan's rise to power in 2003 accelerated this rapprochement, which was fraught with contradictions. In the 2000s, Turkey moved up to seventh place among Russia's bilateral national trading partners. In 2010, during Medvedev's official visit to Ankara, the two countries signed an agreement for the construction of a nuclear power plant in Akkuyu, on the Mediterranean coast directly north of the island of Cyprus, by Russia's Rosatom (construction started in 2018 and is slated for completion in 2023) and for the abolishment of visa requirements for short-term trips. Turkey quickly became the leading destination for Russian tourists abroad. Unquestionably, the proximity of views between Erdoğan and Putin on conservative values and the limited exercise of democracy favors a friendship consolidated by multiple meetings and the common rejection of US pressure in these areas.

This rapprochement, which is cause for embarrassment throughout the rest of NATO, has not been without its share of twists and turns. The Turks have always had important relations with the Abkhazians in Georgia and with the Crimean Tatars, and in both cases, they have strongly criticized Moscow's recognition of Abkhazian independence in 2008 and the annexation of Crimea in 2014. But Russian support for the Turkish president during the July 2016 coup attempt facilitated renewed cooperation, and in 2017 Turkey provoked Washington's fury by announcing the purchase of the Russian S-400 missile defense system. Despite all this, neither of the two states, anxious to consolidate its own regional influence, hesitates to test the limits of the other while taking care not to provoke a definitive rupture.[70]

This marriage of convenience allows for a certain latitude in negotiations with other strategic partners such as the EU or NATO (in the case of Turkey), or China. The Kremlin continues to support the Syrian president to counter Turkish encroachments, and Moscow and Ankara have competing interests surrounding the Nagorno-Karabakh conflict between Armenians and Azeris. The decision, as part of the November 11, 2020 agreement, to reestablish a land route between Azerbaijan and its landlocked exclave of Nakhichevan through Armenian territory, is a victory for Turkey and a weakening of the Russian position in the South Caucasus.

## The New Russian Contest in Africa

Russia has also gradually reconquered some of its vanished Soviet influence in Africa, especially in the French-speaking regions. One of the most visible diplomatic successes of Russia's "return" to Africa was the first Russian-African summit, held in Sochi in collaboration with Egyptian president Abdel Fattah el-Sisi, organized in October 2019. Forty-one African countries were represented, thirteen of them by their head of state or prime minister—a real masterstroke of Russian diplomacy. This success was built on the long-standing relations between the Soviet Union and Africa. After the fall of the USSR, cooperation became rarer, but several Russian companies continued to invest in the mining sector of many sub-Saharan countries. The 2019 summit marked a completely different stage in which Moscow capitalized on the resentment accumulated by some African elites and populations

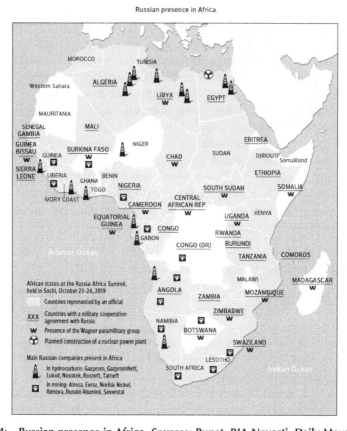

Russian presence in Africa.

Map 6.4: **Russian presence in Africa.** *Sources:* **Runet, RIA Novosti, Daily Maverick.**

against former European colonial powers and their paternalistic relations with the African continent. Even without Washington's or Beijing's financial means, the Russians have not fallen behind.

While most African leaders remain cautious about Moscow's interests, the final declaration calls for the consolidation of cooperation with the BRICS in order to strengthen "the collective mechanisms of global governance within a multipolar system of international relations, with developing countries and emerging market economies playing a significant role."[71] Conflict resolution on the continent must follow the principle of "African solutions to African problems."[72] The declaration also called for "[opposing] political dictatorship and financial blackmail" and rejecting the "extraterritorial application of national law by States in violation of international law"[73]—a clear reference to US policy in this area. As one Moroccan participant stated, "Russia can be for us a partner that restores a balance, more attentive to our specificities, and that gets us out of a closed-door relationship with the West or China."[74]

The situation on the ground grows increasingly tense because the means deployed by France or other traditional partners in the Sahel region (between the Sahara Desert and the rest of the continent), in particular, has failed to stem the pressure of jihadist groups, and several regimes in the region have called on Russian mercenaries from the Wagner Group to secure their territories and regimes: the CAR, Sudan, Mali, and probably Burkina Faso. A recent Russian war film complacently shows the action of mercenaries from the Wagner Group officially charged with training the CAR army.[75] Russian presence is criticized in the West for its multiple interventions in support of authoritarian governments and for the questionable practices of its agents, yet one may wonder if the *Françafrique* acted differently, as it consistently supported notoriously corrupt regimes and rarely succeeded in developing virtuous democratic circles. The Second Russo-African Summit (July 2023) will tell just how consistent this new cooperation is.

## The BRICS and the Search for a New Global Order

Not limiting itself to the relationship with the West, to its dominant role in Eurasia, and to reactivating Soviet-era influences in the Global South, Russia also intends to play a global role, primarily through its active participation in the BRICS.[76] Taking into account their rapid growth, the combined GDP of these "emerging" countries is supposed to equal that of the G7 by 2050, and at purchasing power parity, China already overtook the United States in 2017. The first formal summit of the original four BRIC members was held in Yekaterinburg in 2009. Beyond economic cooperation, the five countries (see map 6.5) agreed to make the BRICS "a large-scale mechanism for intervention on the main issues of the global economy and politics," as formulated by Dmitry Medvedev at the group's New Delhi summit in 2012. The five member states seek to mobilize the "other world" that is excluded from the G7—a position that, obviously, fits very well Russia's situation.[77]

Although recent economic turmoil and COVID-related lockdowns have reduced the BRICS's collective weight on the international economic scene, the agenda they have proposed is vast, and Russian leaders, in cooperation with China, actively promote it. Russia's BRICS policy framework is generally popular in both domestic and non-Western public opinion. Though many of the BRICS's declarations will probably never become realities, long-term global battles are already visible, as demonstrated by Beijing's head-on opposition to the Trans-Pacific Partnership Washington sought to secure while excluding China and Russia. China's counterproposal, the Asian Infrastructure Investment Bank, received support not only from Moscow, but also from several European states (France, Britain, and Germany) despite US opposition.[78]

BRICS.

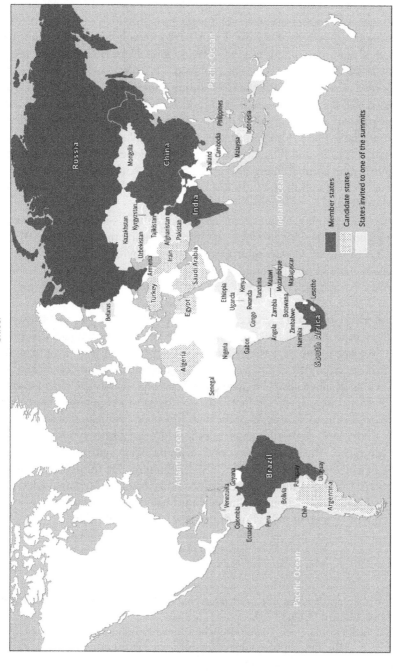

Map 6.5:  BRICS. *Source:* http://infobrics.org.

One of the strengths of the BRICS is the inclusion of partners around the five member states. At meetings, each leader invites other states from its continent in a Global South development format, which offers the possibility of South–South partnerships. From 2017 onward, this approach has been systematized under the formula of BRICS Outreach or BRICS+. The summit that was held by video conference in June 2022 discussed the new tensions that arose as a result of the war in Ukraine and how to adapt to them. Putin stressed that his country was redirecting its foreign trade to "reliable international partners, foremost the BRICS countries."[79] On the eve of the fourteenth summit, the Chinese foreign minister proposed enlarging the group and discussing its norms and procedures, a way to strengthen BRICS representation and influence among emerging and developing countries. Five states have officially expressed their desire to join: Argentina, Iran, Turkey, Egypt, and Saudi Arabia.

While this young organization remains fragile vis-à-vis the G7 and the stranglehold of the United States and its allies on international trade, BRICS, like the Shanghai Cooperation Organization, provides a major avenue for Russia in diversifying its foreign trade, and proof that it may be isolated from the West but not from "the rest."

The world is becoming less centered on the Atlantic Ocean, and Moscow's own "pivot to Asia," although still in its early days, syncs with a wider global shift. Yet one of the core issues for the sustainability of Russia's global outreach is its ability to compensate for the substantial loss of credibility and power that resulted from its invasion of Ukraine, widely criticized even by some of its closest allies. Unquestionably, Russia's foreign policy has become more brittle due to the effects of the war. However, the claim that the Kremlin now finds itself isolated seems questionable, because the issues at stake remain in flux. Russia may be at odds with the West, but its global outreach has not collapsed. The Fifteenth BRICS Summit, set for Johannesburg in August 2023, with Putin's expected attendance having been announced prior to The Hague International Criminal Court having released a warrant for his arrest, will be a good indication of the new global equilibrium.

## NOTES

1. We are not counting the brief intervention of Russian paratroopers at Pristina airport in Kosovo in June 1999.

2. Barack Obama, press conference with Prime Minister Rutte of the Netherlands, March 25, 2014, https://obamawhitehouse.archives.gov/the-press-office/2014/03/25/press-conference-president-obama-and-prime-minister-rutte-netherlands.

3. Mary Elise Sarotte, *Not One Inch: America, Russia, and the Making of Post–Cold War Stalemate* (New Haven, CT: Yale University Press, 2021), 80–81.

4. See the comment on Sputnik News, "Paranoia Over 'Imminent Russian Invasion of Poland' Gives Analysts a Good Laugh," *Sputnik*, July 28, 2016, https://sputniknews.com/politics/20160728/1043716396/analysts-commentary-polish-russian-threat.html.

5. SDC (State Department Cable) 1993-Warsaw-12734, September 1, 1993. Cited by Sarotte, *Not One Inch*, 164.

6. Vladimir Putin, interview by David Frost, *Breakfast with Frost*, BBC, March 5, 2000, http://news.bbc.co.uk/hi/english/static/audio_video/programmes/breakfast_with_frost/transcripts/putin5.mar.txt.

7. James Baker, letter to Helmut Kohl, February 10, 1990. See Sarotte, *Not One Inch*, 365, n. 1.

8. Zbigniew Brzezinski, *The Grand Chessboard: American Primacy and Its Geostrategic Imperatives* (New York: Basic Books, 1998).

9. Maria Repnikova and Harley Balzer, "Chinese Migration to Russia: Missed Opportunities," WWICS *Eurasian Migration Paper*, no. 3 (2010), https://www.wilsoncenter.org/sites/default/files/No3_ChineseMigtoRussia.pdf.

10. Mark Kramer, "The Myth of a No-NATO-Enlargement Pledge to Russia," *Washington Quarterly* 32, no. 2 (April 2009): 39–61, esp. p. 54.

11. Yuri Slezkine, "The USSR as a Communal Apartment, or How a Socialist State Promoted Ethnic Particularism," *Slavic Review* 53, no. 2 (July 1994): 414–52.

12. Gerald Toal, *Near Abroad: Putin, the West and the Contest over Ukraine and the Caucasus* (Oxford: Oxford University Press, 2017).

13. Petr Vail, "Itogi sammita SNG v Kishineve," Radio Svoboda, October 8, 2002, http://www.svoboda.org/a/24193749.html.

14. See the site GUAM Organization for Democracy and Economic Development, http://guam-organization.org.

15. "Russia Says 3 MiG Warplanes with Hypersonic Missiles Moved to Kaliningrad Region- Media," Reuters, August 18, 2022, https://www.reuters.com/world/europe/russia-says-3-mig-warplanes-with-hypersonic-missiles-moved-kaliningrad-region-2022-08-18. See also Frank Tétart, *Géopolitique de Kaliningrad* (Paris: Presses de l'université Paris-Sorbonne, 2007).

16. This facility was closed in 2005 at Moscow's request during the Astana summit of the Shanghai Cooperation Organization (SCO).

17. Isabelle Facon, *La nouvelle stratégie de sécurité nationale de la Fédération de Russie* (Paris: Fondation pour la recherche stratégique, 2016), https://www.frstrategie.org/publications/notes/la-nouvelle-strategie-de-securite-nationale-de-la-federation-de-russie-2016-05.

18. On this complex question, see Stephen Blank, ed., *Russia and the Current State of Arms Control* (Carlisle, PA: Strategic Studies Institute, 2012); from the Russian perspective, Aleksei Arbatov, Vladimir Dvorkin, and Sergei Oznobishchev, eds., *Rossiia i dilemmy iadernogo razoruzheniia*, 2nd ed. (Moscow: IMEMO, Russian Academy of Sciences, 2012).

19. See Jacob W. Kipp, "Russia's Future Arms Control Agenda and Posture," in Blank, ed., *Russia and the Current State of Arms Control*, 1–62.

20. "Voennaia doktrina Rossiiskoi Federatsii," approved by presidential edict February 5, 2010, http://kremlin.ru/supplement/461; "Voennaia doktrina Rossiiskoi Federatsii," approved by presidential edict December 26, 2014, http://kremlin.ru/events/president/news/47334.

21. The list of sixty Russian officials under sanction (visa prohibition) continues the tradition of the Jackson-Vanik amendment, which tied trade with the Soviet Union to the right of Soviet Jews to emigrate.

22. See Eric Ehrmann, "Washington, WikiLeaks and Russian Soft Power," *Russian International Affairs Council*, August 23, 2013, http://russiancouncil.ru/en/blogs/eric-ehrmann/?id_4=628.

23. Richard Sokolsky, "Not Quiet on NATO's Eastern Front," Carnegie Endowment for International Peace, June 29, 2016, http://carnegieendowment.org/2016/06/29/not-quiet-on-nato-s-eastern-front-pub-63984.

24. "Russia Suspends Joint Consultations on Treaty on Conventional Armed Forces in Europe," ITAR-TASS, March 10, 2015, http://tass.com/russia/781973; "NATO Strategic Communications Center Unveiled in Riga," Latvian Public Broadcasting, August 20, 2015, http://www.lsm.lv/en/article/societ/society/nato-strategic-communications-center-unveiled-in-riga.a142243; "NATO Opens Training Center in Georgia," Radio Free Europe/Radio Liberty, August 27, 2015, http://www.rferl.org/a/georgia-nato-training-center/27212128.html.

25. The notion of the Great Game refers to the competition between the Tsarist and British empires in their conquest of Central and South Asia at the end of the nineteenth century. See Vicken Cheterian, *War and Peace in the Caucasus: Ethnic Conflict and the New Geopolitics* (New York: Columbia University Press, 2008); and Maria-Raquel Freire and Roger E. Kanet, eds., *Key Players and Regional Dynamics in Eurasia: The Return of the "Great Game"* (New York: Palgrave, 2010).

26. Susanne Nies, "Nabucco et South Stream: Des gazoducs trop politisés?" Institut Français des relations internationales, January 4, 2008, https://www.ifri.org/fr/publications/editoriaux/edito-energie/nabucco-south-stream-gazoducs-politises.

27. Putin eventually proposed completely ending the export of oil via the Baltic republics' ports by 2018. See Liudmila Podobedova and Natal'ia Derbysheva, "V Pribaltiku ni truboi," RBK, September 12, 2016, http://www.rbc.ru/newspaper/2016/09/13/57d6c5779a7947b83d50f2d3.

28. See the Nord Stream 2 website, https://www.nord-stream.com/ru.

29. Aleksei Topalov, "Obnulit' ukrainskii tranzit," *Gazeta.ru*, January 23, 2015, https://www.gazeta.ru/business/2015/01/22/6383865.shtml.

30. See more in Marlene Laruelle and Sebastien Peyrouse, *The "Chinese Question" in Central Asia: Domestic Order, Social Changes and the Chinese Factor* (London and New York: Oxford University Press and Hurst, 2012).

31. Peter Ferdinand, "Westward Ho: The China Dream and 'One Belt, One Road': Chinese Foreign Policy under Xi Jinping," *International Affairs* 92, no. 4 (2016): 941–57. See also Marlene Laruelle, ed., *China's Belt and Road Initiative (BRI) and Its Impact in Central Asia* (Washington, DC: George Washington University's Central

Asia Program, 2017), http://centralasiaprogram.org/wp-content/uploads/2017/12/ OBOR_Book_.pdf.

32. Yeltsin met with Belarusian president Stanislaw Shushkevich and Ukrainian president Leonid Kravchuk near the Belarusian capital of Minsk on December 8, 1991. The leaders who had not been invited insisted that a second summit be organized in Kazakhstan at Alma-Ata on December 18. Apart from the three already mentioned, representatives also came from Moldova, Armenia, and Azerbaijan as well as the five Central Asian states. No one came from Georgia because its president, Zviad Gamsakhurdia, was overthrown the very same day. Georgia only joined the CIS in October 1993 under Eduard Shevardnadze's presidency.

33. Zbigniew Brzezinski and Paige Sullivan, eds., *Russia and the Commonwealth of Independent States: Documents, Data, and Analysis* (Armonk, NY: M. E. Sharpe, 1997), 41.

34. Yann Breault, Pierre Jolicœur, and Jacques Lévesque, *La Russie et son ex-empire: Reconfiguration géopolitique de l'ancien espace soviétique* (Paris: Presses de Sciences Po, 2003).

35. Begun in 1992, negotiations were concluded in 1997 with the leasing of this strategic base for twenty years; Kyiv reserved for itself the use of one of the base's bays.

36. This was one of the interpretations spread in the Russian newspaper *Izvestiia* on December 9, 1991, under an article titled "Three Slavic Leaders Have Decided the Union's Destiny." The interpretation is easily misleading.

37. "US Army Trainers Land in Georgia," BBC, May 19, 2002, http://news.bbc.co .uk/2/hi/europe/1996833.stm.

38. Katya Kalandadze and Mitchell A. Orenstein, "Electoral Protests and Democratization beyond the Color Revolutions," *Comparative Political Studies* 42 (2009): 1403–25; Joshua Tucker, "Enough! Electoral Fraud, Collective Action Problems, and Post-Communist Colored Revolutions," *Perspectives on Politics* 5 (3): 537–53; Lucan Way, "The Real Causes of the Color Revolutions," *Journal of Democracy* 19, no. 3 (2008): 55–69.

39. Vladimir Putin, speech and following discussion at the Munich Conference on Security Policy, Kremlin, February 10, 2007, http://en.kremlin.ru/events/president/ transcripts/24034.

40. Vladimir Putin, "Vystuplenie i diskussiia na Miunkhenskoi konferentsii po voprosam politiki bezopasnosti," Kremlin, February 10, 2007, http://kremlin.ru/ events/president/transcripts/24034.

41. Manfred Wörner, "The Atlantic Alliance and European Security in the 1990s," address to the Bremer Tabaks Collegium, May 17, 1990, https://www.nato.int/docu/ speech/1990/s900517a_e.htm.

42. Vladimir Putin, "Vystuplenie i diskussiia na Miunkhenskoi konferentsii po voprosam politiki bezopasnosti," Kremlin, February 10, 2007, http://kremlin.ru/ events/president/transcripts/24034.

43. "Bucharest Summit Declaration," NATO, April 3, 2008, https://www.nato.int/ cps/en/natolive/official_texts_8443.htm.

44. "Blok NATO razoshelsia na blokpakety," *Kommersant*, April 7, 2008, https://www.kommersant.ru/doc/877224.

45. Steven Erlanger and Steven Lee Myers, "NATO Allies Oppose Bush on Georgia and Ukraine," *New York Times*, April 3, 2008, http://www.nytimes.com/2008/04/03/world/europe/03nato.html; Paul Gallis, "The NATO Summit at Bucharest, 2008," Congressional Research Service, May 5, 2008, https://www.fas.org/sgp/crs/row/RS22847.pdf; Steven Erlanger, "Georgia and Ukraine Split NATO Members," *New York Times*, October 30, 2008, http://www.nytimes.com/2008/11/30/world/europe/30iht-nato.4.18268641.html; Judy Dempsey, "U.S. Pushing to Bring Ukraine and Georgia into NATO," *New York Times*, November 3, 2008, http://www.nytimes.com/2008/02/13/world/europe/13iht-nato.4.10021504.html.

46. Toal, *Near Abroad*, 160.

47. See the EU's "Tagliavini Report": Independent International Fact-Finding Mission on the Conflict in Georgia, "Report," Vol. 1, September 2009, http://news.bbc.co.uk/2/shared/bsp/hi/pdfs/30_09_09_iiffmgc_report.pdf; Toal, *Near Abroad*.

48. See Pascal Marchand, *Géopolitique de la Russie* (Paris: Presses Universitaires de France, 2014).

49. See, for example, Putin's explicit articulation of this position and these resentments in his "Crimean Speech": Vladimir Putin, "Obrashchenie Prezidenta Rossiiskoi Federatsii," Kremlin, March 18, 2014, http://kremlin.ru/events/president/news/20603.

50. Cooley, *Scripts of Sovereignty*.

51. Piotr Dutkiewicz and Richard Sakwa, eds., *Eurasian Union: The View from Within* (London: Routledge, 2015).

52. Samuel Charap and Timothy Colton, *Everyone Loses: The Ukraine Crisis and the Ruinous Contest for Post-Soviet Eurasia* (London: Routledge, 2017).

53. Paul Stronski and Richard Sokolsky, *The Return of Global Russia: An Analytical Framework* (Washington, DC: Carnegie Endowment for International Peace, 2017), http://carnegieendowment.org/2017/12/14/return-of-global-russia-analytical-framework-pub-75003.

54. See Dmitry Gorenburg, "The Southern Kuril Islands Dispute," PONARS *Eurasia Policy Memo*, no. 226 (September 2012), https://www2.gwu.edu/~ieresgwu/assets/docs/ponars/pepm_226_Gorenburg_Sept2012.pdf.

55. "Rossiia i Iaponiia dogovorilis' o sovmestnom ispol'zovanii Kuril'skikh ostrovov," *Nastoiashchee vremia*, December 15, 2016, http://www.currenttime.tv/a/28178217.html.

56. Marcin Kaczmarski, *Russia-China Relations in the Post-Crisis International Order* (London: Routledge, 2015).

57. Ferdinand, "Westward Ho."

58. Joint Statement of the Russian Federation and the People's Republic of China on the International Relations Entering a New Era and the Global Sustainable Development, http://en.kremlin.ru/supplement/5770.

59. Kira Latukhina, "S gazom!," *Rossiiskaia gazeta*, May 22, 2014, https://rg.ru/2014/05/21/gaz-site.html.

60. Elena Domcheva, "Rossiia naladit innovatsionnoe sotrudnichestvo s Kitaiem," *Rossiiskaia gazeta*, July 9, 2016, https://rg.ru/2016/07/09/rossiia-naladit -innovacionnoe-sotrudnichestvo-s-kitaem.html.

61. "Russia: Trade Statistics," UN Comtrade via GlobalEdge, Michigan State University, https://globaledge.msu.edu/countries/russia/tradestats.

62. "Backing Ukraine's Territorial Integrity, UN Assembly Declares Crimea Referendum Invalid," UN *News Centre*, March 27, 2014, https://news.un.org/en/story /2014/03/464812; Voting Record of "Item 33(b) A/68/L.39 Draft Resolution Territorial Integrity of Ukraine, Resolution 68/262," https://digitallibrary.un.org/record /767565; "UN Security Council Action on Crimea Referendum Blocked," UN *News Centre*, March 15, 2014, http://www.un.org/apps/news/story.asp?NewsID=47362# .WMLR00eltVo.

63. China's Position on Political Settlement of Ukraine Crisis, February 24, 2023, https://news.cgtn.com/news/2023-02-24/Full-text-China-s-Position-on-Political -Settlement-of-Ukraine-Crisis-1hG2dcPYSNW/index.html.

64. Henry Plater-Zyberk and Andrew Monaghan, *Strategic Implications of the Evolving Shanghai Cooperation Organization* (Carlisle, PA: Strategic Studies Institute and US Army War College Press, 2014).

65. With India and Pakistan, the SCO now has eight member states, four observers (Afghanistan, Belarus, Iran, and Mongolia), and six dialogue partners (Armenia, Azerbaijan, Cambodia, Nepal, Sri Lanka, and Turkey).

66. Marlene Laruelle, "Russia at War and the Muslim World," *Russie.NEI. Visions*, no. 127, Ifri, January 2023, https://www.ifri.org/en/publications/notes-de-lifri/russia -war-and-islamic-world.

67. Iurii Bogdanov and Mikhail Moshkin, "Rossiia trebuiet zashchity khristian na Blizhnem Vostoke," *Vzgliad*, April 6, 2015, https://vz.ru/politics/2015/4/6/738064 .html.

68. "Shoigu dolozhil Putinu o vyvode voisk iz Sirii," RIA Novosti, December 22, 2017, https://ria.ru/20171222/1511531277.html.

69. The Turkish Straits, consisting of the Dardanelles to the southwest and the Bosporus to the northeast, link the Mediterranean to the Black Sea. They are governed by the Montreux Convention (1936), which ensures the free movement of commercial ships but introduces specific conditions for military ships or the fleets of states not bordering the Black Sea.

70. Iliya Kusa, "Russia's Turkey Foreign Policy Objectives," *Focus Ukraine* (blog), Kennan Institute, Wilson Center, September 7, 2022, https://www.wilsoncenter.org/ blog-post/russias-turkey-foreign-policy-objectives.

71. "Deklaratsiia pervogo sammita Rossiia—Afrika," Kremlin, October 24, 2019, http://kremlin.ru/supplement/5453.

72. "Deklaratsiia pervogo sammita Rossiia—Afrika," Kremlin, October 24, 2019, http://kremlin.ru/supplement/5453.

73. "Deklaratsiia pervogo sammita Rossiia—Afrika," Kremlin, October 24, 2019, http://kremlin.ru/supplement/5453.

74. Vitkine, "À Sotchi, la Russie se pose en défenseure."

75. *The Tourist*, directed Andrei Batov (2021), was shot entirely in the CAR. According to several sources, it was financed by the Russian oligarch Yevgeny Prigozhin, godfather of the Wagner Group.

76. Jim O'Neill, "Building Better Global Economic BRICs," Global Economics Paper No. 66, Goldman Sachs, November 30, 2001, https://www.goldmansachs.com/insights/archive/archive-pdfs/build-better-brics.pdf.

77. Recall that Russia, invited to join the G8 in 1997, was expelled from it in 2014. It is remarkable that when the Australian prime minister (a member of the G7) wanted to exclude Russia from the G20 summit in Brisbane in November 2014, he was confronted by a general outcry from "emerging nations" that forced him to backpedal.

78. Brice Pedroletti, "La Chine façonne son nouvel ordre mondial," *Le Monde*, January 9, 2015, http://www.lemonde.fr/asie-pacifique/article/2015/09/01/la-chine-faconne-son-nouvel-ordre-mondial_4742315_3216.html.

79. Ignat Dalakian, "Putin zaiavil, chto RF aktivno zanimaietsia pereorientatsiei ekonomicheskikh potokov na nadiozhnykh partnyorov," *Zvezda*, June 22, 2022, https://tvzvezda.ru/news/20226221445-VtyAl.html.

# 7

# Russia and the World
# in a Time of War

## *Besieged Fortress and New Crusader*

Until the Russo-Ukrainian War, Western perspectives on Russian foreign policy could roughly be divided into two points of view. Some saw a country in decline, one that has failed to integrate into the Western world and has missed the chance to fundamentally reform. Such a country has no choice but to take refuge in militarist and nationalist withdrawal and engage in aggression toward its neighbors. Others saw a changing country engaged in a conservative and authoritarian way that was still battling with its past and managing thirty years of unprecedented societal ruptures. Seeking its place in the world, this country was not satisfied with following rules that it believes others have developed to serve their own interests and dreamt of shifting the modus operandi of the international community, without knowing if it will fail or succeed. With the war, a large portion of Western narratives radicalized to describe Russia as a new evil empire. The war has been depicted as a battle between good and evil, democracy and totalitarianism, enlightenment and darkness.[1] A small minority of observers think, on the contrary, that the war launched by Moscow is the product of three decades of misunderstandings and of systemic imbalances in the world order.[2]

This dual image of Russia, produced in the West, is quite symmetrical to the depiction the Russian media and the Kremlin themselves produce. They present Russia to their own public as a besieged fortress that has no other choice but to defend itself against the coordinated attacks of its internal and external enemies and would otherwise want nothing more than to be left in peace. At the same time, they show Russia as a conquering country, taking steps that wreak havoc on the "political correctness" of the international community, offering alternatives to the failures of the West, and building a new world order that will rebalance power in favor of emerging players. It is interesting to note that Western, especially US, and Russian discourses, ignorant of one another, still mirror each other.[3]

A critical component of this discussion relies on how we interpret the interaction between Russia and the West. Is Russia's trajectory on the international scene the product of a predestined path resulting from its past or the careers of its leaders, or has it been developing in tenuous interaction with the way the Russian leadership interpreted the West's own actions? While they cannot justify the full-scale war launched by Putin in February 2022, decisions made *outside* Russia may have been as important as any internal predestination of the regime.

## RUSSIA'S TOOLKIT OF POWER, HARD AND SOFT

Like any state that claims to play a major international role, and similar to the Soviet Union before it, Russia uses the full range of tools available to it to project power. The Soviet authorities never hesitated to deploy military means to defend strategically important areas of the empire, as seen in Eastern Europe (Budapest in 1956 and Prague in 1968) and Asia (the Soviet–Chinese conflict over the Amur River boundary in 1969 and the invasion of Afghanistan in 1979). They also excelled in the use of propaganda, carefully presenting their achievements in all areas in order to attract foreign sympathizers well beyond Communist circles and mastering a kind of soft power long before the term came into common usage.

In this sense, the 1990s marked a break. Preoccupied with other foreign and domestic concerns, and limited by the country's impoverishment, the new Russian leaders seemed to abandon the previously vaunted merits of foreign policy planning. Even before the Soviet Union collapsed in late 1991, Moscow had to abandon some of the symbols of its power. The fall of the Berlin Wall in 1989 and the dissolution of the Warsaw Pact in 1991 were followed by other setbacks. The repatriation of Soviet troops from East Germany and other socialist states, the loss of the Baltic states, and the closure of bases at Lourdes in Cuba and Cam Ranh in Vietnam in 2001 are milestones that mark the loss of a strategic system that had been organized over the course of the twentieth century, as well as the weakening of Moscow's role as a global superpower. For over twenty-five years, from Gorbachev to Medvedev, Moscow's policy was almost exclusively oriented toward Europe and the Atlantic, but its immediate scope was singularly limited to the post-Soviet space. Around Putin's third term, the Kremlin moved toward a more global outreach, gaining in influence in several parts of the world.

## Modernizing the Army

First the Kremlin had to perform a drastic reset of its own armed forces. The two Chechen Wars and the Russian–Georgian conflict in 2008 highlighted the weaknesses of a bloated army often equipped with obsolete weapons. Its structural defects have long been known: a command imbalance with a lack of junior officers that facilitates the mistreatment of conscripts (*dedovshchina*), and units plagued by corruption and irresponsibility, causing the proliferation of serious incidents such as explosions on military bases.[4] Even the nuclear forces are implicated, as illustrated by the *Kursk* submarine accident in 2000 and repeated failures in the development of the Bulava missile and the GLONASS program (intended to compete with the American GPS).

From 2008 onward, Putin has undertaken comprehensive reforms to upgrade the entire Russian military. He greatly increased the defense budget and brought order to the military-industrial complex to secure his country's place in the international arms trade. He also fundamentally changed the territorial and operational organization of the troops to a more professional, better-paid, and better-equipped army.[5] While Russia continues to lag behind in areas such as surface ships, drones, and automated control systems, it remains ahead of NATO in anti-ship missiles, ground-based antiair defense, and the nuclear sector, both military and civilian, and it is narrowing the gap in areas such as precision-guided munitions.[6]

The Syrian intervention helped a Russian army in full transformation to experiment firsthand on a real war theater: according to defense minister Sergey Shoigu, about 90 percent of Russian officers and equipment saw at least one rotation in Syria, and new armaments types, such as Kalibr cruise missiles, were tested in real-world conditions.[7] In some ways, the demonstration of force in Syria was intended to show NATO leaders that the Russian military was ready to fulfill commitments beyond the post-Soviet space. Yet it seems that the Syrian experience created a surplus of confidence in the Russian military and in its leadership. The nature of the war in Ukraine, as well as the resistance from the Ukrainian Army and society, are on a totally different scale from the Syrian conflict and have broken the trust placed in the Russian Army and its strategic and logistical capacities.

Beyond strictly military responses, Moscow has been using a range of methods to exert pressure. All relations within the CIS have been marked by constant bilateral negotiations in which each country tries to obtain this concession or that exchange. As already mentioned in the case of gas prices, Russia negotiates on a case-by-case basis, rewarding "good allies" and punishing the recalcitrant. Numerous industrial cooperation agreements show how Russian negotiators deal with individual partners, always striving to obtain the transfer of elements of strategic interest in exchange for debt forgiveness or assistance. Thus, after years of pressure, large Russian companies own all or large parts of the gas and power-generation networks in Belarus and Armenia, chemical and metallurgical plants in Central Asia, and shares in many other companies.[8] Some of these acquisitions are based on pure industrial and commercial bases and should not call for special attention. Others generate ample controversy in the countries concerned, given the often opaque conditions of acquisition or the new owners' noncompliance with their investment commitments. These battles sometimes lead to the eruption of anti-Russian demonstrations, as in Armenia in 2015, when the population rebelled against the mismanagement of the country's power grid by its Russian owner.[9]

## Rebuilding Soft Power

While Russia invested massively in modernizing its military power and used its economic dominance over its neighbors to secure allegiances, it has also rediscovered the virtues of soft power. The abrupt weakening of the Russian state's institutions and finances in the early 1990s disrupted the powerful public diplomacy that the Soviet Union had conducted. Fraternal nations such as Cuba saw assistance from Russia reduced to a trickle; Communist parties around the world lost funding and logistical support; associations promoting world peace and other fellow travelers of socialism disappeared from the international scene or had to reinvent themselves, often as anti-globalization movements. Tools such as Moscow Radio, translated editions of Soviet publications from Progress Publishers, and art tours organized by the USSR Ministry of Culture became obsolete; many of the cultural events that continued to be exported relied on support from their host countries. Even the influence of the Russian language was left in the rearview mirror, with no institutions supervising the important network of Russian-language universities and programs that operated in many countries, in the CIS as well as in the "far abroad."

During the 1990s, Russia had either no voice on the international scene or was silent by virtue of sharing the Western point of view. It was not until the Yugoslav Wars and the bombing of the Serbian capital of Belgrade in 1999 that a Russian voice reemerged in protest. Yet from the early 1990s onward, many "political technologists"—the term used to describe the new specialists in political communication—began to surround the Kremlin, supporting Yeltsin in his 1995–1996 reelection campaign and selling their services to other Russian and post-Soviet politicians. Gleb Pavlovsky, an adviser to the presidential administration until 2011, was the iconic figure among these public relations specialists; Russian speakers internalized the term *PR* so much that they Russified it as *piar*. Within a few years, Russia would take marketing techniques designed for private firms and apply them to the political sector and to the country's own branding.

It took a few years for these marketing techniques to find a place in Russia's foreign policy toolkit and become part of Putin's narrative. During his election campaign in 2012, the Russian president openly invoked soft power, mentioning the "set of tools and methods to achieve foreign policy objectives without use of weapons."[10] It was the crop of color revolutions, especially the Orange Revolution in Ukraine in 2004, that pushed the Kremlin to reinvest in its soft power aimed at the "near abroad." A presidential directorate for interregional and cultural relations was created, charged with rethinking Moscow's relationship to its near abroad and developing new tools of influence. It required boosting the new multilateral institutions and avoiding bilateral relationships with colonial overtones; developing academic, cultural, and linguistic cooperation; and financing media, NGOs, and local political parties with pro-Russian interests. In parallel, Moscow implemented a policy of "passportization"—the issuing of Russian passports to secessionist minorities in neighboring countries—to further Russia's legal right to protect "compatriots."[11]

The Kremlin also wanted to reach the international community, especially Western public opinion. In 2004, at the peak of his international popularity, Putin launched the Valdai Club, an annual meeting of global experts on Russia, based on the Davos model, to build the image of a globalized Russia dialoguing with the rest of the world and displaying a diversity of political perspectives. In 2007, Moscow founded two chapters of the Institute for Democracy and Cooperation, one in Paris and one in New York (both closed their doors a decade later) to promote the Russian concept of "sovereign democracy"—then an in-vogue term developed by the Kremlin's "gray eminence," Vladislav Surkov, that signified Russia's right to reject Western interference. In 2010, the Kremlin created the Alexander Gorchakov Public Diplomacy Fund, which funds projects to promote Russia and Russian culture abroad, and the Russian Council on International Affairs, in charge of international cooperation between scholars.

That same year, Moscow started the Rossotrudnichestvo International Cooperation Agency, whose mission is to oversee the soft-power projects Russia funds in the so-called near abroad, Latin America, and the Middle East, complemented by the launch of RosAid, a Russian humanitarian aid agency modeled after the US Agency for International Development (USAID), which oversees the humanitarian and emergency aid that Russia delivers worldwide.[12] As part of this new, soft-power toolkit, the Kremlin also invested massively in mega-events: in 2007, the selection of Sochi to host the 2014 Winter Olympics fit perfectly with the objective of rehabilitating Russia's image as a modern and attractive country, even if the results have been overshadowed by Crimea's annexation.[13] The 2018 FIFA World Cup was unable to reach the same level of impact, happening at a time of renewed tensions between Russia and the West surrounding the Syrian theater of war and the Salisbury poisoning affair (Sergei Skripal, a former Russian military officer and double agent for the British intelligence agencies, and his daughter were poisoned with a Novichok nerve agent in an attempted assassination), which resulted in the biggest collective expulsion of Russian diplomats in history.[14]

Russia has also drawn upon the legacy of Soviet-era soft power. Contacts with Communist or former Communist political parties have been reactivated in Europe. The most striking example was, for a few years, Die Linke, the German far left party, but there was a similar strategy at play with leftist circles in Greece—for instance, around Syriza—or in France, with the friendly positions expressed sometimes by two key figures of the Left: Jean-Luc Mélenchon and former minister Jean-Pierre Chevènement.[15] Although Russia no longer represents the ideals of the Left, its stance in favor of national, economic, and cultural sovereignty, its anti-American and anti-NATO geopolitical positioning, and its rejection of neoliberal multilateralism in favor of traditional nation-states were convincing elements for many anti-globalization movements.

Moscow has also rebuilt ties with countries that identify or used to identify as socialist in various ways, including Cuba, Vietnam, North Korea, Syria, and Venezuela. But it was also able to move beyond these usual suspects and develop more innovative relationships with countries that were traditional allies of Washington during the Cold War, such as the Gulf monarchies and Egypt. (See map 6.1 for an illustration of Putin's impressive array of trips abroad.) Finally, as discussed in chapter 6, Moscow plays on the concept of the BRICS, a valuable calling card for Russia because it anchors the country within a broader, non-Western-centered, future world equilibrium.

The increasing importance of world public opinion and nation branding was another lesson that Russian leaders learned from the color revolutions and the conflict with Georgia. They became seriously concerned that the deterioration of their country's image had become an overall source of weakness. At the peak of the Orange Revolution in Ukraine from late 2004 to early 2005, Sergei Markov, a professor at the Moscow State Institute of International Relations (also known as MGIMO University) known for his pro-Kremlin positions, verbalized what the Russian political establishment had been thinking: Russia had lost its control over Georgia and Ukraine because its political communication technologies were inferior to those of the West.[16]

Since then, the topic of an information war organized by the West against Russia has come up in almost all debates about the country's interaction with the rest of the world.[17] Moscow believed that it lost its influence in the world due to its inability to master new information technologies capable of guiding public opinion by providing only one side of the story. Russian authorities therefore decided to invest massive sums in catching up with the latest information technologies, taking advantage of the entry into the labor market of a generation of young Russians bottle-fed from the internet and social media.

In 2005, Russia launched its own television channel, Russia Today (then renamed the more neutral RT), modeled on CNN or Al Jazeera, and broadcasting in Russian, English, Arabic, Spanish, and French. RT's strategy, as expressed by Putin himself, is to "break the Anglo-Saxon monopoly on information flows"[18]—that is, not only to promote the Russian worldview but also (and more importantly) to give voice to the "dissidents" in Western societies. All the evils of the West are put in the spotlight: racist violence and social inequality in the United States, Europe's failure to integrate migrants, and dissonant voices that do not find expression in mainstream Western media. Russia has an impressive budget, increasing from US $30 million in 2005 to US $300 million in 2015 and around US $400 million per year in 2021 and 2022[19]—more than the BBC's World Service, the largest news agency in the world.[20] These funds allowed the Russian channel to recruit famous international journalists and open national newsrooms tailored to each audience.

These bureaus were launched in the United States in 2010, where over two million people were said to regularly tune in, in Britain in 2015, and in France in 2017. RT has also broken into the Argentinian market, where it has been included in the package of public channels accessible to everyone.[21] The former Voice of Russia news agency, renamed Sputnik, has developed a similar strategy on the internet and social media. Published in more than thirty languages, its business model (no royalties for republication) has helped it become an important source of reposting for many cheap outlets, especially in the Global South.[22]

While from one perspective, Russia is simply modernizing the tools of influence that were created during the Soviet era, the Kremlin sees itself as replicating the influence strategies that the United States has itself built. The media outlets of Voice of America and Radio Free Europe/Radio Liberty, along with the financial support of USAID, the National Endowment for Democracy, and other state-sponsored institutions and NGOs are among the mechanisms of US influence that, from Moscow's perspective, were used to weaken Russia, create internal dissent, and shape information to advance the US point of view. Russia believes it must turn these tools to its advantage, offering an alternative version that denounces Western lies and double standards—an element explained by Putin himself in the series of extended, high-profile interviews he gave from 2015 to 2017 to American film producer Oliver Stone for the Showtime Network.[23]

This information war, a war for the hearts and minds of public opinion, has grown to unprecedented levels from the 2014 crisis to the full-scale invasion of 2022. It has been characterized by the use of all the instruments of power, to the point that some observers have created a model of a new type of conflict, "hybrid war," to take account of all the means of modern propaganda brought to bear on a conflict. The concept of a hybrid war has been challenged for its blurriness and also for its politicization.[24] The perception of a powerful Russia mastering hybrid warfare reached a new level in the United States with "Russiagate," a complex, heated, and overblown mix of accusations of collusion between the Russian government and the main figures of the Trump campaign, meddling in the 2016 US presidential election, hacking the Democratic National Committee, and Russian social media presence in the United States. Yet recent research has found no evidence of a meaningful relationship between exposure to the Russian foreign influence campaign and changes in attitudes, polarization, or voting behavior among US citizens.[25]

## Russia as the Standard-Bearer of Conservative Values

Russia's positions on several societal topics concerning sexuality, gender, and family have allowed it to build a new international brand as the standard-bearer of conservative values and the last defender of Europe's Christian heritage.[26] Putin has cultivated his image as a European leader with the courage of his convictions, expressing out loud what many European citizens think, but do not dare to say in the face of the political correctness of European institutions. At the Valdai Club's 2013 summit, he offered a long ideological statement on what authentic European values should be:

We can see how many of the Euro-Atlantic countries are rejecting their roots, including Christian values, which form the basis of Western civilization. They are trying to deny moral principles and their traditional identity: national, cultural, religious, and even sexual. They put in place policies that equate large families with homosexual families, and make faith in God equal to belief in Satan. . . . In many European countries, people are embarrassed to talk about their religion. . . . I believe that this opens a direct path to degradation and primitivism, leading to a profound demographic and moral crisis. What else but the loss of the capacity to reproduce could be the best evidence of this moral crisis? Today, almost all developed nations are no longer capable of assuring their demographic renewal, even with the assistance of immigration. Without the values present in Christianity and the other religions of the world, without the moral standards that have formed over thousands of years, people inevitably lose their human dignity. We see it as right and natural to defend these values. It is necessary to respect the right of each minority to be different, but the rights of the majority should not be called into question.[27]

Although this framing reached its peak in the 2010s, it has been part of Russia's foreign policy toolkit since the mid-2000s. Moscow became aware of this untapped soft-power potential during the reconciliation process between the Moscow Patriarchate and the Russian Orthodox Church Outside of Russia (ROCOR), born during the White emigration (referring to the opponents of the Communist Reds in the civil war that followed the Bolshevik Revolution of 1917), which resulted in the canonical communion (reunification) between the two churches in 2007.[28] While debates rage around gay marriage in several European countries, and Catholic and Protestant churches face many questions on whether to accept societal changes (divorce, homosexuality, abortion, etc.), the Kremlin realized it could build new ideological alliances with European actors as the preeminent defender of so-called traditional values by means of anti-homosexual laws and pro-natalist propaganda.

The Moscow Patriarchate has been at the forefront of this strategy for years. One of its main representatives, Hilarion Alfeev, was, for instance, sent to discuss Russia's perspectives with Pope Francis as well as with the American religious Right. In 2010, he gave a speech in front of thousands of Evangelicals in Dallas, Texas, calling for a strategic alliance between all those who defend Christian values, and met in person with former US president George W. Bush.[29] A part of the American Evangelical Right recognized Vladimir Putin as an ally in its war against what it saw as Barack Obama's excessively liberal presidency. Republican figures such as Reagan-era White House communications director Pat Buchanan, Tea Party members, and pro-life activists celebrated the Russian president and his defense of Christian values.

The World Congress of Families, which includes all the radical associations on the Right that defend the "natural family," praised Russia and even planned to hold its global meeting in Moscow in 2014 before the Ukrainian crisis forced its cancellation.[30] The issue of connections between Russia and part of the US Far Right became a critical one with the election of Donald Trump, especially during the few months Steve Bannon, the editor of the Far Right news portal Breitbart, worked as White House chief strategist (January to August 2017). The US Alt-Right, or Alternative Right, did not hide its admiration for Russia, but contacts on both sides are tenuous and revolve around a few marginal figures, not impacting high politics.[31]

In Europe, Russia's ideological successes were even more visible: Moscow won the support of traditional religious circles and illiberal groups, as well as some of the more mainstream conservative parties in Europe, at least until the full-scale war started. In France, Marine Le Pen and her revamped National Rally party (formerly known as the National Front under her father, Jean-Marie) were for several years seen as the darling of Moscow, before preference was given to the Matteo Salvini's Lega Nord party, as well as other figures close to former conservative prime minister Silvio Berlusconi in Italy. Russia also developed strong relations with the Freedom Party of Austria (FPÖ), the AfD (Alternative for Germany) in Germany, and an array of smaller parties in Belgium, the Netherlands, and Britain.[32]

At the regime level, both Prime Minister Viktor Orbán's Hungary and President Aleksandar Vučić's Serbia have defended softer positions toward Russia. This informal alliance between Moscow and the European populists and radical Right first came to light during the 2014 Ukrainian crisis, as most of the parties expressing some degree of support for Russia were from the national-conservative camps in their respective countries. The committee of European observers who visited Crimea to validate the March 16, 2014 "referendum" on joining Russia was, for instance, composed mostly of representatives of the Europe's extreme right wing.[33]

But Russia's full-scale invasion of Ukraine has dramatically reshaped European illiberal leaders' positioning toward Moscow. In fall 2022, Giorgia Meloni became the new Italian prime minister on a platform that featured classic far-right policies but an anti-Russian and pro-NATO stance.[34] The Swedish Democrats are now the second-largest party in parliament and will be able to influence the government coalition, yet they support their country's entry into NATO and will likely seek to transform other aspects of Swedish foreign policy—such as its feminism—rather than build a pro-Russian narrative.

However, Russia's soft power with the European Right did not rely solely on its conservative values agenda; it also banked on other, equally important elements that were more geopolitical than moral. Moscow has been a steady and vocal critic of European integration and holds Brussels's supranational institutions responsible for Europe's so-called submission to US interests. Putin has called for a Europe of nations that would pursue a "continentalist" rather than an "Atlanticist" policy. Moscow also plays an ambiguous game on questions of national identity and immigration. The Russian media highlights the alleged failure of multiculturalism in Europe and advances an ethnic interpretation of social tensions related to immigrants and their descendants while calling for the protection of Europe's "white" and Christian identity against an uncontrolled invasion of migrants.[35] All these components constitute a genuinely shared vision between Russia and several European actors on the Right—and, for its geopolitical component, with some on the Left—of the political spectrum.

The revival of a certain Russian messianism under the guise of conservative values has required Russian authorities to pull off a delicate balancing act. The Kremlin has denounced the "fascist junta" that supposedly came to power in Kyiv and complains that Europe has purposely forgotten the Soviet Union's role in the victory in 1945. At the same time, Moscow openly sympathizes ideologically with—and even sometimes supports financially—the Far Right groups that are the direct or indirect heirs of the former enemies of the Soviet Union. This apparent contradiction can be explained by Russia's desire to work toward a new world order in which all the enemies of the liberal order, whatever their convictions, are rediscovered as allies.

## RUSSIA IN SEARCH OF A NEW WORLD ORDER

Even before the full-scale invasion of Ukraine, it had become commonplace for those in Western policy and media circles to accuse Russia of being a revisionist power. The notion of revisionism remains poorly conceptualized, but at present, it is used mostly to denounce a rogue country that rejects the so-called liberal world order and opposes liberal democracies as a matter of policy. Yet one could also define Russia as a counter-revisionist, or "neo-revisionist," power that seeks to resist US-led revisionism with its own revisionism.[36] After all, the world order has evolved dramatically since the collapse of Communism in Europe and Eurasia, transforming into a liberal, internationalist order defined by multilateralism, a belief in supranational institutions, a trade-based vision of peace, and humanitarian interventionism.[37] The West's liberal internationalism lies at the core of the ideological conflict between the West and Russia over the future of Europe and its security architecture.

### Global South against Collective West?

Seen from Moscow, which takes the 1945 wartime meeting between Stalin, Churchill, and Roosevelt at Yalta on the Crimean Peninsula as the model of great powers reigning over their respective spheres of influence as its preferred yardstick for the international order, the liberal world order is itself revisionist. As argued by Richard Sakwa, Russia wanted to join a *transformed* West, not an *expanded* one, and has therefore gradually distanced itself from the existing European/transatlantic institutions, as it has not been given the status of cocreator of this new European order.[38] In the Russian view, the world order as it stands is directly subject to Washington's decisions. Indeed, Moscow reads the international scene based on old realpolitik—the theory that, by nature, states are selfish organizations that defend their own strategic interests.[39]

According to Russian discourse, the United States has used idealistic and moralistic rhetoric to assert an illusory regime of human rights and a concept of international governance embodied by the right to intervene, when in reality Washington is simply pursuing its strategic interests as a great power.

This is particularly the case for the large financial structures of the Bretton Woods Agreements of 1944 that created the World Bank and the International Monetary Fund, and for the "Washington Consensus" of 1989, which pushes for property rights regimes, lowering trade and investment barriers, and avoiding excessive fiscal deficits and high debt-to-GDP ratios. US supremacy over European interests in transatlantic institutions, such as NATO and the OSCE, is likewise rejected. Russia condemns the United States's repeated breaches of this world order that they themselves created and now police with a double standard: America's friends are supported by their protector even when they violate international norms (such as the case with Israel) and are exempted from US activism in the cause of human rights (for example, the Gulf states, particularly Saudi Arabia).

Russia's distrust of the world order is reflected in its gradual questioning of all the instruments that have governed the global balance of power since 1945, with the exception of the UN General Assembly (based on the principle of "one state, one vote"), which Russia considers the only legitimate body representing world opinion. In many international institutions, representatives of Russia propose amendments that would introduce formulas calling for respecting every state's legislation and traditions rather than the supremacy of human rights principle, which they feel paves the way for foreign intervention. In Moscow's view, states are the ultimate players on the international scene; nonstate actors—transnational corporations, anti-globalization movements, and civil society—are regarded as instruments of dominant states.

This explains Moscow's firm refusal to acknowledge popular street movements, like the color revolutions, which it sees as inevitably manipulated by foreign interests and not expressing genuine support for democracy. Of course, one can argue that this position suits the Russian authorities, who are concerned with their own survival and who have sometimes welcomed the overthrow of leaders with whom they are unhappy—as in the case of Kyrgyz president Kurmanbek Bakiyev, who was forced out of office in 2010, or what they were hoping to do in Ukraine by overthrowing the Zelenskyy government.

On many occasions, and often in association with Beijing, Moscow has used its veto on the UN Security Council to oppose Western resolutions to intervene in any country—as noted in Iraq and in Syria, where the Kremlin has been engaged as Assad's main defender (together with Iran and, to a lesser extent, China). Several reasons have been invoked to explain this policy, which the West denounces as a conservative blocking strategy. Russian and Chinese leaders have always pointed out that they are much closer to these sources of tension and therefore more likely to suffer the effects of contagion. However, it is also clear that in defending regimes embroiled in internal conflict, Moscow and Beijing are disputing the very principle of foreign interference in the internal affairs of states. They see a risk that this principle could one day be applied to their own countries during a global or regional political crisis, for example, in the North Caucasus for Russia, or Tibet or Xinjiang for China. Moscow and Beijing accuse the United States of double-talk and abuse of its dominant position, by which it ignores the UN Security Council (e.g., Kosovo and Iraq) or twists its resolutions to suit Washington's will (e.g., Libya).[40]

Russia's position goes beyond criticism or rejection of the world order. Since the second half of the 2000s, and more actively since 2014, Moscow has worked to institute collective resistance, or more-or-less credible alternatives. Hence the Kremlin's assertive promotion of the BRICS, as Russia's economy cannot challenge the world order without more powerful allies. In the financial sector, Russia is reliant on China in particular, and the BRICS as a whole, to advance alternatives to US-led financial capitalism. The launch of the BRICS New Development Bank and the creation of a BRICS Contingent Reserve Arrangement (a reserve fund) in 2014 were intended to openly challenge the roles of the International Monetary Fund and the World Bank. Although both institutions depend on China's financial power and are based in Shanghai, all the member states have an equal stake and an equal vote. In 2015, the BRICS also discussed the creation of their own international rating agency, which could compete with the existing US-based agencies by establishing other methods to assess the health of global economies that would be more deferential to domestic social conditions.

Moscow and Beijing have also discussed converting contracts to rubles or yuan in order to start moving away from the domination of the US dollar. Already in 2014, after the first Western sanctions, the Bank of Russia proposed to create a new interbank transfer system alternative to the SWIFT, something the BRICS discussed a year later. This has resulted in two alternative systems: one Chinese, the Cross-Border Interbank Payment System, launched in 2015; the other Russian, the *Sistema bystrykh platezhei* (SPB), launched in 2019. The de-dollarization of the Russian economy will be accelerating now that the decoupling with the West is more pronounced.

Russia has also become proactive in the digital realm as it criticizes US supremacy in internet management: the servers of the cloud and major domains (.com, .org, etc.) are based in the United States, and large US technology companies are accused of sharing information about their users at the behest of Washington. The Edward Snowden and WikiLeaks cases, multiple revelations of illegal mass surveillance conducted by US government bodies, such as the National Security Agency (NSA), and the end of net neutrality have strengthened Russian suspicions that Washington uses the internet as a weapon to protect its strategic and economic interests. But obviously, Russian authorities are not themselves without ulterior motives: like China, though to a lesser extent, the Kremlin wants to take control over its "national segment" of the internet in order to protect itself from possible coercive measures and to silence its domestic opposition.

This dual strategy of both criticizing the West's hegemony in globalized instruments and simultaneously building for itself the same autonomous instruments is in evidence in multiple sectors. One example was the decision made in 2015 that all Russian state institutions stop using Western software in favor of Russian alternatives. With the onset of the full-scale war in Ukraine, Russia has been left with very few options other than import substitution and reinventing the technological tools it is now being deprived of. On the international scene, the Global South is now Moscow's main territory for power projection and strategic alliances.

## The Post–February 24 Dilemmas of Russia's Soft Power

Russia's soft power in Europe has been largely destroyed by its use of hard power in Ukraine: the war has cut short the honeymoon between Moscow and many European illiberal politicians, who had to follow the massive denunciation of Russia's violence by European leaders and public opinion. Russia has lost its media tools of foreign influence with the banning of RT and Sputnik from many European countries. Entrepreneurs of influence who were in charge of cultivating links with European illiberal forces, such as Russian media mogul Konstantin Malofeev, the former Russian Railways director Vladimir Yakunin (sanctioned by the West since Crimea's annexation), and the infamous Yevgeny Prigozhin of the Wagner Group, have now been hit by a barrage of sanctions: they will not be able to travel to Europe to meet with their counterparts, and some of their assets have been seized or frozen. Everything associated with Russia has become highly toxic, forcing even European illiberal figures to keep their distance, and in Central and Eastern European countries, even Russian culture is seen with suspicion.

Yet Russia's ability to speak to foreign audiences and to be seen as a role model for conservative or illiberal ideologies and governance has not totally disappeared. First, there is not unanimity in Europe: the French National Rally, Italian Lega Nord, and AfD parties continue to promote a moderate line favorable to Russia, and in the United States, the pro-Trump camp, with media figures such as former Fox News anchor Tucker Carlson and right-wing commentator Candace Owens, continue to exhibit a pro-Russian stance.

Second, some Western countries cultivate strategic ambiguity toward Russia. Hungary's ambivalent stance is a result of Viktor Orbán's own illiberal regime and the need to counterbalance EU pressures, even if Hungarian public opinion is almost evenly split between Orbán voters, who support Russia, and his opponents, who criticize Budapest's relationship with

Moscow. Serbia's stance is more consensual: its impressive Russophilia is explicable by reference not only to its sense of shared Slavic history and Orthodox culture but also to Moscow's support for Belgrade on the issue of Kosovo's independence and bitter disappointment with the EU owing to the stalled accession talks.[41]

Israel's position has been more nuanced, in an attempt to maintain a relationship with both sides. Israeli politicians have made both critical and supportive statements on Russia, with changes in positioning explicable mostly by Tel Aviv's need to secure Moscow's role in Syria.[42] But the decision to not deliver weapons to Kyiv is highly contested within Israel itself. And last but not least, Turkey is without doubt the country in the Middle East that most exemplifies an ostensible policy of refusing to take sides. Ankara now finds itself in a comfortable position to balance between all actors; it has been able to bolster its international prestige and play up its "crossroads" identity and multipronged foreign policy. In all four cases, an ideological and personal affinity between national leaders (Orbán, Vučić, Netanyahu, and Erdoğan) and Putin plays an important role in the country's geopolitical posture.

Third, and this is a central point, the war has a strong Eurocentric focus. The West's framing of the war in Ukraine as a fight for democracy against authoritarianism does not resonate with many regimes for whom democracy is a synonym for chaos and foreign interference.[43] The framing of the war would have had a better chance of success if it had been construed as a defense of Ukraine's sovereignty and territorial integrity. Many countries in the Global South share similar values with Russia, which makes them cautious toward Western narratives of democracy: looking at the list of countries that have abstained from UN resolutions condemning Russia's full-scale invasion of Ukraine (see map 5.2, page 145), one can, for instance, notice that they tend to lean toward survival values and traditional sources of authority, and away from self-expression values and secular-rational sources of authority, per the World Values Survey.[44] The emphasis on survival values indicates that these nations are most concerned with physical and economic security and feature lower levels of interpersonal trust and tolerance of dissenting views and practices. The clustering around traditional values conveys their embrace of traditional family values, deference to authority, and the like.[45]

Furthermore, seen from the South, the war is largely interpreted as belonging to the Global North, pitting US and European normative imperialism against Russia's own imperialism in its "near abroad." While many people in the South may have been shocked by Russia's blatant violations of international law, the Global South has painful memories of what it sees as US unilateralism and military interventionism. Memories of the US invasion of Iraq, the management of the Libyan crisis, and the failed twenty-year NATO presence in Afghanistan, as well as accumulated resentment against former

European colonial powers such as France or the UK, have all shaped public opinion, with the result that the Western narrative on the war in Ukraine does not really resonate with many of them.

Supporting Moscow, or at least not punishing it, allows for countries in the Global South to counterbalance the US-dominated world order. It by no means suggests submission to Russia's own interests (except in cases where the regime is heavily dependent on Moscow, as is the case with Syria), but rather it allows these states to promote their own interests on the international scene by playing several transactional alliances—of which their relationship with Russia is one—off against each other. Moreover, national economic interests dominate, and no one in the Global South wants to aggravate their domestic economic situation in the name of sanctioning Russia to please the West.

When one disaggregates the world data of perception of Russia into big regions, an important North–South gap appears. Russia's highest level of favorability comes from sub-Saharan Africa—confirming the importance of the Soviet legacy there—followed by Asia, Latin America, and the Middle East and North Africa (MENA) region. With the war, this gap between the Global North and Global South has increased: while favorable opinions of Russia in the West have fallen to between 5 percent and 16 percent on average, Foa et al. have found that "the real terrain of Russia's international influence lies outside of the West: 75% of respondents in South Asia, 68% in Francophone Africa, and 62% in Southeast Asia continued to view the country positively," in spite of the war.[46]

With its miscalculated war, Russia has been destroying many of the successes it had secured over the last three decades. It will have to reinvent its soft power if it wants to restore a positive image of itself in target European audiences. Because Russia's new post–February 24, 2022, identity is still in flux, it is difficult to export such a swiftly changing brand. But once the war either comes to an end or reaches the point of stalemate, Russian actors, such as state-funded media for foreign audiences, public-diplomacy institutions such as Rossotrudnichestvo, and myriad entrepreneurs of influence in charge of exporting ideological frameworks that resonate with foreign audiences will try to rebuild some networks and shared language. Obviously, they will have to work in a more hostile environment, with less chance of success and a smaller budget available to "lubricate" these relationships. In Central Europe, radical measures of shunning Russian culture as well, along with Russian citizens as being held equally responsible for the war, will likely impact, for a long time to come, local public policies in their relationship to everything Russian.

But the dream expressed by some Western experts of turning Russia into a giant North Korea–type pariah state, that is, one that is totally autarkic, is misguided: Russia may have become toxic in the West but not to the "rest," and even in the West, there will remain some pro-Russian voices, even if they are marginalized. More importantly, culture wars do not just disappear, because they are embedded in local realities and agendas. What we will see is a partial decoupling of being pro-Russian from the taking of a populist, Euroskeptic, or illiberal stance. Francis Fukuyama's idea that "a Russian defeat will make possible a new birth of freedom"[47] appears particularly naive: the toxicity of today's Russia does not erode the structural reasons for illiberal politics to prosper and resonate with more anxious parts of world societies.

Russia may be down, but it is not out. Its decline is resulting in a retrenchment strategy—that is, a redefinition of Russia's objectives to core commitments, drawing down everything that is nonessential, to deal with its geopolitical decline and newly exposed weaknesses. Russia's retrenchment may be seen as a victory for the West in Europe itself, but there is no Western victory in the Global South; on the contrary, the war is accelerating the fragmentation of the world, the deglobalization and regionalization of strategic blocs and economic ties. Regional powers are learning their lessons from the way the West is leading its economic warfare against Russia and will seek to reinforce their own autonomy from Western institutions and pressure points, especially in relation to the dollar's extraterritoriality and the United States' digital supremacy. This provides confirmation, if any was still needed, that the war may result in a reconsolidated "collective West" in the Global North, whereas outside of the West, the war is accelerating the multipolarization of the world and its de-Westernization.

## NOTES

1. Timothy Snyder, "Ukraine Holds the Future: The War Between Democracy and Nihilism," *Foreign Affairs* (September/October 2022), https://www.foreignaffairs .com/ukraine/ukraine-war-democracy-nihilism-timothy-snyder.

2. "John Mearsheimer on Why the West Is Principally Responsible for the Ukrainian Crisis," *The Economist*, March 19, 2022, https://www.economist.com/by-invitation /2022/03/11/john-mearsheimer-on-why-the-west-is-principally-responsible-for-the -ukrainian-crisis.

3. Andrei Tsygankov, *The Dark Double: US Media, Russia, and the Politics of Values* (Oxford: Oxford University Press, 2019).

4. See Françoise Daucé, *L'État, l'armée et le citoyen en Russie post-soviétique* (Paris: L'Harmattan, 2001).

5. See Dmitry Gorenburg, "Midrats: Russia's Invasion of Ukraine," *Russian Military Reform* (blog), April 14, 2022, https://russiamil.wordpress.com/author/gorenbur; as well as Isabelle Facon, *La Nouvelle Armée russe* (Paris: L'Inventaire, 2021).

6. Dmitry Gorenburg, "Russia's Military Modernization Plans: 2018–2027," PONARS *Eurasia Policy Memo*, no. 495, November 2017, https://www.ponarseurasia.org/russia-s-military-modernization-plans-2018-2027.

7. "Minoborony podvelo itogi operatsii v Sirii," TASS, August 22, 2018, https://tass.ru/armiya-i-opk/5479447.

8. Jakov Hedenskog and Robert L. Larsson, *Russian Leverage on the* CIS *and the Baltic States* (Stockholm: FOI, Swedish Defence Research Agency, 2007).

9. "'Inter RAO' ne vyderzhalo armianskikh dram," *Kommersant*, June 29, 2015.

10. Vladimir Putin, "Russia's Place in a Changing World" (English translation), *Moskovskie novosti*, February 27, 2012, https://web.archive.org/web/20120613180122/worldmeets.us/Moskovskiye.Novosti000001.shtml.

11. Kristopher Natoli, "Weaponizing Nationality: An Analysis of Russia's Passport Policy in Georgia," *Boston University International Law Journal* 28 (2010): 389–417, https://www.bu.edu/law/journals-archive/international/documents/natoli_weaponizingnationality.pdf.

12. Anna Brezhneva and Daria Ukhova, "Russian as a Humanitarian Aid Donor," Oxfam Discussion Paper, July 2013, https://www.oxfam.org/en/research/russia-humanitarian-aid-donor.

13. Robert Orttung and Sufian Zhemukhov, *Putin's Olympics: The Sochi Games and the Evolution of Twenty-First Century Russia* (London: Routledge, 2017).

14. Andrey Makarychev, "The Legacies of the 2018 FIFA World Cup in Russia: Three Facets of Mega-Events' Biopolitics," in *Mega Events, Urban Transformation, and Social Citizenship*, ed. Naomi Hanakata, Filippo Bignami, and Niccolo Cuppini (London: Routledge, 2022).

15. See Patrick Moreau and Stéphane Courtois, eds., *En Europe, l'éternel retour des communistes 1989–2014* (Paris: Vendémiaire, 2014).

16. Quoted by Sinikukka Saari in "Russia's Post-Orange Revolution Strategies to Increase Its Influence in the Former Soviet Republics: Public Diplomacy *po russki*," *Europe-Asia Studies* 66, no. 1 (2014): 50–66.

17. Eliot Borenstein, *Plots against Russia: Conspiracy and Fantasy after Socialism* (Ithaca, NY: Cornell University Press, 2019).

18. Simon Shuster, "Inside Putin's On-Air Machine," *Time*, March 5, 2015, https://time.com/rt-putin.

19. "Gosudarstvennyi telekanal Russia Today poluchit iz biudzheta pochti 29 mlrd rublei v sleduiushchem godu," *Ekho Moskvy*, December 23, 2021, https://web.archive.org/web/20220216141635/https://echo.msk.ru/news/2956368-echo.html.

20. Shuster, "Inside Putin's On-Air Machine."

21. Maxime Audinet, *Russia Today: Un media d'influence au service de l'Etat russe* (Paris: I.N.A., 2021).

22. Maxime Audinet and Kevin Limonier, "Le dispositif d'influence information-nelle de la Russie en Afrique subsaharienne francophone: un écosystème flexible et composite," *Questions de communication* 41, no. 1 (2022): 129–48.

23. Available at https://www.sho.com/the-putin-interviews.

24. Ofer Fridman, *Russian Hybrid Warfare: Resurgence and Politicisation* (Oxford: Oxford University Press, 2018), chapter 6.

25. Gregory Eady et al., "Exposure to the Russian Internet Research Agency For-eign Influence Campaign on Twitter in the 2016 US Election and Its Relationship to Attitudes and Voting Behavior," *Nature Communications* 14, no. 62 (2023), https://www.nature.com/articles/s41467-022-35576-9.

26. Kristina Stoeckle and Dmitry Uzlaner, *The Moralist International: Russia in the Global Culture Wars* (New York: Fordham University Press, 2022).

27. "Meeting of the Valdai International Discussion Club," *Kremlin*, September 19, 2013, http://en.kremlin.ru/events/president/news/19243.

28. The Russian Orthodox Church Outside of Russia (ROCOR) is the name given to the Russian Orthodox Church of the emigration, which left the fold of the Moscow Patriarchate during the Soviet era in protest of the church's submission to an atheist power and the religious repression of the Soviet state.

29. Adam Federman, "How US Evangelicals Fueled the Rise of Russia's 'Pro-Family' Right," *The Nation*, January 7, 2014, https://www.thenation.com/article /archive/how-us-evangelicals-fueled-rise-russias-pro-family-right.

30. Miranda Blue, "Globalizing Homophobia, Part. 1: How The American Right Came to Embrace Russia's Anti-Gay Crackdown," *Right Wing Watch*, October 3, 2013, https://www.rightwingwatch.org/post/globalizing-homophobia-part-1-how-the -american-right-came-to-embrace-russias-anti-gay-crackdown; Miranda Blue, "Glo-balizing Homophobia, Part 2: Today the Whole World Is Looking at Russia," *Right Wing Watch*, October 3, 2013, https://www.rightwingwatch.org/post/globalizing -homophobia-part-2-today-the-whole-world-is-looking-at-russia.

31. Peter Stone et al., "Donald Trump and Russia: A Web That Grows More Tangled All the Time," *The Guardian*, July 30, 2016, https://www.theguardian.com/ us-news/2016/jul/30/donald-trump-paul-manafort-ukraine-russia-putin-ties.

32. More in Anton Shekhovtsov, *Russia and the Western Far Right: Tango Noir* (London: Routledge, 2017); and Marlene Laruelle, ed., *Eurasianism and the Euro-pean Far Right: Reshaping the Europe-Russia Relationship* (Lanham, MD: Lexing-ton, 2015).

33. Anton Shekhovtsov, "Pro-Russian Extremists Observe the Illegitimate Crimean 'Referendum,'" *Anton Shekhovtsov's Blog*, March 17, 2014, https://anton-shekhovtsov .blogspot.com/2014/03/pro-russian-extremists-observe.html.

34. Marc Lazar, "Italy Putin's Russia, and Ukraine," Illiberalism Studies Program, October 5, 2022, https://www.illiberalism.org/italy-putins-russia-and-ukraine.

35. Stephen Hutchings, *Projecting Russia in a Mediatized World: Recursive Nationhood* (London: Routledge, 2022).

36. Richard Sakwa, *Russia against the Rest: The Post-Cold War Crisis of World Order* (Cambridge, UK: Cambridge University Press, 2017).

37. G. John Ikenberry, "The Liberal International Order and its Discontents," *Millennium: Journal of International Studies* 38, no. 3 (2010): 509–21.

38. Sakwa, *Russia against the Rest*, 4–5.

39. John Mearsheimer, The Great Delusion: Liberal Dreams and International Realities (New Haven, CT: Yale University Press, 2018).

40. "Putin: nevozmozhno bez otvrashcheniia smotret' na kadry ubiistva Kaddafi," RIA *Novosti*, October 26, 2011, https://ria.ru/20111026/471693000.html.

41. Helena Ivanov, Marlene Laruelle, Henry Jackson Society.

42. Steven A. Cook, "The Deeper Reason Netanyahu Won't Arm Ukraine Against Russia," *Foreign Affairs*, February 6, 2023.

43. Kelly A. Grieco, and Marie Journal, "Democracy vs. Autocracy Is the Wrong Framing for the War in Ukraine," *World Politics Review*, June 14, 2022, https://www.worldpoliticsreview.com/democracy-vs-autocracy-is-the-wrong-framing-for-ukraine-war.

44. See the 2023 WVS Cultural Map of the World here, https://www.worldvaluessurvey.org/images/MAP20232.png.

45. Mariya Omelicheva, "United We Stand (with Russia)? How Moscow's Soft Power Shaped Views on the War," *PONARS Eurasia Policy Memo*, no. 10, November 14, 2022, https://www.ponarseurasia.org/united-we-stand-with-russia-how-moscows-soft-power-shaped-views-on-the-war.

46. Roberto Foa et al., *A World Divided: Russia, China, and the West*, Centre for the Future of Democracy, October 2022, https://bennettinstitute.cam.ac.uk/wp-content/uploads/2023/01/A_World_Divided.pdf, 2.

47. Rachel Sharp, "Francis Fukuyama Says Russian Defeat in Ukraine will 'Make Possible a New Birth of Freedom,'" *The Independent*, March 14, 2022, https://www.independent.co.uk/news/world/americas/russia-ukraine-invasion-francis-fukuyama-b2035413.html.

# Conclusion

Since the full-scale invasion of Ukraine by Russia on February 24, 2022, and the West's imposition of a historic wave of sanctions, it has often been said that Russia is isolated and its leadership caught in a strategic deadlock. A more careful analysis, however, demonstrates that this is largely a Western-centric perception.

Yes, Russian aggression was largely condemned by the UN General Assembly vote on March 2 (141 of 193 member states condemned it, 47 abstained or did not take part, and only 5 supported it, namely, Russia, Belarus, North Korea, Syria, and Eritrea), but many non-Western states have refused to apply sanctions, even under pressure from Washington. It is not that the Global South is pro-Russian per se, but it is largely opposed to a Western or US domination of the world order and does not like to be lectured and given orders. Seen from the South, Russia embodies a resistance to the West that is worth supporting or at least not marginalizing. Indeed, Russia's blending of conservative values, distrust of liberal international institutions, and status as a rebellious power against the United States has been a successful trademark of its foreign policy, allowing Russia to find common ground with many non-Western countries.

At the same time, the way the Russian Army is conducting the war has provoked widespread indignation and has troubled even its most supportive partners. Not only has Russia massively attacked civilian infrastructure but revelations coming from liberated, occupied territories indicate the occurrence of systematic looting, rape, torture, and the deportation of adults and children to filtration camps and then to Russia. The low morale of the Russian Army and its disorganization, at least in the first months of the war, are largely responsible for these violations, yet they seem to have been also consciously used as part of the toolkit of the Russian "way of war." Moscow can still cultivate influence and recognition by criticizing the liberal West and strengthening its outreach in the Global South, but the Russian Army's war crimes and the possible charges of genocide before the International

Criminal Court in The Hague have strongly impacted Russia's image, even among its allies.

One can look at the war through several lenses, each with different temporal and spatial scales.[1] First, it is a local conflict, a Russian war of imperial reconquest aimed at reintegrating Ukraine into Russia against a Ukrainian war of national liberation. Second, the war is a new stage of a broader geopolitical conflict between Russia and the transatlantic community in reshaping the post–Cold War European security architecture. This geopolitical conflict could potentially engage the West as a cobelligerent in the war, even if there are key tensions between the "old" and the "new" Europe about the degree of risk to be accepted and the place of Russia in the future of the continent. Last but not least, it is a conflict about the legitimacy of the West in punishing those who do not respect the established international order through economic sanctions and multilayered "cancellation"—a legitimacy that many in the Global South view with suspicion.

Consideration of Russia's desire to emerge as an alternative power to the Western-led world order raises several questions. The main one is whether Russia has the capacity to fulfill its ambitions. It seems obvious that without the common will of the BRICS—and especially a partnership with China—Russia cannot credibly seek to modify the international order. Its economic and financial strength is minimal: the country represents about 2 percent of world GDP and lacks dominance in any innovative sectors. Even if the Russian economy is more resilient than many Western observers predicted, the country will emerge weakened from the conflict. Any alternative economic and financial order could only come from China or from a coalition of emerging countries in which Russia will look like an aging economy based on raw materials exports. It risks being confined to junior status behind Beijing, which will cause knock-on security concerns for Moscow in the coming decades.

Moreover, Moscow will have to deal with the consequences of its aggression even among its closest allies. Its long-term partners, such as Kazakhstan, have become distanced, using the current situation to step further out from under Russia's umbrella. Even India and, in a more ambiguous manner, China refuse to side openly with Moscow with regard to the war, and they have called for a diplomatic solution; for rejecting the use of nuclear, chemical, or biological weapons; and for respect for Ukraine's sovereignty. They will not apply sanctions or second Western criticisms, but Russia's international branding and its army's reputation have been damaged in the long run. Whatever the future holds for Russia, the country will enter into an era of retrenchment, requiring it to rethink its priorities in foreign policy and its ability to influence and to adapt to a decoupling with the West in a context of its partial economic decline.[2]

The war is unlikely to dramatically impact the relationship between Russia and China. Even if the elites of both countries do harbor mutual distrust, the strategic partnership is based on a convergence of strategic fundamental interests that will not disappear, because they are rooted in a worldwide global rebalancing. Moreover, both countries are economically complementary (raw materials from Russia; financial and technological power from China), cooperate militarily, and share a common ideological background (authoritarian leadership and denunciation of US hegemony—even if the doctrinal frameworks and power projection toolkits are different). Regardless of how the war ends, China will benefit from Russia's weakening and will be able to impose its economic conditions on its partner more easily. Chinese strategic elites are also learning in real time from Russia's failure at conquering Ukraine and from the magnitude of Western sanctions, and will apply this knowledge to their own goals, especially toward Taiwan. But seen from China (as with the rest of the Global South), Russia is "too big to fail": its total defeat or collapse is perceived as a danger for the waves of instability it would generate and for the imbalance in the world order it would create.

Without sending its own troops to the battlefield, the United States is also among the main beneficiaries of the war: it plays a critical role in Ukraine's resistance, hopes to take advantage of Putin's strategic mistake to weaken Russia over the long term,[3] and benefits from consolidating its strategic and economic influence over Europe. Even if the support given to Ukraine may be criticized by a part of US public opinion and part of the Republican Party, Russia's war has offered Washington both economic benefits (Europe's energy dependence) and strategic ones (NATO's relegitimization and enlargement, reinforcement of Poland's and the Baltic states' influence inside the EU framework against Germany and France). Also, the US military-industrial complex is guaranteed years of generous funding and many new clients with growing military budgets.

One should not celebrate too readily Russia's strategic miscalculations and military challenges as a victory for the West. The solutions brought by the United States to the conflict are a double-edged sword. The EU could find itself locked into years of economic stagnation. Many European countries, first and foremost Germany, will pay a heavy price for the unexpected change of energy policy, with potential social and political consequences. The distance being kept by European national-populist parties from Russian leaders does not diminish the erosion of liberal democracy in Europe. On the global scene, challenges lie ahead. The United States could find itself tied down dealing with increased Russian-Chinese penetration in the Middle East and Africa. Beijing and Global South elite centers are closely studying the way Western sanctions are deployed and how Russia builds its circumvention strategies in response, and they will be sure to prepare themselves similarly.

Criticisms leveled at the extraterritoriality of US laws and the dominance of the dollar, as well as attempts at breaking down the Western and especially US levers of control in the world banking system (by devising means of getting around SWIFT) and on the internet will grow. And the war has caused many Western countries to backslide on key environmental issues.

If the West becomes strategically consolidated by the war, the gap between the "West and the rest" will continue to increase. The refusal by the West to seriously consider the multiple (climate-, energy-, and food-related) vulnerabilities of the South will raise tensions that both China and a weakened Russia will exploit. The West misreads the impact that the collapse of the Soviet Union had on itself: if Russia is struggling to accept its status as a diminished great power, the United States, too, is also grappling with recognizing that it cannot impose its vision and values on the rest of the world.

Obviously, a weakened Russia will have to readjust the way it sees itself and its place on the world scene. Its dependence on China will increase, and even Ankara and Tehran have secured more room to maneuver toward Moscow than before. Even North Korea seems to have become a much more important partner for Russia than it was before. Russian authorities now have to cooperate with "small" countries that were once seen as clients but are now considered allies, to compensate for the collapse of its relations with the West.

Some in the West wish for Russia to be dismembered as the Soviet Union was. The American anti-kleptocracy journalist Casey Michel stated, "The West must complete the project that began in 1991. It must seek to fully decolonize Russia."[4] The Nobel Peace Prize laureate and former Polish president, Lech Wałęsa, too, has advocated for the "60 peoples who got colonized by Russia" to break away so that Russia would be reduced to a country of about 50 million people (as opposed to one of over 140 million).[5] A League of Free Nations as well as a Forum of the Free Peoples of Russia have staged meetings in Central Europe and called for "freeing imprisoned nations"—a formulation that harkens back to the Tsarist period, when opponents derided Russia as a "prison for nations," and from the CIA-sponsored Anti-Bolshevik Bloc of Nations during the Cold War. Chechen opponents of the Kadyrov regime hope to reopen the domestic front and heavily support Ukraine in its resistance.[6]

Yet dreaming that dismembering Russia would solve the West's "Russia problem" fails to consider that a Russian breakup could also be disastrous for international security.[7] Importantly, Russia will not evolve independent of the global context. The question of the permanence of its current ideological quest, hesitation between isolationism and engagement, between besieged fortress and new crusade, will largely be shaped by parallel developments in other major international players, especially Western countries. For Central and Eastern European countries that find themselves on the frontline of the conflict, such as Poland or the Baltic states, the war is a transformative experience that will shape anti-Russian policies for years to come and impact the EU's internal equilibriums. Ukraine itself will become a significant voice in the debate: its status as a victim, its heroic resistance, its potential place in the EU and NATO frameworks, de jure or de facto, and its powerful and modernized army will have a major say in how things proceed.

And last but not least, Russia's place on US foreign policy chessboards will also impact the construction of a collective future. Reestablishing channels of communication between Washington and Moscow to prevent any escalation, especially in the potential for nuclear confrontation, and a collective debate about how, when, and under which conditions to reintegrate Russian voices on issues of global importance, such as Arctic affairs, climate change, and space cooperation, are very much needed, even more so now that the war seems to have entered into a long, drawn-out phase.

Domestically, Russia's future looks somber, but Western forecasts have failed to capture the country's resilience. The future of Russia's economy is one of decline, shaped by a dramatic change in its export of energy and the loss of access to Western technologies, but with pockets of growth linked to the war, an ability to get by with outdated economic mechanisms, and a reorientation toward the Global South in terms of trade and soft power. The population has entered a phase of defensive consolidation that will help the regime stabilize, even if there are still too many unknown impacts of the war on Russian society to predict the future with any certainty: the number of soldiers dying or being wounded, the brain drain, a heavier indoctrination, a decline in standards of living and state capacity to provide social services, dissatisfaction in ethnic republics, the paramilitarization of society, among other developments, may challenge already fragile domestic equilibriums.

What role will the political regime play in the changes affecting Russia as a state and a nation? How much room for maneuver does the Kremlin have in order to cope with these structural challenges? It is problematic to answer such a question, since the longevity of the Putin regime has obscured our perceptions of alternate futures for the country. What would they look like? If Putin were to leave power, would his successor be more amenable to negotiations and ready to end the war under conditions unfavorable to Russia? Is there a risk of a transformation of Russia into a mercenary state or a military dictatorship in which civilian elites would have lost control over decision-making mechanisms? Can the Russian military's defeats on the ground lay the groundwork for a regime change, as we have seen with Prigozhin's attempted coup? In the case of a stalemate on the ground, can Moscow decide to renew some forms of dialog with the West, and will the West be interested in talking? Can Russia reinvent itself with a more democratic regime without reproducing the mistakes of the 1990s and incurring new, massive societal traumas? Or should we consider that new traumas are a painful but necessary phase to go through to re-create a new political culture? Can the country promote a form of genuine, decentralized federalism without risking secessionism?

Even if the political field reopens to a greater diversity of opinion, the desire to promote a "Russian voice" in the world, whatever its content, and to play a role on the global stage will remain. Many elements of the contemporary ideological toolkit—messianism, conservative values, Russia as an autonomous civilization between East and West—could be easily adapted to other political contexts, including more liberal ones. The country could become more liberal economically without being liberal politically. Equally, Russia could become more politically liberal without advancing a pro-Western agenda. A new Russia will emerge at a certain point once the regime has exhausted its alternatives for ensuring its "survivability." Yet it remains for Russians themselves, the countries around Russia, and the West to reimagine a collective future.

## NOTES

1. Michel Foucher, "Ukraine. Les échelles d'une guerre de libération nationale," *Ramses 2023*, https://www.ifri.org/sites/default/files/atoms/files/ramses2023_foucher .pdf.

2. Ivan U. Klyszcz, "Prepare for Russia's Coming Retrenchment," *PONARS Eurasia Policy Memo*, no. 812 (November 2022).

3. Trita Parsi, "No, Weakening Russia Is Not 'Costing Peanuts' for the U.S.," *New Republic*, January 20, 2023.

4. Casey Michel, "Decolonize Russia," *The Atlantic*, May 27, 2022.

5. "Guerre en Ukraine: Lech Walesa suggère de 'ramener' la Russie à 'moins de 50 millions d'habitants,'" *Le Figaro*, July 10, 2022.

6. Marat Ilyasov, "The Chechen Footprint During Russian Wartime," *PONARS Eurasia Policy Memo*, no.816 (December 16, 2022), https://www.ponarseurasia.org/ the-chechen-footprint-during-russian-wartime.

7. Marlene Laruelle, "Putin's War and the Dangers of Russian Disintegration," *Foreign Affairs*, December 2022.

# Selected Bibliography

Ablaev, Ildar. "Innovation Clusters in the Russian Economy: Economic Essence, Concepts, Approaches." *Procedia Economics & Finance* 24 (2015): 3–12. http://www.sciencedirect.com/science/article/pii/S221256711500605X.

"Abramovich, Roman." *Lenta.ru.* https://lenta.ru/lib/14161457.

Agadjanian, Alexander. "Religious Pluralism and National Identity in Russia." *International Journal on Multicultural Societies* 2, no. 2 (2000): 97–124.

Aitamurto, Kaarina. "Reviving the Native Faith: Nationalism in Contemporary Slavic Paganism Rodnoverie." *Forum für osteuropäische Ideen und Zeitgeschichte* 1, no. 2 (2011): 167–84.

Andreff, Wladimir. *Économie de la transition. La transformation des économies planifiées en économies de marché.* Paris: Bréal, 2007.

Arnold, Richard. "Testing Constructivism: Why Not More 'Cossacks' in Krasnodar Kray?" *Post-Soviet Affairs* 30, no. 6 (2014): 481–502.

———. "Visions of Hate: Explaining Neo-Nazi Violence in the Russian Federation." *Problems of Post-Communism* 57, no. 2 (2010): 37–59.

Aslund, Anders. *Russia's Crony Capitalism: The Path from Market Economy to Kleptocracy.* New Haven, CT: Yale University Press, 2019.

*Atlas religii i natsional'snostei Rossii.* 2012. http://sreda.org/arena/maps.

Audinet, Maxime. *Russia Today: Un media d'influence au service de l'Etat russe.* Paris: I.N.A., 2021.

Audinet, Maxime, and Kevin Limonier. "Le dispositif d'influence informationnelle de la Russie en Afrique subsaharienne francophone: Un écosystème flexible et composite." *Questions de communication* 41, no. 1 (2022): 129–48.

Avdeyeva, Olga A. "Policy Experiment in Russia: Cash-for-Babies and Fertility Change." *Social Politics: International Studies in Gender, State & Society* 18, no. 3 (2011): 361–86.

Avrutin, Eugene. *Racism in Modern Russia: From the Romanovs to Putin.* London: Bloomsbury, 2022.

Baidakova, Anna. "Gennadii Gudkov: 'Natsional'nuiu gvardiiu gotoviat k podavleniiu sotsialnogo protesta." *Novaia gazeta*, April 6, 2016. https://www.novayagazeta.ru/articles/2016/04/06/68105-gennadiy-gudkov-171-natsionalnuyu-gvardiyu-gotovyat-k-podavleniyu-sotsialnogo-protesta-187.

Balzer, Harley. "Vladimir Putin's Academic Writings and Russian Natural Resource Policy." *Problems of Post-Communism* 53, no. 1 (2006): 48–54.

Bantekas, Ilias. "Bilateral Delimitation of the Caspian Sea and the Exclusion of Third Parties." *International Journal of Marine & Coastal Law* 26, no. 1 (2011): 47–58.

"Baza dannykh: akty nasiliia." Sova Center. https://www.sova-center.ru/database/violence.

Bertrand, Eva. "Pouvoir, catastrophe et représentation: Mise(s) en scène politique(s) des incendies de l'été 2010 en Russie occidentale." PhD diss., Sciences Po, Paris, 2016.

Blank, Stephen, ed. *Russia and the Current State of Arms Control.* Carlisle, PA: Strategic Studies Institute, 2012.

Borenstein, Eliot. *Plots against Russia: Conspiracy and Fantasy after Socialism.* Ithaca, NY: Cornell University Press, 2019.

Bortsov, Andrei. "Russko-kitaiskii samolet sotrudnichestva vzletaet vse vyshe." *Politicheskaia Rossiia,* June 27, 2016. http://politrussia.com/world/o-russko-kitayskom-dalnemagistralnom-602.

Breault, Yann, Pierre Jolicœur, and Jacques Lévesque. *La Russie et son ex-empire: Reconfiguration géopolitique de l'ancien espace soviétique.* Paris: Presses de Sciences Po, 2003.

Brezhneva, Anna, and Daria Ukhova. "Russian as a Humanitarian Aid Donor." Oxfam Discussion Paper, July 2013. https://www.oxfam.org/en/research/russia-humanitarian-aid-donor.

"Britaniia ozabochena resheniem po 'Sakhalinu-2.'" BBC Russia, September 20, 2006. http://news.bbc.co.uk/hi/russian/russia/newsid_5363000/5363114.stm.

Brubaker, Rogers. "Between Nationalism and Civilizationism: The European Populist Moment in Comparative Perspective." *Ethnic and Racial Studies* 40, no. 8 (2017): 1191–1226.

Brudny, Yitzhak M. *Reinventing Russia: Russian Nationalism and the Soviet State, 1953–1991.* Cambridge, MA: Harvard University Press, 2000.

Brzezinski, Zbigniew. *The Grand Chessboard: American Primacy and Its Geostrategic Imperatives.* New York: Basic Books, 1998.

———, and Paige Sullivan, eds. *Russia and the Commonwealth of Independent States: Documents, Data, and Analysis.* Armonk, NY: M. E. Sharpe, 1997.

Casamayou, J. P. "Sukhoï investit en Sibérie pour son Superjet-100." *Air & Cosmos,* May 1, 2007.

*CCI France Russie.* https://www.youtube.com/c/ccifrancerussie.

Charap, Samuel, and Timothy Colton. *Everyone Loses: The Ukraine Crisis and the Ruinous Contest for Post-Soviet Eurasia.* London: Routledge, 2017.

Cheterian, Vicken. *War and Peace in the Caucasus: Ethnic Conflict and the New Geopolitics.* New York: Columbia University Press, 2008.

Connolly, Richard, and Philip Hanson. "Russia's Accession to the World Trade Organization: Commitments, Processes, and Prospects." *Eurasian Geography & Economics* 53 (2012): 479–501.

Cooley, Alexander. "Scripts of Sovereignty: The Freezing of the Russia–Ukraine Crisis and Dilemmas of Governance in Eurasia." *Center on Global Interests,* January 30, 2015.

"Dagestanu ponadobilos' 900 millionov na pereselenie lezgin iz Azerbaidzhana." Lenta.ru, December 26, 2012. https ://lenta.ru/news/2012/12/26/resettlement.

Dalakian, Ignat. "Putin zaiavil, chto RF aktivno zanimaietsia pereorientatsiei ekonomicheskikh potokov na nadiozhnykh partnyorov." *Zvezda,* June 22, 2022. https://tvzvezda.ru/news/20226221445-VtyAl.html.

Dal'gren, Lennart. *Vopreki absurdu, ili kaki ia pokorial Rossiiu, a ona—menia: Vospominaniia byvshego general'nogo direktora IKEA v Rossii.* Moscow: Al'pina Biznes Buks, 2010.

"Dat volnuiu Femide: retsepty reformirovaniia sudebnoi sistemy ot Alekseia Kudrina i Borisa Titova." *Real'noe vremia,* March 24, 2017. https://realnoevremya.ru/articles/60123-recepty-reformirovaniya-sudebnoy-sistemy-ot-kudrina-i-titova.

Daucé, Françoise. *L'État, l'armée et le citoyen en Russie post-soviétique.* Paris: L'Harmattan, 2001.

Dawisha, Karen. "Vladislav Surkov, 1964–." In *Russia's People of Empire: Life Stories from Eurasia, 1500 to the Present,* edited by Stephen Norris and Willard Sunderland, 339–49. Bloomington: Indiana University Press, 2012.

De Tinguy, Anne. *La grande migration.* Paris: Plon, 2004.

Désert, Myriam, and Gilles Favarel-Garrigues. "Les capitalistes russes." *Problèmes politiques et sociaux,* no. 789 (August 1997).

Dollbaum, Jan Matti, Marvan Lallouet, and Ben Noble. *Navalny: Putin's Nemesis, Russia's Future?* 2nd ed. London: Hurst Publishers, 2021.

Dutkiewicz, Piotr, and Richard Sakwa, eds. *Eurasian Union: The View from Within.* London: Routledge, 2015.

Eady, Gregory, Tom Paskhalis, Jan Zilinsky, Richard Bonneau, Jonathan Nagler, and Joshua A. Tucker. "Exposure to the Russian Internet Research Agency Foreign Influence Campaign on Twitter in the 2016 US Election and Its Relationship to Attitudes and Voting Behavior." *Nature Communications* 14, no. 62 (2023), https://www.nature.com/articles/s41467-022-35576-9.

Ehrmann, Eric. "Washington, WikiLeaks and Russian Soft Power." *Russian International Affairs Council,* August 23, 2013.

"Elektoral'nyi reiting politicheskikh partii." VTsIOM. https://wciom.ru/news/ratings/elektoralnyj_rejting_politicheskix_partij.

Eltchaninoff, Michel. *Inside the Mind of Vladimir Putin.* New York: Hurst, 2018.

Evans, Alfred B. "Protests and Civil Society in Russia: The Struggle for the Khimki Forest." *Communist and Post-Communist Studies* 45, no. 3–4 (2012): 233–42.

Fabry, Mikulas. "The Contemporary Practice of State Recognition: Kosovo, South Ossetia, Abkhazia, and Their Aftermath." *Nationalities Papers: Journal of Nationalism & Ethnicity* 40, no. 5 (2012): 661–76.

Facon, Isabelle. *La Nouvelle Armée russe.* Paris: L'Inventaire, 2021.

———. *La nouvelle stratégie de sécurité nationale de la Fédération de Russie.* Paris: Fondation pour la recherche stratégique, 2016. https://www.frstrategie.org

/publications/notes/la-nouvelle-strategie-de-securite-nationale-de-la-federation-de -russie-2016-05.

Favarel-Garrigues, Gilles. *La verticale de la peur. Ordre et allégeance en Russie poutinienne.* Paris: La découverte, 2023.

Ferdinand, Peter. "Westward Ho: The China Dream and 'One Belt, One Road': Chinese Foreign Policy under Xi Jinping." *International Affairs* 92, no. 4 (2016): 941–57.

Foa, Roberto, Margot Mollat, Han Isha, Xavier Romero-Vidal, David Evans, and Andrew J. Klassen. *A World Divided: Russia, China, and the West.* Centre for the Future of Democracy, October 2022. https://bennettinstitute.cam.ac.uk/wp-content /uploads/2023/01/A_World_Divided.pdf.

Foucher, Michel. "Ukraine: Les échelles d'une guerre de libération nationale." *Ramses 2023,* https://www.ifri.org/sites/default/files/atoms/files/ramses2023_foucher.pdf.

Freire, Maria-Raquel, and Roger E. Kanet, eds. *Key Players and Regional Dynamics in Eurasia: The Return of the "Great Game."* New York: Palgrave, 2010.

Fridman, Ofer. *Russian Hybrid Warfare: Resurgence and Politicisation.* Oxford: Oxford University Press, 2018.

Gaddy, Clifford G., and Barry W. Ickes. "Resource Rents and the Russian Economy." *Eurasian Geography & Economics* 46, no. 8 (2005): 559–83.

———. "Russia's Declining Oil Production: Managing Price Risk and Rent Addiction." *Eurasian Geography & Economics* 50, no. 1 (2009): 1–13.

Gel'man, Vladimir. "The Rise and Decline of Electoral Authoritarianism in Russia." *Demokratizatsiya* 22, no. 4 (2014): 503–22.

Gerber, Theodore. "Beyond Putin? Nationalism and Xenophobia in Russian Public Opinion." *Washington Quarterly* 37, no. 3 (2014): 113–34.

Giuliano, Elise. *Constructing Grievance: Ethnic Nationalism in Russia's Republics.* Ithaca, NY: Cornell University Press, 2011.

Gloriozova, Ekaterina, and Aude Merlin, eds. "Sotchi-2014: La Russie à l'épreuve de ses Jeux, les Jeux à l'épreuve du Caucase." *Connexe, les espaces post-communistes en question(s),* no. 2 (December 2016).

Goldman, Marshall I. "The 'Russian Disease.'" *International Economy* 19, no. 3 (2005): 27–31.

Gorenburg, Dmitry. "Regional Separatism in Russia: Ethnic Mobilization or Power Grab?" *Europe-Asia Studies* 51, no. 2 (1999): 245–74.

"Gosudarstvennaia programma 'Patrioticheskoe vospitanie grazhdan Rossiiskoi Federatsii na 2001–2005 gg.'" Gosudarstvennaia sistema pravovoi informatsii. http: //pravo.gov.ru/ipsdata/?doc_itself=&collection=1&backlink=1&nd=201006229 &page=1&rdk=0#I0.

"Gosudarstvennaia programma 'Patrioticheskoe vospitanie grazhdan RF na 2006– 2010 gody.'" Gosudarstvennaia sistema pravovoi informatsii. http://pravo.gov.ru/ proxy/ips/?docbody=&nd=102098946&intelsearch=1233+03.11.1994.

Greene, Samuel. *Moscow in Movement: Power and Opposition in Putin's Russia.* Stanford, CA: Stanford University Press, 2014.

Grieco, Kelly A., and Marie Journal. "Democracy vs. Autocracy Is the Wrong Framing for the War in Ukraine." *World Politics Review,* June 14, 2022. https://

www.worldpoliticsreview.com/democracy-vs-autocracy-is-the-wrong-framing-for
-ukraine-war.

Gudkov, Lev D. "Ethnic Phobias in the Structure of National Identification." *Russian Social Science Review* 39, no. 1 (1998): 89–103.

Gudkov, Lev. "Pamiat' o voine i massovaia identichnost' rossiian." *Neprikosnovennyi zapas*, no. 40–41 (2005).

Guillot, Michel, Natalia Gavrilova, and Tetyana Pudrovska. "Understanding the 'Russian Mortality Paradox' in Central Asia: Evidence from Kyrgyzstan." *Demography* 48, no. 3 (2011): 1081–1104.

Hale, Henry, and Marlene Laruelle. "Rethinking Civilizational Identity from the Bottom Up: A Case Study of Russia and a Research Agenda." *Nationalities Papers* 48, no. 3 (2020): 585–602.

Hale, Henry, Maria Lipman, and Nikolay Petrov. "Russia's Regime-on-the-Move." *Russian Politics* 4, no. 2 (2019): 168–95.

Hanson, Philip. *Russian Economic Policy and the Russian Economic System Stability versus Growth*. Chatham House, December 2019. https://www.chathamhouse.org/sites/default/files/CHHJ7799-Russia-Economics-RP-WEB-FINAL.pdf.

Hedenskog, Jakov, and Robert L. Larsson. *Russian Leverage on the CIS and the Baltic States*. Stockholm: FOI, Swedish Defence Research Agency, 2007.

Henriksen, Tore, and Geir Ulfstein. "Maritime Delimitation in the Arctic: The Barents Sea Treaty." *Ocean Development & International Law* 42, no. 1–2 (2011): 1–21.

Holland, Edward, and Eldar Eldarov. "'Going Away on Foot' Once Again: The Revival of Temporary Labour Migration from Russia's Dagestan." *Central Asian Survey* 31, no. 4 (2012): 379–93.

Hutchings, Stephen. *Projecting Russia in a Mediatized World: Recursive Nationhood*. London: Routledge, 2022.

Ikenberry, G. John. "The Liberal International Order and Its Discontents." *Millennium: Journal of International Studies* 38, no. 3 (2010): 509–21.

Ilyasov, Marat. "The Chechen Footprint during Russian Wartime." *PONARS Eurasia Policy Memo*, no. 816 (December 16, 2022). https://www.ponarseurasia.org/the-chechen-footprint-during-russian-wartime.

*Insights of the French-Russian Observatory*. Paris, 2013–. http://obsfr.ru/fr/le-rapport-annuel.html.

"'Inter RAO' ne vyderzhalo armianskikh dram." *Kommersant*, June 29, 2015.

"Izmenenie chislennosti naselenie po variantam prognoza," "Demograficheskii prognoz do 2036 goda." Rosstat, 2021. https://rosstat.gov.ru/storage/mediabank/progn1.xls.

Jurczyszyn, Lukasz. "Russian Radical Nationalist Interpretation of the French Riots of November 2005." *Demokratizatsiya: Journal of Post-Soviet Democratization* 19, no. 3 (2011): 277–85.

Kaczmarski, Marcin. *Russia-China Relations in the Post-Crisis International Order*. London: Routledge, 2015.

Kaganskii, Vladimir. *Kul'turnyi landshaft i sovetskoe obytaemoe prostranstvo: sbornik statei* Moscow: NLO, 2001.

Kalandadze, Katya, and Mitchell A. Orenstein. "Electoral Protests and Democratization beyond the Color Revolutions." *Comparative Political Studies* 42 (2009): 1403–25.

Kappeler, Andreas. *Russes et Ukrainiens, les frères inégaux*. Paris: CNRS Éditions, 2022.

Karpova Galina G., and Maria A. Vorona. "Labour Migration in Russia: Issues and Policies." *International Social Work* 57, no. 5 (2014): 535–46.

Kastoryano, Riva, ed. *Les codes de la différence. Race, origine, religion. France, Allemagne, États-Unis*. Paris: Presses de Sciences Po, 2005.

Kasyanov, Mikhail. *Bez Putina. Politicheskie dialogi s Evgeniem Kiselevym*. Moscow: Novaia gazeta, 2009.

Kavykin, Oleg. *"Rodnovery": Samoidentifikatsiia neo-iazychnikov v sovremennoi Rossii*. Moscow: Institut Afriki RAN, 2007.

Kernen, Beat. "Putin and the Parliamentary Election in Russia: The Confluence (Slijanie) of Russian Political Culture and Leadership." *East European Quarterly* 38, no. 1 (2004): 85–107.

Klyszcz, Ivan U. "Prepare for Russia's Coming Retrenchment." *PONARS Eurasia Policy Memo*, no. 812 (November 2022).

Kochergina, Ekaterina. "Predstavleniia o gendernykh roliakh i gendernom ravnopravii v Rossii. Analiz dannykh massovykh oprosov za 30 let." *Vestnik obschestvennogo mneniia Dannye. Analiz. Diskussii* 3–4 (2018).

Kolosov, Vladimir, and Olga Vendina, eds. *Rossiisko-ukrainskoe pogranich'e. Dvadtsat' let razdelennogo edinstva*. Moscow: Novyi Khronograf, 2011.

Kolstø, Pål. "Marriage of Convenience? Collaboration between Nationalists and Liberals in the Russian Opposition 2011–12." *Russian Review* 75, no. 4 (2016): 645–63.

Kondakov, Alexander. "The Silenced Citizens of Russia: Exclusion of Non-Heterosexual Subjects from Rights-Based Citizenship." *Social & Legal Studies* 23, no. 2 (2014): 151–74.

"Konflikt s Ukrainoi: otsenki dekabria 2022ogo goda." Levada Center, December 23, 2022. https://www.levada.ru/2022/12/23/konflikt-s-ukrainoj-otsenki-dekabrya -2022-goda.

Kragh, Martin. "Conspiracy Theories in Russian Security Thinking." *Journal of Strategic Studies* 45, no. 3 (2022): 334–68.

Kramer, Mark. "The Myth of a No-NATO-Enlargement Pledge to Russia." *Washington Quarterly* 32, no. 2 (April 2009): 39–61.

Kuboniwa, Masaaki. "Diagnosing the 'Russian Disease': Growth and Structure of the Russian Economy." *Comparative Economic Studies* 54, no. 1 (2012): 121–48.

Laruelle, Marlene. "Alexei Navalny and Challenges in Reconciling 'Nationalism' and 'Liberalism.'" *Post-Soviet Affairs* 30, no. 4 (2014): 276–97.

———. "Commemorating 1917 in Russia: Ambivalent State History Policy and the Church's Conquest of the History Market." *Europe-Asia Studies* 71, no. 2 (2019): 249–67.

———, ed. Eurasianism and the European Far Right: Reshaping the Europe-Russia Relationship. Lanham, MD: Lexington, 2015.

————. "A Grassroots Conservatism? Taking a Fine-Grained View of Conservative Attitudes among Russians." *East European Politics* (March 2022).

————. *In the Name of the Nation: Nationalism and Politics in Contemporary Russia.* New York: Palgrave Macmillan, 2009.

————. "Indigenous Peoples, Urbanization Processes, and Interactions with Extraction Firms in Russia's Arctic." *Sibirica* 18, no. 3 (2019): 1–8.

————. *Is Russia Fascist? Unraveling Propaganda East and West.* Ithaca, NY: Cornell University Press, 2021.

————. "Russia as a 'Divided Nation,' from Compatriots to Crimea: A Contribution to the Discussion on Nationalism and Foreign Policy." *Problems of Post-Communism* 62, no. 2 (2015): 88–97.

————. "Russia as an Anti-Liberal European Civilization." In *The New Russian Nationalism: Between Imperial and Ethnic*, edited by Pål Kolstø and Helge Blakkisrud, 275–97. Edinburgh: Edinburgh University Press, 2016.

————. "Russia at War and the Muslim World." In *Russie.NEI.Visions.* Paris: IFRI, 2023.

————, Ivan Grek, and Sergey Davydov. "Culturalizing the Nation: A Quantitative Approach to the Russkii/Rossiiskii Semantic Space in Russia's Political Discourse." *Demokratizatsiya: The Journal of Post-Soviet Democratization*, no. 1 (2023): 3–28.

————, and Sophie Hohmann. "Biography of a Polar City: Population Flows and Urban Identity in Norilsk." *Polar Geography* 40, no. 4 (2017): 306–23.

————, and Sophie Hohmann. "Polar Islam: Muslim Communities in Russia's Arctic Cities." *Problems of Post-Communism* 67, no. 4–5 (2020): 327–37.

————, and Natalia Yudina. "Islamophobia in Russia: Trends and Societal Context." In *Religious Violence in Russia*, edited by Olga Oliker and Jeffrey Mankoff. Washington, DC: CSIS, 2018.

Lieven, Anatol. *Chechnya: Tombstone of Russian Power.* New Haven, CT: Yale University Press, 1999.

Limanov, Aleksandr. "Vsio luchshee–detiam." *Novoe vremia*, no. 21 (206), June 18, 2011.

Lynch, Allen C. "Russia's 'Neopatrimonial' Political System, 1992–2004." In *How Russia Is Not Ruled: Reflections on Russian Political Development*, 128–65. Cambridge: Cambridge University Press, 2005.

Magun, Vladimir, and Maksim Rudnev. "Basic Values of Russians and Other Europeans: (According to the Materials of Surveys in 2008)." *Problems of Economic Transition* 54, no. 10 (2012): 31–64.

Makarychev, Andrey. "The Legacies of the 2018 FIFA World Cup in Russia: Three Facets of Mega-Events' Biopolitics." In *Mega Events, Urban Transformation, and Social Citizenship*, edited by Naomi Hanakata, Filippo Bignami, and Niccolo Cuppini. London: Routledge, 2022.

Malinova, Olga. "The Embarrassing Centenary: Reinterpretation of the 1917 Revolution in the Official Historical Narrative of Post-Soviet Russia." *Nationalities Papers* 46, no. 2 (2018): 272–89.

Mälksoo, Lauri. "Which Continuity? The Tartu Peace Treaty of 2 February 1920, the Estonian-Russian Border Treaties of 2005, and the Legal Debate about Estonia's Status in International Law." *Archiv des Völkerrechts* 43, no. 4 (2005): 513–24.

Mandraud, Isabelle. "A Moscou, le Comité d'enquête, bras judiciaire de Poutine." *Le Monde*, February 25, 2015. http://www.lemonde.fr/international/article/2015/02/05/a-moscou-le-bras-arme-de-poutine_4570142_3210.html.

Mearsheimer, John. *The Great Delusion: Liberal Dreams and International Realities*. New Haven, CT: Yale University Press, 2018.

Mendras, Marie. *Russie: Le débat sur l'intérêt national*. Paris: La Documentation française, 1992.

Minchenko, Ievgenii. "Sistemnye riski komandy Putina." *Nezavisimaia gazeta*, December 2, 2014. http://www.ng.ru/ng_politics/2014-12-02/9_risks.html.

Mingazov, Sergei. "Schetnaia palata otchitalas' o roste neftegazovykh dokhodov biudzheta v 1,7 raza." *Forbes*, August 30, 2022. https://www.forbes.ru/finansy/475741-scetnaa-palata-otcitalas-o-roste-neftegazovyh-dohodov-budzeta-v-1-7-raza.

Mitrokhin, Nikolai. *"Russkaia partiia": dvizhenie russkikh natsionalistov v SSSR 1953–1985 gg.* Moscow: NLO, 2003.

Moreau, Patrick, and Stéphane Courtois, eds. *En Europe, l'éternel retour des communistes 1989–2014*. Paris: Vendémiaire, 2014.

Morris, Jeremy. *Everyday Post-Socialism: Working-Class Communities in the Russian Margins*. London: Palgrave Macmillan, 2016.

———. "Russians in Wartime and Defensive Consolidation." *Current History* 121, no. 837 (2022): 258–63.

———, and Masha Garibyan. "Russian Cultural Conservatism Critiqued: Translating the Tropes of 'Gayropa' and 'Juvenile Justice' in Everyday Life." *Europe-Asia Studies* 73, no. 8 (2021): 1487–1507.

Motyl, Alexander. "Putin's Russia as a Fascist Political System." *Communist & Post-Communist Studies* 49, no. 1 (2016): 25–36.

Narochnitskaia, Nataliia. "Za chto nas ne liubiat." Interview. *Story*, August 2013. https://pravoslavie.ru/63668.html.

Natoli, Kristopher. "Weaponizing Nationality: An Analysis of Russia's Passport Policy in Georgia." *Boston University International Law Journal* 28 (2010): 389–417.

Naumov, Aleksandr. "Perspektivy razvitiia rossiiskogo avtoproma." *Mirovoe i natsional'noe khoziaistvo*, no. 2 (2010): 51–59.

Nemtsov, Boris, and Vladimir Milov. *Putin. Itogi. 10 let*. Moscow: Solidarsnost,' 2010.

Nikitina, Viktoriia. "Dorogi RF v 38 raz dorozhe i v 2 raza 'nezhnee' kanadskikh." *Argumenty i fakty*, June 8, 2011. http://www.aif.ru/money/25863.

"Nostal'giya po SSSR." Levada Center, December 19, 2018. https://www.levada.ru/2018/12/19/nostalgiya-po-sssr-2/?fromtg=1.

"Nuzhno-li patrioticheskoe vospitanie?" FOM, July 20, 2020. https://fom.ru/TSennosti/14411.

"Obshchaia chislennost pensionerov v Rossiiskoi Federatsii." Rosstat, 2022. https://rosstat.gov.ru/storage/mediabank/sp_2.1.docx.

*Obshchestvennoie mnenie—2013*. Moscow: Levada Center, 2014.

*Obshchestvennoie mnenie—2014*. Moscow: Levada Center, 2015.

*Obshchestvennoie mnenie—2020*. Moscow: Levada Center, 2021.

*Obshchestvennoie mnenie—2021*. Levada Center, 2021. https://levada.ru/cp/wp-content/uploads/2022/04/OM-2021.pdf.

O'Dwyer, Connor. "Gay Rights and Political Homophobia in Postcommunist Europe: Is There an EU Effect?" In *Global Homophobia: States, Movements, and the Politics of Oppression*, edited by Meredith Weiss and Michael Bosia. Champaign: University of Illinois Press, 2013.

Omelicheva, Mariya. "United We Stand (with Russia)? How Moscow's Soft Power Shaped Views on the War." *PONARS Eurasia Policy Memo*, no. 10 (November 14, 2022). https://www.ponarseurasia.org/united-we-stand-with-russia-how-moscows-soft-power-shaped-views-on-the-war.

O'Neill, Jim. *The Growth Map: Economic Opportunity in the BRICs and Beyond*. London: Penguin Books, 2011.

Orttung, Robert, and Sufian Zhemukhov. *Putin's Olympics: The Sochi Games and the Evolution of Twenty-First Century Russia*. London: Routledge, 2017.

"Otnosheniie rossiian k LGBT liudiam." Levada Center, October 15, 2021. https://www.levada.ru/2021/10/15/otnoshenie-rossiyan-k-lgbt-lyudyam.

Parsi, Trita. "No, Weakening Russia Is Not 'Costing Peanuts' for the U.S." *New Republic*, January 20, 2023.

Perevoshchikova, Mariia. "Moll da dorog: v Rossii mozhet zakrytsia kazhdyi vtoroi torgovyi tsentr." *Izvestiia*, November 30, 2022. https://iz.ru/1433209/mariia-perevoshchikova/moll-da-dorog-v-rossii-mozhet-zakrytsia-kazhdyi-vtoroi-torgovyi-tcentr.

Petrov, Nikolai, and Darrell Slider. "Putin and the Regions." In *Putin's Russia: Past Imperfect, Future Uncertain*, 2nd ed., edited by Dale Herspring, 75–98. Lanham, MD: Rowman & Littlefield, 2005.

Peyrouse, Sebastien. "Former 'Colonists' on the Move? The Migration of Russian-Speaking Populations." In *Migration and Social Upheaval as the Face of Globalization in Central Asia*, edited by Marlene Laruelle, 215–38. London: Brill, 2013.

Piketty, Thomas. "La Russie poutinienne se caractérise par une dérive kleptocratique sans limites." *Le Monde*, April 7, 2018. http://www.lemonde.fr/idees/article/2018/04/07/piketty-la-russie-poutinienne-se-caracterise-par-une-derive-kleptocratique-sans-limites_5282016_3232.html.

Pilkington, Hilary, Elena Omel'chenko, and Al'bina Garifzianova. *Russia's Skinheads: Exploring and Rethinking Subcultural Lives*. London: Routledge, 2010.

Plater-Zyberk, Henry, and Andrew Monaghan. *Strategic Implications of the Evolving Shanghai Cooperation Organization*. Carlisle, PA: Strategic Studies Institute and U.S. Army War College Press, 2014.

Podobedova, Liudmila, and Natal'ia Derbysheva. "V Pribaltiku ni truboi." *RBK*, September 12, 2016. http://www.rbc.ru/newspaper/2016/09/13/57d6c5779a7947b83d50f2d3.

"Polozhitel'naia ekologicheskaia ekspertiza proekta 'Sakhalin-2' otmenena." RIA Novosti, September 19, 2006. https://ria.ru/20060919/54059888.html.

"Pravitelstvo RF vydelit okolo 44 mlrd rublei na proizvodstvo aviadvigatelei." *Kommersant,* November 14, 2022. https://www.kommersant.ru/doc/5667456.

Pribylovskii, Vladimir. *Kooperativ Ozero i drugie proekty Putina.* Moscow: Algoritm, 2012.

Radvanyi, Jean. "Quand Vladimir Poutine se fait géographe." *Hérodote* 3–4, no. 166–167 (2017): 113–32.

———. *La Russie face à ses régions: Problèmes politiques et sociaux.* Paris: La Documentation française, 1994.

———. *Russie, un vertige de puissance.* Paris: La Découverte, 2023.

———, and Nicolas Beroutchachvili. *Atlas géopolitique du Caucase.* Paris: Autrement, 2010.

Reeves, Madeleine. "Clean Fake: Authenticating Documents and Persons in Migrant Moscow." *American Ethnologist* 40, no. 3 (2013): 508–24.

Robertson, Graeme. "The Election Protests of 2011–2012 in Broader Perspective." *Problems of Post-Communism* 60, no. 2 (2013): 11–23.

Rogov, Kirill. "Putin's Reelection: Capturing Russia's Electoral Patterns." *PONARS Eurasia,* June 7, 2018. https://www.ponarseurasia.org/putin-s-reelection-capturing -russia-s-electoral-patterns-a-discussion-with-kirill-rogov.

Rousselet, Kathy. "Butovo: La création d'un lieu de pèlerinage sur une terre de massacres." *Politix* 20, no. 77 (2007): 55–78.

Saari, Sinikukka. "Russia's Post-Orange Revolution Strategies to Increase Its Influence in the Former Soviet Republics: Public Diplomacy *po russki.*" *Europe-Asia Studies* 66, no. 1 (2014): 50–66.

Sabitov, Richat. *Le fédéralisme russe contemporain et la République du Tatarstan.* Paris: Fondation Varenne, 2013.

Sagers, Matthew. "The Regional Dimension of Russian Oil Production: Is a Sustained Recovery in Prospect?" *Eurasian Geography & Economics* 47, no. 5 (2006): 505–45.

———. "Russia's Energy Policy: A Divergent View." *Eurasian Geography & Economics* 47, no. 3 (2006): 314–20.

Sakwa, Richard. "Putin's Leadership: Character and Consequences." *Europe-Asia Studies* 60, no. 6 (2008): 879–97.

———. *The Quality of Freedom: Khodorkovsky, Putin, and the Yukos Affair.* Oxford: Oxford University Press, 2009.

———. *Russia against the Rest: The Post–Cold War Crisis of World Order.* Cambridge: Cambridge University Press, 2017.

"Sanktsii zapada." Levada Center, June 8, 2022. https://www.levada.ru/2022/06/08/ sanktsii-zapada.

Sapir, Jacques. "Stratégie industrielle russe." *Hypotheses* (blog), May 30, 2015, http: //russeurope.hypotheses.org/3879.

Sarotte, Mary Elise. *Not One Inch: America, Russia, and the Making of Post–Cold War Stalemate.* New Haven, CT: Yale University Press, 2021.

Schenk, Caress. "Controlling Immigration Manually: Lessons from Moscow (Russia)." *Europe-Asia Studies* 65, no. 7 (2013): 1444–65.

———. "Open Borders, Closed Minds: Russia's Changing Migration Policies: Liberalization or Xenophobia?" *Demokratizatsiya: Journal of Post-Soviet Democratization* 18, no. 2 (2010): 101–21.

Schroeder, Gertrude. "Dimensions of Russia's Industrial Transformation, 1992 to 1998: An Overview." *Post-Soviet Geography & Economics* 39, no. 5 (1998): 243–70.

Scicchitano, Dominic. "The 'Real' Chechen Man: Conceptions of Religion, Nature, and Gender and the Persecution of Sexual Minorities in Postwar Chechnya." *Journal of Homosexuality* 68, no. 9 (2021): 1545–62.

Sell, Louis. "Embassy under Siege: An Eyewitness Account of Yeltsin's 1993 Attack on Parliament." *Problems of Post-Communism* 50, no. 4 (2003): 43–64.

Sharafutdinova, Gulnaz. "Paradiplomacy in the Russian Regions: Tatarstan's Search for Statehood." *Europe-Asia Studies* 55, no. 4 (2003): 613–29.

———. "The Pussy Riot Affair and Putin's Demarche from Sovereign Democracy to Sovereign Morality." *Nationalities Papers: Journal of Nationalism & Ethnicity* 42, no. 4 (2014): 615–21.

———. *The Red Mirror: Putin's Leadership and Russia's Insecure Identity*. Oxford: Oxford University Press, 2020.

Sharp, Rachel, "Francis Fukuyama Says Russian Defeat in Ukraine Will 'Make Possible a New Birth of Freedom.'" *The Independent*, March 14, 2022. https://www.independent.co.uk/news/world/americas/russia-ukraine-invasion-francis-fukuyama-b2035413.html.

Shekhovtsov, Anton. *Russia and the Western Far Right: Tango Noir*. London: Routledge, 2017.

Shevel, Oxana. "The Politics of Citizenship Policy in Post-Soviet Russia." *Post-Soviet Affairs* 28, no. 1 (2012): 111–47.

———. "Russian Nation-Building from Yeltsin to Medvedev: Ethnic, Civic, or Purposefully Ambiguous?" *Europe-Asia Studies* 63, no. 1 (2011): 179–202.

Shnirel'man, Victor. "Arkaim: arkheologiia, ezotericheskii turizm i natsional'naia ideia." *Antropologicheskii forum*, no. 114 (2014): 134–67.

Silaev, Nikolai. "Chechen Nation-Building under Kadyrov: A Belated 'Korenizatsiya'?" *Problems of Post-Communism* (July 2022).

Slezkine, Yuri. "The USSR as a Communal Apartment, or How a Socialist State Promoted Ethnic Particularism." *Slavic Review* 53, no. 2 (1994): 414–52.

Smyth, Regina. "How the Kremlin Is Using the Moscow Renovation Project to Reward and Punish Voters." *PONARS Eurasia Policy Memo*, no. 513 (March 6, 2018). https://www.ponarseurasia.org/how-the-kremlin-is-using-the-moscow-renovation-project-to-reward-and-punish-voters.

Snegovaya, Maria, and Kirill Petrov. "Long Soviet Shadow: The Nomenklatura Ties of Putin Elites." *Post-Soviet Affairs* 38, no. 4 (2022): 329–48.

Snyder, Timothy. *The Reconstruction of Nations: Poland, Ukraine, Lithuania, Belarus, 1569–1999*. New Haven, CT: Yale University Press, 2004.

Soboleva, Irina, and Yaroslav Bakhmetjev. "Political Awareness and Self-Blame in the Explanatory Narratives of LGBT People amid the Anti-LGBT Campaign in Russia." *Sexuality & Culture* 19, no. 2 (2015): 275–96.

Soldatov, Andrei, and Irina Borogan. *The Red Web: The Kremlin's Wars on the Internet*. New York: Public Affairs, 2017.

Solov'eva, Ol'ga. "Vmesto pervoi piaterki Rossiia popala v glubokuiu zastoinuiu iamu." *Nezavisimaia Gazeta*, November 27, 2018. https://www.ng.ru/economics /2018-11-27/1_7449_crisis.html.

Solzhenitsyn, Alexander. *Rebuilding Russia*. London: Harvill, 1991.

Sonnenfeld, Jeffrey A., Steven Tian, Franek Sokolowski, Michal Wyrebkowski, and Mateusz Kasprowicz. "Business Retreats and Sanctions Are Crippling the Russian Economy." Yale University, July 19, 2022. https://papers.ssrn.com/sol3/papers.cfm ?abstract_id=4167193.

*Sotsial'nyi atlas rossiiskikh regionov*. Moscow: Nezavisimyi institut sotsial'noi politiki, 2017. http://www.socpol.ru/atlas/overviews/social_sphere/kris.shtml.

"Statistika vyezda rossiian za rubezh v 2019 godu. Ofitsialnye dannye." Association of Tour Operators of Russia, February 17, 2020. https://www.atorus.ru/news/press -centre/new/50475.html.

Stella, Francesca. "The Right to Be Different? Sexual Citizenship and Its Politics in Post-Soviet Russia." In *Gender, Equality and Difference during and after State Socialism*, edited by Rebecca Kay, 146–66. London: Palgrave Macmillan, 2007.

Stoeckle, Kristina, and Dmitry Uzlaner. *The Moralist International: Russia in the Global Culture Wars*. New York: Fordham University Press, 2022.

Stolberg, Eva-Maria. "The Siberian Frontier between 'White Mission' and 'Yellow Peril,' 1890s–1920s." *Nationalities Papers: Journal of Nationalism & Ethnicity* 32, no. 1 (March 2004): 165–81.

Sullivan, Charles. "Motherland: Soviet Nostalgia in Post-Soviet Russia." PhD diss., George Washington University, 2014.

Suny, Ronald Grigor, and Terry Martin, eds. *A State of Nations: Empire and Nation-Making in the Age of Lenin and Stalin*. New York: Oxford University Press, 2001.

Suslov, Mikhail. *Geopolitical Imagination*. Stuttgart, Germany: Ibidem Verlag, 2020.

Tabata, Shinichiro. "Observations on Russian Exposure to the Dutch Disease." *Eurasian Geography & Economics* 53, no. 2 (2012): 231–43.

Taylor, Bryan. *The Code of Putinism*. Oxford: Oxford University Press, 2018.

Tétart, Frank. Géopolitique de Kaliningrad. Paris: Presses de l'université Paris-Sorbonne, 2007.

Tetruashvily, Esther. "How Did We Become Illegal? Impacts of Post-Soviet Shifting Migration Politics on Labor Migration Law in Russia." *Region* 1, no. 1 (2012): 53–74.

Thorez, Julien. "*Khorosho, gde nas net*. L'émigration des 'Russophones' d'Asie centrale." *EchoGéo*, no. 9 (2009): 1–25.

Tishkov, Valerii. *Rossiiskii narod. Istoriia i smysl natsional'nogo samosoznaniia*. Moscow: Nauka, 2013.

Toal, Gerard. *Near Abroad: Putin, the West, and the Contest over Ukraine and the Caucasus.* Oxford: Oxford University Press, 2017.

Tompson, William. "Back to the Future? Thoughts on the Political Economy of Expanding State Ownership in Russia." *Les Cahiers Russie,* no. 6 (2008).

Tsukhlo, Sergei. "Importozameshchenie: mify i realnost.'" In *Ezhegodnyi doklad Franko-rossiiskogo tsentra Observatorii Rossiia-2016,* edited by Arnaud Dubien, 92–103. Paris: Le Cherche-Midi, 2016.

Tsygankov, Andrei. *The Dark Double: US Media, Russia, and the Politics of Values.* Oxford: Oxford University Press, 2019.

Tucker, Joshua. "Enough! Electoral Fraud, Collective Action Problems, and Post-Communist Colored Revolutions." *Perspectives on Politics* 5 (3): 537–53.

Tumarkin, Nina. *The Living and the Dead: The Rise and Fall of the Cult of World War II in Russia.* New York: Perseus Books, 1994.

Turaeva, Rano. "Imagined Mosque Communities in Russia: Central Asian Migrants in Moscow." *Asian Ethnicity* 20, no. 2 (2019): 131–47.

"UN Security Council Action on Crimea Referendum Blocked." UN News Centre, March 15, 2014. http://www.un.org/apps/news/story.asp?NewsID=47362#.WMLR00eltVo.

United Nations Population Division. "Replacement Migration." http://www.un.org/esa/population/publications/ReplMigED/RusFed.pdf.

"Velikii post i religioznost.'" Levada Center, March 3, 2020. https://www.levada.ru/2020/03/03/velikij-post-i-religioznost.

Vercueil, Julien. "Russie: la 'stratégie 2020' en question." *Revue d'études comparatives Est-Ouest* 44, no. 1 (2013): 169–94.

———. *Transition et ouverture de l'économie russe: Pour une économie institutionnelle du changement.* Paris: L'Harmattan, 2000.

Voting Record of "Item 33(b) A/68/L.39 Draft Resolution Territorial Integrity of Ukraine, Resolution 68/262." https://papersmart.unmeetings.org/media2/2498292/voting-record.pdf.

Way, Lucan. "The Real Causes of the Color Revolutions." *Journal of Democracy* 19, no. 3 (2008): 55–69.

White, Stephen. "Soviet Nostalgia and Russian Politics." *Journal of Eurasian Studies* 1, no. 1 (2010): 1–9.

Wilson, Jeanne. *Strategic Partners: Russian–Chinese Relations in the Post-Soviet Era.* Armonk, NY: M. E. Sharpe, 2004.

Witte, John, and Michael Bourdeaux. *Proselytism and Orthodoxy in Russia: The New War for Souls.* Ossining, NY: Orbis Books, 1999.

Yablokov, Ilya. *Fortress Russia: Conspiracy Theories in the Post-Soviet World.* New York: Polity Press, 2018.

Yarlykapov, Akhmet. "Divisions and Unity of the Novy Urengoy Muslim Community." *Problems of Post-Communism* 67, no. 4–5 (2020): 338–47.

Yeltsin, Boris. Speech to Canadian Parliament, June 19, 1992. http://www.lipad.ca/full/1992/06/19/13.

"Yeltsin o natsional'noi idee." *Nezavisimaia gazeta,* July 13, 1996.

Yurchak, Alexei. *Everything Was Forever, Until It Was No More: The Last Soviet Generation.* Princeton, NJ: Princeton University Press, 2005.
Zaionchkovskaya, Zhanna, ed. *Migranty v Moskve.* Moscow: Tri kvadrata, 2009.

# Index

Made in United States
North Haven, CT
09 July 2024